THE
FAILED PROMISE

ALSO BY ROBERT S. LEVINE

Race, Transnationalism, and Nineteenth-Century American Literary Studies

The Lives of Frederick Douglass

The Norton Anthology of American Literature
(general editor)

A Companion to American Literary Studies
(editor, with Caroline F. Levander)

The Works of James M. Whitfield
(editor, with Ivy Wilson)

Dislocating Race and Nation

Frederick Douglass and Herman Melville
(editor, with Samuel Otter)

Hemispheric American Studies
(editor, with Caroline F. Levander)

Martin R. Delany: A Documentary Reader
(editor)

Martin Delany, Frederick Douglass, and the Politics of Representative Identity

Conspiracy and Romance

THE
FAILED
PROMISE

RECONSTRUCTION,
FREDERICK DOUGLASS,
and the IMPEACHMENT *of*
ANDREW JOHNSON

Robert S. Levine

W. W. NORTON & COMPANY
Independent Publishers Since 1923

For information about permission to reproduce selections from this book,
write to Permissions, W. W. Norton & Company, Inc., 500 Fifth Avenue,
New York, NY 10110

For information about special discounts for bulk purchases, please contact
W. W. Norton Special Sales at specialsales@wwnorton.com or 800-233-4830

Manufacturing by Lake Book Manufacturing
Book design by Brooke Koven
Production manager: Anna Oler

Library of Congress Cataloging-in-Publication Data

Names: Levine, Robert S. (Robert Steven), 1953– author.
Title: The failed promise : Reconstruction, Frederick Douglass, and the
impeachment of Andrew Johnson / Robert S. Levine.
Other titles: Reconstruction, Frederick Douglass, and
the impeachment of Andrew Johnson
Description: First edition. | New York, NY : W. W. Norton & Company, [2021] |
Includes bibliographical references and index.
Identifiers: LCCN 2021005132 | ISBN 9781324004752 (hardcover) |
ISBN 9781324004769 (epub)
Subjects: LCSH: Reconstruction (U.S. history, 1865–1877) | Douglass, Frederick,
1818–1895. | United States—History—Civil War, 1861–1865—Influence. |
Johnson, Andrew, 1808–1875—Impeachment. | United States—Politics and
government—1865–1877. | United States—Social conditions—1865–1918. |
United States—Race relations—History—19th century.
Classification: LCC E668 .L683 2021 | DDC 973.8—dc23
LC record available at https://lccn.loc.gov/2021005132

W. W. Norton & Company, Inc., 500 Fifth Avenue, New York, N.Y. 10110
www.wwnorton.com

W. W. Norton & Company Ltd., 15 Carlisle Street, London W1D 3BS

1 2 3 4 5 6 7 8 9 0

In Memory of My Beloved Sister Karen Levine (1960–2020)

CONTENTS

LIST OF ILLUSTRATIONS

INTRODUCTION

ANDREW JOHNSON took the oath of office and assumed the presidency on April 15, 1865, hours after Abraham Lincoln died from his assassin's bullet. Almost three years later, on February 24, 1868, Johnson was impeached by the U.S. House of Representatives for "high crimes and misdemeanors." It was an event no one would have predicted on the day of his inauguration.

Johnson was an anomaly among southern political leaders. He had opposed southern secession after the 1860 election of Lincoln, and during the Civil War he had called for the end of slavery. In 1864, as military governor of Tennessee, he announced to a large gathering of Blacks in Nashville that he had ended slavery in his home state. Seemingly more radical and progressive than the president himself, Johnson looked like the ideal person to serve as Lincoln's vice president.

When the Civil War ended, the country was poised for great changes. Slavery had been abolished by the Thirteenth Amendment to the Constitution. Hope abounded, at least in the North, about the possibility of bringing forth a more egalitarian nation through what was already being called "Reconstruction." Lincoln's Republican Party took the main responsibility for Reconstruction after his death, and those on the party's most progressive wing—such as Senator Charles Sumner of Massachusetts, Congressman Thaddeus Stevens of Pennsylvania, and Senator Benjamin Wade of Ohio—hoped to transform the erstwhile slave South into a region where the freedpeople could vote, find work, own property, and have the same rights and privileges as white people. These leaders, the Radical Republicans, initially regarded Andrew Johnson as the best possible president to lead the nation. But they soon learned that Johnson had an altogether different understanding of Reconstruction. Johnson believed that the president, not Congress, should be overseeing the process, and that the main goal of Reconstruction should be to restore the ex-Confederate states to the national body with no essential changes mandated by the federal government, except for the abolition of slavery.

The conflict between Johnson and the Radical Republicans on the meaning of Reconstruction began less than a year after Johnson's inauguration. It quickly dominated national political debate, and it culminated in the first impeachment of a U.S. president. When the impeachment trial concluded in May 1868 with the acquittal of Johnson, three years had passed since the end of the Civil War. By then, the odds of creating a reconstructed United States as imagined by the Radical Republicans had greatly diminished.

May 1868 lay far in the distance on Johnson's inauguration day. Even with the shock and mourning at the assassination of Lincoln, Republicans had high hopes. But the promise of Reconstruction began to fade just a few months into Johnson's presidency, and by late 1868 one could already talk about its failure.[1] This book charts the course of Reconstruction, from the optimism of the spring of 1865 to the increasing pessimism of the late 1860s and 1870s, from the perspective of a man who was not a senator or congressman, and was not directly involved with the political conflict between the president and Congress. That man is the great African American leader Frederick Douglass.

Douglass was forty-seven years old in 1865, when Johnson took office. He was actively advancing his own vision of Reconstruction.

Like the Radical Republicans, Douglass argued for Black male suffrage and federal programs that would help the freedpeople gain education, employment, property, and equal rights as U.S. citizens. He viewed the Radical Republicans as the friends and supporters of Black people, though he became wary when they didn't move quickly or boldly to address racial inequities. For a few months in 1865, he may well have considered Johnson as potentially the right leader for the times. But by late summer of 1865, Douglass was disillusioned, and as the Johnson presidency wore on, he gave numerous lectures and published essays challenging Johnson. He even met with the president at the White House to make a case for Blacks' civil rights.

During the Johnson years, Douglass undertook a series of rescue missions in an effort to sustain the kind of Reconstruction that he thought would best serve the interests of Black people. These missions—lectures, meetings, strategic publications—meant constantly watching, or shadowing, Johnson, which Douglass did for the full four years of Johnson's presidency. Johnson did the same for Douglass, for he recognized that he could not ignore this prominent Black critic of his administration. I've intertwined Douglass's career with Johnson's presidency to provide a new view of Johnson's impeachment and the promise and failure of Reconstruction itself.

When I began this book on Douglass and the impeachment of Andrew Johnson, I noticed that even the very best works on the impeachment focus mainly on the Radical Republicans. Black voices are almost entirely absent, with Douglass providing only occasional cameos. But Douglass had a sustained interest in Johnson from 1865 to the time of the impeachment, and his perspective wasn't always in accord with that of the Radical Republicans. It is certainly worth celebrating the idealistic Republican congressmen who defied the president in order to bring equal rights to the freedpeople.[2] That is a compelling story, but it's not the full or only story that we can tell about the impeachment. We need to consider Douglass's perspective more fully. Among other things, it helps us to see some of the limits of the Republicans.

Douglass was not the only African American leader who called for a radical, multiracial Reconstruction and contested Johnson's limited, top-down vision. Because of the attention given to the Radical Republicans, the voices of other African Americans, not just Douglass's, have been neglected.[3] Many of these Black leaders collaborated with Douglass at Black conventions, spoke with him at lecture venues, and wrote for newspapers and periodicals. This book emphasizes Douglass's responses to Johnson, but it also includes discussion of other key African American critics of Johnson, such as George T. Downing, Frances Harper, Douglass's sons Lewis Henry Douglass and Charles Remond Douglass, Philip A. Bell, and the anonymous contributors to the *Christian Recorder*, the most widely read African American newspaper of the period. I also consider Black leaders such as John Langston and Martin R. Delany, who thought Johnson wasn't all that bad, at least for a white president.

African American leaders had called for a transformative Reconstruction since the beginning of the Civil War. As I became interested in recovering a Black perspective on the impeachment of Johnson, the book grew beyond its initial focus on the impeachment. I wound up telling a more comprehensive story of Douglass's and other African Americans' efforts to articulate what they saw as the promise of Reconstruction and the problem with Johnson.

Johnson's impeachment remains central to this book. I follow Johnson's career as it unfolds from the day of his inauguration, and I trace the engagement of Douglass and his African American contemporaries with the events leading to the impeachment. In doing so, I attempt to move African Americans from the background to the foreground of the four years of Reconstruction under Johnson. At an 1865 meeting of the American Anti-Slavery Society, the veteran Black abolitionist Charles Lenox Remond (the namesake of Frederick Douglass's son Charles Remond) remarked that it was "utterly impossible for our white friends, however much they have tried, fully to understand the Black man's case in this nation."[4] Through Douglass and his compatriots, I have tried to convey African Americans' case against

Johnson, and even the Radical Republicans, in the years immediately after the Civil War.

According to the Radical Republicans, Johnson resisted their version of Reconstruction by undermining their legislated programs. According to Douglass and other Black writers and speakers, Johnson was an immoral president who had blood on his hands. But most African Americans had larger concerns than Johnson during the late 1860s. They lived with pervasive anti-Black racism across the nation, and they regarded that racism as even more insidious than Johnson. After all, that racism sanctioned Johnson, who retained his popularity well into his presidency. The idea of Johnson as an extreme or exemplary racist didn't make sense to most African American commentators.

Douglass was well aware of racism in the Republican Party, particularly after he was nearly excluded from a Republican meeting in September 1866 because he was Black. To Douglass, that racism, although nothing like Johnson's, contributed to the narrow way that the Republicans framed Johnson's eventual impeachment. The Republicans' articles of impeachment said nothing explicit about the harm the president did to Black people; the eleven articles said nothing about race. During the impeachment trial, there was not a single allusion to a Black voice or perspective. The Republicans may have been idealistic, but they were pragmatic politicians. From Douglass's point of view, they were at times compromised politicians as well.

Douglass was a skillful organizer of social protest, a charismatic leader, and one of the greatest orators and writers of his time. His speeches and writings are central to this work. As a literary historian by training, I confess to my obsession with his masterful rhetoric. Douglass was brilliant with shaping arguments for different occasions and audiences. He was "a man of words," writes David W. Blight, his most recent biographer.[5] We need to attend to Douglass's words if we want to fully capture his evolving views of Johnson and Reconstruction.

Douglass is not the only man of words in this book. Johnson, too, was a skilled rhetorician. He is typically described as one of the worst presidents we've ever had and as an irredeemable racist. Why bother to look closely at the words of such a man? Johnson certainly was a bad president, but the more I examined his writings and speeches (and the Johnson Papers are massive), the more I began to think we have overlooked his complexity, especially in the early years of his political life. Johnson was a wide reader with a special interest in the writings of the nation's Founders. He interpreted the Constitution in ways that many of us would reject (and which many politicians of his time did reject), but he always supported his political positions through sustained and informed analysis. Like Douglass, Johnson was renowned as an orator. When he made the bold decision as a southerner to reject southern secession, he offered precedents to explain himself. When he championed antislavery as a southerner—at the risk of his life—he developed his critique using contemporary and historical examples in the fashion of a northern abolitionist. As he became more embattled and reactionary during his presidency, he directed his speeches more narrowly toward his supporters. But he was a politician to be reckoned with, and even when his positions come across as wrong-headed, or racist, his words remain an important part of the story. I attend to Johnson's language in order to better understand the shifts and turns in his career, his contradictory positions, and even his failed promise, while not losing sight of his racism.

My close attention to language goes hand in hand with my chosen method of telling the story of Douglass and Johnson as it unfolds over time. We know what happened in the Johnson presidency, and it is tempting to tell even the early story of 1865 through the lens of the impeachment of 1868. But the actual historical participants made choices on a day-to-day basis without knowing what the outcomes would be. At times I anticipate the impeachment, but I do not view every moment from the time of Johnson's inauguration as inevitably leading to impeachment. That said, we can certainly see the likelihood of impeachment increasing as conflict between Congress and the president intensified. Douglass watched this drama develop, but he also acted in it. He posed challenges to both Johnson and Congress in the many speeches he delivered to Black, white, and mixed-race audiences. And he was not always focused on Johnson. In 1867, he began to focus more specifically on the flaws of the American Constitution that he believed paved the way for Johnson's actions.

More needs to be said about Johnson's racism. Douglass retrospectively presented Johnson in his 1881 *Life and Times of Frederick Douglass* as a reflexive racist. For many commentators then and now, Johnson's racism explains his behavior as president. But racism was everywhere in white America during this time. Even Radical Republicans like Thaddeus Stevens of Pennsylvania and Benjamin Wade of Ohio, who worked staunchly for Blacks' rights in the South, equivocated when it came to advocating Blacks' civil rights in the North, in part because they knew their own constituents were racist. Stevens was unhappy about Douglass attending a convention of southern Republican supporters, fearing that Douglass's participation would lead the white people of Pennsylvania to vote against Republicans. African American leaders agitated for the vote continually during the late 1860s, but every Black suffrage bill that appeared on ballots in the North and Midwest during the Johnson presidency went down to defeat. Wade had his own problems with racism. In 1851, during a visit to the South, he wrote his wife that he couldn't bear "the Nigger smell" and that he hated eating food "cooked by Niggers until I can smell and taste the Nigger." Twenty-two years later, after battling against Johnson for Radical Reconstruction, he wrote his wife, "I am sick and tired of niggers." Historian Eric Foner tells us that Abraham Lincoln "never became a full-fledged racial egalitarian. In private, he continued to use words like 'nigger' and 'darky' and tell racially inflected stories."[6] As president, Lincoln voiced support for colonization programs that would have deported African Americans to Central and South America.

Johnson's racism partly explains his resistance to Reconstruction. His reading of the Constitution as limiting the federal government's oversight of the states had a significant impact as well. It's worth noting that some Blacks of the time, most notably John Langston—who would become the first dean of Howard University's law school—admired Johnson, and Johnson had numerous positive interactions with other African Americans during 1865 and 1866. After Douglass and a Black delegation confronted Johnson at the White House in February 1866, the Black nationalist Martin R. Delany wrote Douglass and his associates with a caution about turning against Johnson too quickly. "Do not expect too much of him—as black men, I mean," Delany advised. "Do not forget that you are black and he is white. Make large allowances for this, and take this as the stand-point."[7]

Johnson's whiteness informs a strange and paradoxical aspect of a great many of his speeches. A racist, he thought of himself as a leader of Black people. He even regarded himself as their savior. This bizarre self-conception originated in an 1864 speech he delivered to Blacks in Nashville, Tennessee. When he announced that he was ending slavery in the state, he assumed the mantle of a Moses who would lead African Americans to their freedom. Johnson never let go of that self-conception. He bragged about his Moses-like status to Douglass, an actual African American leader. Even when Johnson came under political siege and gave vent to reactionary rhetoric, he continued to describe himself as Blacks' Moses. He was self-deceived, but at times that self-deception led him toward insight. In the interstices of his many references to himself as Moses, Johnson suggested that he regarded Blacks as equal to whites, or at least worth leading to freedom. But his actions never lived up to his favorite metaphor. Even the Blacks of Tennessee who initially embraced him as their leader came to view him as an oppressor.

Heeding Delany's cautions about not being overly judgmental of Johnson, I have struggled to resist the temptation to put Johnson on trial myself. Johnson was a white man from the slave South, and I've tried to meet him on that ground, not our own. During the Civil War, Johnson was brave and in his own way idealistic, as John Langston observed when he met with him both before and after Johnson became president. But because I am also telling this story from the perspective of Douglass, I have been guided by his judgments as well. Douglass saw a president who was driven by racism and whose actions led directly to the suffering and death of African Americans. He saw a president who had the opportunity to transform the United States into a multiracial democracy and, at great and lasting national cost, chose not to. In short, Douglass saw a president who contributed to the failed promise of Reconstruction. History has borne Douglass out.

But even as Douglass placed some of the blame on Johnson for the failure of Reconstruction, he never closed his eyes to how the nation's long history of slavery had led so many white Americans to regard Black people as not fully human. In Douglass's view, Republicans and other white Americans needed to confront that history as much as they needed to do battle with Johnson. "Slavery has left its poison behind it," Douglass wrote in 1870, "both in the veins of the slave and in those of the enslaver."[8] That poison made the achievement of any sort of egalitarian Reconstruction program all the more difficult.

Reconstruction has never captured the public imagination in the way of the Civil War, partly because it's so complicated. The cast of characters—senators, representatives, jurists, and many others—is enormous. Ongoing debates in Congress produced bill after bill, many of which were vetoed by Johnson. Meanwhile, the ex-Confederate states attempted to establish new governments, with conflict ensuing over matters both large and small concerning their proposed state constitutions. Even with the lasting achievement of the Thirteenth, Fourteenth, and Fifteenth Amendments—which ended slavery, guaranteed birthright citizenship, and gave the vote to Black men— Reconstruction can seem like a legal and legislative morass.

We are now witnessing a resurgence of interest in Reconstruction— and a change in the stories we're telling about it. Early generations of historians saw Reconstruction as a bad idea that was badly executed. Led by Eric Foner, today's historians of the period see Reconstruction as an era of tragically unfulfilled promise, a "second founding" that failed to realize its noble vision.[9] It was also a time when African

Americans were terrorized and murdered so regularly that racial violence, and Black resistance to that violence, became part of everyday life.

Viewed from the perspective of Douglass and other African Americans of the post–Civil War years, Reconstruction wasn't all that complicated. It was a quest, as Douglass regularly reminded his auditors and readers, for dignity and equality for Black people in a racist nation that hadn't yet lived up to the egalitarian promise of 1776. Reconstruction, he said in January 1865, was simply "an act of justice to the American bondmen or freedmen."[10] The crucial moment right after the Civil War offered the prospect for achieving such justice, but the time for action was limited and would not be available for long. The story of Douglass and the impeachment of Johnson addresses the hopes and frustrations of Reconstruction during the moment of opportunity and crisis that was the Johnson presidency. The story begins at Lincoln's second inauguration.

PART ONE

---·---

Douglass, Johnson, Lincoln

Prologue

LINCOLN'S SECOND
INAUGURATION

I T WAS A festive day in Washington, D.C., on March 4, 1865.
Boardinghouses and inns were filled to capacity. Many visitors
to the capital slept in hallways or wherever they could find space at
local taverns. Recent Union army victories, led by generals Ulysses
S. Grant and William Tecumseh Sherman, added to the celebratory
mood of the thousands in attendance for Abraham Lincoln's second
inauguration, making it seem like a national holiday. The spirited
revelers were not discouraged by the rains that flooded the city's dirt
streets, creating what some observers measured as ten inches of mud.
Nor were they daunted by the sight of wounded soldiers, a fixture
in the city. The District's massive open-air hospitals, packed with
soldiers who had lost limbs and were struggling to stay alive, made
clear that the bloody war had not yet come to an end. Still, the Union
seemed close to winning the war, so the festivities went on. Civic
groups, local bands, Republican supporters, and military men—
including four companies of Black troops representing the approximately two hundred thousand African Americans who fought in the
Union army—paraded through the muddy downtown streets, as the

Abraham Lincoln delivering his second inaugural address as president of the
United States, Washington, D.C., March 4, 1865. Photograph by Alexander
Gardner. (*Courtesy of the Library of Congress, Prints and Photographs Division.*)

crowd assembling outside the White House eagerly awaited hearing
from the president.[1]

Among the wet celebrants was Frederick Douglass, the nation's
most famous Black man, who had become friendly with Lincoln after
meeting with him at the White House in 1863 and 1864. Lincoln
had invited Douglass to the inauguration as his special guest. While
Douglass and thousands of onlookers huddled in the rain, something
almost mystical happened: the rain abruptly stopped and the sun at
long last appeared.

Lincoln then stepped forth, took the oath of office from Chief Justice Salmon P. Chase, and gave his short and powerful second inaugural address. Douglass considered the president's words "to contain

more vital substance than I have ever seen compressed in a space so narrow." Lincoln finished his speech solemnly:

> With malice toward none, with charity for all, with firmness in the right as God gives us to see the right, let us strive to finish the work we are in, to bind up the nation's wounds, to care for him who shall have borne the battle, and for his widow and his orphans, to do all which may achieve and cherish a just and lasting peace among ourselves and with all nations.

Douglass recalled in his 1881 *Life and Times of Frederick Douglass* that he was so moved by the speech that he wanted to convey his compliments directly to the president. He attempted to enter the White House for the evening reception, but two policemen stopped him at the entrance, convinced that he was an intruder. He protested and refused to depart, when one of Lincoln's guests recognized Douglass and led him past the guards. As soon as he entered the reception area, Lincoln hurried over to greet "my friend Douglass," took him by the hand, and asked for Douglass's assessment of his speech, saying for all to hear: "There is no man in the country whose opinion I value more than yours. I want to know what you think of it?" Without hesitation, Douglass responded, "Mr. Lincoln, that was a sacred effort," to which the president replied, "I am glad you liked it!" Douglass "passed on, feeling that any man, however distinguished, might well regard himself honored by such expressions, from such a man."[2]

Douglass's glowing account of President Lincoln contrasts sharply with his description of Vice President Andrew Johnson. Douglass and Johnson did not exchange words at the inauguration, just glances. Yet those glances, as Douglass presented the moment, were enough for him to know the man:

> I was standing in the crowd by the side of Mrs. Thomas J. Dorsey, when Mr. Lincoln touched Mr. Johnson and pointed me out to him. The first expression which came to his face, and which I

think was the true index of his heart, was one of bitter contempt and aversion. Seeing that I observed him, he tried to assume a more friendly appearance, but it was too late; it is useless to close the door when all within has been seen. His first glance was the frown of the man; the second was the bland and sickly smile of the demagogue. I turned to Mrs. Dorsey and said, "Whatever Andrew Johnson may be, he certainly is no friend of our race."[3]

In the context of his 1881 autobiography, this passage could be taken as an insightful, indeed prophetic evaluation of the man who would soon become president. For Douglass, Johnson's glance at him and Louise Tobias Dorsey, a Black woman, revealed Johnson as an inveterate racist. That glance, in short, anticipated that a Reconstruction program bringing full rights of citizenship to the freedpeople would be extraordinarily difficult to achieve under a Johnson presidency (the office he would assume one month later). That glance, to some extent, also anticipated the impeachment of Johnson, which was motivated, at least in part, by the Radical Republicans' anger about his racist policies.

But Douglass's narrative of Lincoln's second inauguration should be viewed with some skepticism. Douglass told this story twenty-five years later, with full knowledge of the course of Johnson's presidency. In hindsight, Douglass, as he describes himself that inauguration day, appears prescient in his assessment of Johnson, but anyone could have been prescient by the time Douglass wrote this version of his autobiography.

As an autobiographer, Douglass sometimes told stories long after the fact that sidestepped ambiguities or conflicts. Nowhere is his fabulation more on display than in his account of Lincoln in *Life and Times*. There, Douglass describes how he campaigned for Lincoln and reveled in the "triumphant election" of "a man who in the order of events was destined to do a greater service to his country and to mankind than any man who had gone before him in the presidential office."[4] That was a convenient observation to make at a time when Douglass worked as a functionary of the Republican Party and found it advantageous to his own career to link his star with Lincoln's.

But Douglass's writings about Lincoln in real time told a story about a man he often regarded as overly conciliatory to the southern slave power. A month after Lincoln's victory in the November 1860 election, Douglass wrote in his newspaper *Douglass' Monthly*: "Slavery will be as safe, and safer, in the Union under such a President, than it can be under any President of a Southern Confederacy." His concerns about Lincoln were not allayed by the new president's March 1861 inaugural address. As Douglass reported to his readers: "Mr. Lincoln opens his address by announcing his complete loyalty to slavery in the slave States, . . . prostrating himself before the foul and withering curse of slavery." Later that year, Douglass wrote about Lincoln's lack of action on slavery: "We might as well remove Mr. LINCOLN out of the President's chair, and respectfully invite JEFFERSON DAVIS or some other slaveholding rebel to take his place." In September 1862, Douglass remarked that the president's politics had "been calculated . . . to shield and protect slavery from the very blows which its horrible crimes have loudly and persistently invited."[5] Douglass found the Emancipation Proclamation exciting but limited because it failed to liberate the enslaved people of the border states. Despite two good meetings with Lincoln at the White House to discuss Civil War policy, he initially chose not to endorse Lincoln for a second term, preferring the antislavery Republican John C. Frémont. Douglass's celebration of Lincoln as the nation's savior began only after the president's assassination.

Given Douglass's practice of storytelling in his autobiographies, and especially given his uncritical portrayal of Lincoln in *Life and Times*, should we trust that Andrew Johnson looked at him with such racist disdain? After all, Johnson was a southern Democrat who, in ways Douglass would have admired, turned against his party at the time of secession. At considerable political cost, Johnson affirmed his support for the Union and soon called for the abolition of slavery. When Lincoln began to formulate plans for readmitting the former

Confederate states to the Union, Johnson even pressed him to require more stringent loyalty oaths.

The initial meeting between Douglass and Johnson raises a number of questions central to the story of the two men. What were their political positions on the Civil War and Reconstruction when they exchanged glances at the White House? Might there have been possibilities for collaboration? Does Douglass's stark retrospective contrast between Johnson and Lincoln have a basis in fact? To address these questions we need to consider the paths that led Douglass and Johnson to Lincoln's second inauguration.

1

SOUTHERN UNIONIST

ABRAHAM LINCOLN WAS a famously self-made man who rose from obscurity to become president. Andrew Johnson's rise to prominence to become Lincoln's vice president was equally impressive. Born into poverty in 1808 in Raleigh, North Carolina, Johnson lost his father at age three, never attended school, and was apprenticed to a tailor before he was ten years old. With his brother, he moved back and forth between North Carolina and South Carolina, and at age sixteen moved on his own to Greeneville, Tennessee, with a tailor's skills but virtually no money. He opened a tailor's shop there, married at eighteen, and soon dabbled in real estate investments. He had already taught himself to read and write, and he continued his self-education by spending long hours at the Greeneville College library poring over books about politics and history, taking a special interest in the constitutional debates of the Founders. Though he was not a matriculated student at the college, Johnson joined its debating society and gained a reputation as a skillful public speaker. His oratorical skills served him well when he took up politics in Greeneville as a Jacksonian Democrat. He won a seat as a town alderman in 1829, became mayor a few years later, and in 1835 captured a seat in the Tennessee state legislature. In 1841 he moved from the state legislature to the state senate, sold his tailoring business, and invested almost exclusively in real estate. Johnson won a congressional seat in 1843 and began to develop a national reputation. Over the next ten years he served as a Democratic congressman from Tennessee. When he lost the congressional election of 1853 because of district gerrymandering, he successfully ran for governor and held that position for four years. In 1857, before there were direct elections for that office, the Tennessee state legislature elected him a U.S. senator.[1]

Johnson was much admired, and even feared, as a politician during

Andrew Johnson, c. 1865. Photograph by Matthew B. Brady. (*Courtesy of the Library of Congress, Prints and Photographs Division.*)

the years leading up to his election as senator. Central to his appeal was his populism, which he got from his hero, Andrew Jackson. He regularly called for direct elections to the Senate, sponsored homestead bills to make land available to the working classes, supported public education, and in good Jacksonian fashion spoke out against aristocrats. He was also a nationalist who shared Jackson's disdain for those who put their state politics above the U.S. Constitution. In Johnson's view, President Jackson was at his most heroic in 1832 when he resisted South Carolina's efforts to nullify federal tariffs.

Johnson's speaking style added to his popularity. At five feet nine, he was not a big man, but he had a booming voice that seemed to emerge from a much larger body. Observers commented on his black hair, dark eyes, and (not surprising for a former tailor) fine clothes. There was something Byronic about his dark features, and with his Romantic good looks and energy, he enjoyed giving speeches outdoors to large crowds. These speeches, often delivered without notes, could go on for several hours, in the style of the day. Johnson made a name for himself by speaking as a common man, even as he displayed his uncommon knowledge of American history. He also came to be known for the ferocity of his personal attacks on his political opponents.

A profile of Johnson in the 1849 *New York Sunday Times* captured the winning qualities of this emerging national figure in the Democratic Party. The anonymous author claimed to have observed Johnson over his first three terms as a congressman. He admired his populist commitment to "those who get their living by the sweat of the brow," and he found his physical appearance to be compelling. Johnson, he wrote, "looks all over like the self-made man." The author was taken with Johnson's combative speaking style, his ability to wield an "oratorical bowie-knife." The writer provided descriptions of Johnson in action that suggested a man who had learned from his experience in a debating club. "In the course of the six years I have known him in the House," the reporter noted, "I do not recollect ever to have seen him consent to give way for an interruption." Like a good debater, Johnson used "words of many syllables, or of recent foreign derivation" in order to rattle the opposition. His ability to intimidate informed the article's most striking description of him at this early phase of his career:

> He thrusts his opponents through and through, as with a rusty and jagged weapon, tearing a big hole and leaving something behind to fester and be remembered. Woe be unto the luckless wight who offers him a personal indignity—casts a slur upon him, in debate; for if he has to wait two years for the opportunity, when it *does* come, Mr. J. makes the best use of it. . . . Perhaps I may fairly characterize his efforts as being crushingly slashing and slashingly crushing; for he chops to mince-meat and then grinds to powder the men, measures and principles he may be contending against.[2]

This was a man—knowledgeable, passionate—you would want on your side. But this was also a man, the article suggests, who could run into problems when facing opposition that wouldn't back down. Negotiation did not appear to be part of his political vocabulary.

Johnson mostly agreed with the main principles of the Democratic Party in the South during the 1840s and 1850s, with one significant exception: he had mixed feelings about slavery. He believed in the legitimacy of the institution, but as a man who had long struggled financially, he resented the owners of slave plantations, convinced that they constituted an aristocracy detrimental to the working classes. These beliefs placed him in an unusual position during that period as a free-labor advocate in the slaveholding South.

That said, Johnson was a politician, and before he adopted anti-slavery views during the early 1860s, he defended slavery in Congress. In a speech of January 1844, he scoffed at the idea that Congress could abolish slavery in Washington, D.C., and he reviled abolitionists for preparing "to turn over two million of negroes loose upon the country to become a terror and burden to society." During a testy 1848 debate with Massachusetts congressman John Gorham Palfrey, he drew his "oratorical bowie-knife" when he challenged the abolitionist's claim that Black people were becoming refined and educated. Johnson asked Palfrey if he was prepared "with a member of his family—to wit, his own daughter—to give his consent to her being given to this intellectual, interesting, and charming negro boy in wedlock as her companion through life?" (As reported in the *Congressional Globe*, Johnson later offered a public apology to Palfrey, saying "he did not . . . intend to insult the gentleman or his family.") In 1849, Johnson announced in Congress that the South had come under such attack from antislavery forces that he supported taking "timely resistance against any aggression that might be made upon her."[3]

Though he despised the wealthy owners of slave plantations, Johnson was nevertheless willing to own what were then called house slaves. He purchased a fourteen-year-old named Dolly in the late 1830s or early 1840s, and later purchased her half brother Sam. The 1850 census listed Johnson as owning four slaves; he purchased an additional enslaved person in 1857, who may have been related to one of the adults, and made one other purchase before 1860. During the 1850s, Johnson took the conventional view of slavery apologists that chattel slavery in the South was better than the "wage slavery" of the North. Antislavery northerners, he asserted at the 1856 State Democratic Convention in Nashville, had found "white slavery . . . cheaper" for their factories. When Johnson, during his presidency, spoke about himself as a former slaveholder, he would pridefully claim that he had never sold any of his slaves or separated families.[4]

After Johnson became a senator in 1857, he devoted much of his time to developing homestead bills, none of which were ever adopted. As an unconventional populist who depended on slave owners and their sympathizers for support, he also continued to defend slavery. When the antislavery militant John Brown led his October 1859 attack on the federal arsenal at Harpers Ferry, Virginia, hoping to inspire slave rebellions throughout the South, Johnson warned that fanatical abolitionists threatened the South's way of life, and called the

assault on Harpers Ferry "an insurrection or invasion."[5] Fearing that
the North aimed to break up the Union, Johnson committed himself
to what he regarded as the nation's proslavery Constitution.

Less than a year after giving his vitriolic speech against Brown,
Johnson surprised and angered his constituents when he announced
that the South, not the North, posed the greatest danger to the future
of the nation. At this point he revealed himself as the rarest of crea-
tures: a southern Unionist. The intensity of his nationalism, and his
respect for the U.S. Constitution, led him in the strongest possible
terms to reject secession as a legitimate response to the election of
Lincoln. In a passionate and learned speech to Congress, Johnson
declared that even though he voted against Lincoln, the American
people had voted for him and the South needed to respect that democratic decision. He asked his southern colleagues in the Senate: "Shall
we shrink from our duty, and desert the Government as a sinking ship,
or shall we stand by it?" He offered his own answer: "I, for one, will
stand . . . with my shoulder supporting the edifice as long as human
effort can do it."[6]

Johnson's pro-Union speech got so much attention that the Congressional Globe Office printed it up for mass circulation. Senator
Charles Sumner of Massachusetts, who would later become a leader of
Radical Reconstruction and one of President Johnson's most implaca-
ble opponents, ordered five hundred copies. Johnson himself ordered
ten thousand copies to distribute to his constituents.[7]

Standing alone as a southern senator committed to the Union, at
a time when other southern congressmen had gone with the Confederacy, Johnson put himself at notable risk. In March 1861, he was
denounced by the proslavery Democratic senator Joseph Lane of Ore-
gon as a "Black Republican." But when Johnson responded to Lane
that he would have secessionists arrested and killed if found guilty, the
New York Times lauded him as "the greatest man of the age."[8]

During 1861 Johnson gave fiery anti-secessionist speeches in Tennessee and Ohio, moving quickly from place to place in a covered
wagon for fear of being assassinated. He felt particularly vulnerable

in his home state of Tennessee, which seceded from the Union in June 1861. As he traveled, he was even shot at several times by bushwhackers. Increasingly he blamed the advent of the Civil War on the owners of slave plantations, whom he now regarded with open contempt as oligarchs who had little concern for the nation. In a speech delivered in Newport, Kentucky, in September 1861, Johnson took the risky position of saying he would support Lincoln as long as he adhered to the Constitution.[9]

Johnson's anti-secessionism and lack of hostility toward Lincoln contributed to Lincoln's decision to appoint him military governor of Tennessee in March 1862. In that role, Johnson worked with the Lincoln administration over the next three years, at times speaking publicly for both himself and Lincoln. Again and again he lashed out at Jefferson Davis, the president of the Confederate States. In one of his first speeches as military governor, he asked the citizens of Tennessee if they were willing to countenance "the hell of usurpation of JEFF. DAVIS." Davis, he said, was "a traitor to his country and his God, engaged in the most diabolical purpose that ever disgraced the life of man."[10]

Johnson may have hated Davis and southern slave owners, but it took him over a year as military governor before he began to present himself as an abolitionist and supporter of emancipation. He said in spring 1862, "I believe that slaves should be in subordination, and will live and die so believing." Delivering a stump speech in Baltimore in March 1863, he proclaimed to a proslavery crowd: "I am no abolitionist." He would make similar statements over the next several months. As military governor Johnson focused on developing a loyal white citizenry. He insisted on the need to punish secessionist traitors, even as he began to develop an argument that would become central to his presidency: that the Constitution did not allow for the possibility of secession, and for that reason secession had never legally occurred. "I hold to my theory that no State can secede. The Union was to be perpetual," he asserted in a February 1863 speech in Indianapolis.[11] Convinced that the states had never actually seceded, he would maintain during his presidency that they should simply be restored to the Union, not reconstructed.

Johnson was doing more than developing constitutional arguments; he was putting on a show. He may have been anathema in many parts of Tennessee, but he was becoming wildly popular north of the Mason-Dixon Line. His speech in Indianapolis on the fine points of secession is a good example. He had been invited to speak at the statehouse by Governor Oliver Morton, who publicized the upcoming occasion in an effort to mobilize support for the Lincoln administration. According to conservative estimates, Johnson attracted a crowd of at least twenty-five thousand; others put the crowd at over thirty thousand. The *Indianapolis Journal* reported that people began to gather in Indianapolis the day before the speech, and that "train after train swelled the vast assemblage" until "there was not a spare bed . . . in any hotel, nor in many private houses, and hundreds had to sit up all night in hotel parlors sleeping in chairs." The next day Johnson spoke from a podium on the statehouse grounds to an enthusiastic crowd that filled the three stands erected for his visit and overflowed onto adjacent streets. He typically had no problem projecting his voice, but under these circumstances few could hear what he had to say. Still, the excitement of his visit was palpable. According to an observer quoted in the *New York Times*, "faces upturned to the stand, as if their bodies were one huge chunk on which faces had been glued, like shells on a fancy basket, as thickly as they could stick."[12] It's odd to think of Johnson in the company of compelling nineteenth-century orators like Daniel Webster and Frederick Douglass, but his skills as a speaker had helped to build his career, and there were few who were more charismatic during the Civil War.

Early in 1863, Johnson began quietly to raise questions about Lincoln's conduct of the war. Like Douglass and other African American critics of the president, Johnson thought Lincoln moved too slowly in deploying the full force of the Union army against the secessionists. He wanted Lincoln to take charge and "crush the rebellion." Recognizing the need for forceful action, Lincoln, who had been lobbied on the issue by African Americans, decided that northern free Blacks could serve in the Union army. A March 1863 letter from Lincoln to Johnson suggests that the military governor was considering doing something similar in Tennessee. "I am told you have at least *thought* of raising a negro military force," Lincoln wrote Johnson. "If you *have* been thinking of it please do not dismiss the thought."[13]

Johnson hesitated on recruiting African Americans, but in a speech delivered in Nashville in August 1863, he announced for the first time that he was opposed to slavery. Using the vivid language of disease, he asserted that "slavery was a cancer on our society and the scalpel of the statesman should be used not simply to pare away the exterior and leave the roots to propagate the disease anew, but to remove it altogether." He called for "immediate emancipation" even when speaking in Tennessee, a state that had not been covered by Lincoln's Emancipation Proclamation because it was under Union control. Johnson's antislavery position emerged from his anger at the southern slave owners who promoted secession, but adopting antislavery also served his political ambitions. Having seen slavery firsthand, he may have also come to hate the institution, particularly as practiced on plantations. Lincoln in a letter of September 11 praised Johnson for "declar[ing] in favor of emancipation in Tennessee," and urged him once again to recruit Black troops. One week later, Johnson wrote Secretary of War Edwin M. Stanton that he had begun doing exactly that.[14]

Johnson's August 1863 antislavery speech in Nashville circulated widely in newspapers. Republicans admired him for reaching out to African Americans and encouraging white southerners to adjust to a world without slavery, all of which helped to propel him to the vice presidential nomination the next year. In a November 1863 report to the Freedmen's Inquiry Commission, established by Secretary of War Stanton, Johnson stated that he wanted Blacks working for wages, and acknowledged, with irony at his own expense, the heroic work of Tennessee's three regiments of African American troops: "They have performed much better than I expected. I was very agreeably disappointed." In this report and subsequent speeches, Johnson urged whites to hire Blacks as a way of transforming the South. As he explained in a January 1864 speech to whites in Nashville: "Hire your negroes to work for you, and you will find that they will do better labor for you than when they were slaves. By this means you will do your part in this great transition to teach them self-reliance." Speaking in Knoxville several months later, he challenged his white auditors: "What right have I, what right have you, to hold a fellow-man in bondage, except for crime? What right have you to use his labor without compensation?"[15] Johnson's reference to the African American as "fellow-man" signaled how far he had come from the days when he was defending slavery.

In a letter to Lincoln of April 5, 1864, Johnson offered his full and unconditional support for a constitutional amendment abolishing slavery. Two months later, Lincoln made the bold decision to ask a southern Democrat—albeit a Union Democrat—to run as his vice president, replacing the incumbent, Hannibal Hamlin of Maine. Republican Party leaders—who at that time chose the vice presidential as well as the presidential nominee—agreed with Lincoln that a North-South geographic balance would maximize the president's chances in what many believed was going to be a failed bid for a second term. Assistant presidential secretary John Hay noted in his diary Lincoln's pragmatic reason for taking on a new vice president: "Lincoln rather prefers Johnson or some other War Democrat as calculated to give more strength to the ticket."[16]

As Lincoln hoped and expected, Johnson played an important role in adding to the appeal of what the Republicans now temporarily called the National Union Party. Antislavery Republicans admired the way that the southerner Johnson boldly castigated the slave South. When he accepted the vice-presidential nomination, Johnson spoke in no uncertain terms about the need to punish leaders of the Confederacy, an "aristocracy" of slave owners whom he blamed for the crisis of the Civil War. He praised the South's "loyal citizens," and he reiterated his support for emancipation and the principles of free labor. "I desire that all men shall have a fair start and an equal chance in the race of life," he proclaimed to the delegates, "and let him succeed who has the most merit."[17] Johnson's use of the word "equal" is significant here, but does not elucidate how far he believed equality should go.

The themes of Johnson's acceptance speech became staples of his remarks on the campaign trail. He was certainly capable of racist talk about African Americans, but he continued to emphasize the principles of equality, as when he asserted at Gallatin, Tennessee, that he "was for the negro having a chance—a fair chance."[18]

He moved into high gear as he campaigned through towns in the Midwest. Traditionally, vice presidential candidates did not go on the hustings, but Johnson, with his resounding voice and love of addressing large crowds, served the National Union Party well. He regularly drew hundreds if not thousands to his speeches. In Logansport, Indiana, he denounced "Jeff. Davis' war" and rejected any compromise that would sustain slavery in the United States. He had spent his life in a slave state, he told the crowd, but slavery needed to come to an end. Speaking in a state whose whites hardly warmed to its few African Americans, Johnson took risks in asserting that southern Blacks, most of whom were enslaved, deserved fair wages for their work. He even affirmed his commitment to what he called a social "experiment" in cross-racial equality in the marketplace. He said nevertheless, as most white leaders of the South regularly did, that the United States was and should remain "a white man's government."[19] But how long would it remain a white man's government if African Americans had the opportunities he was calling for?

"Your Moses"

Johnson's various remarks on emancipation and Black liberty culminated in his most famous speech on Black liberation. He delivered what became known as his "Moses of the Colored Men" speech on October 24, 1864, outside the capitol in Nashville to several thousand of the city's African Americans, who had marched in a torchlight procession to his residence in a show of support for the Lincoln-Johnson ticket. Assembling outside the capitol, they called on the military governor to speak, and with two weeks remaining before the presidential election, Johnson rose to the occasion. He had a flair for improvisation and, according to reporters on the scene, spoke spontaneously for over an hour, imagining a new day for the Black people of Tennessee. Positioning himself as a radical in relation to the moderate Lincoln, he asserted that the Emancipation Proclamation was limited, that it needed to be applied to border states like Tennessee. Caught up with the excitement of the unscripted occasion and sensing the warmth of those assembled, Johnson made a surprising announcement that he probably hadn't thought about until that very moment. "I, too, without reference to the President or any other person," he said, "have a proclamation to make; and standing here upon the steps of the Capitol, with the past history of the State to witness, I, Andrew Johnson, do hereby proclaim freedom, full, broad and unconditional, to every man in Tennessee!" This was an extraordinary proclamation, and the crowd cheered his every word, surprised and delighted by what was essentially an "illegal" action of unilaterally offering freedom to all Blacks in Tennessee before consulting with Lincoln.[20]

In this emancipation speech, Johnson also offered an insightful analysis of the evils of slavery that echoed the critiques of Harriet Beecher Stowe and other notable antislavery writers. As was typical of his recent orations, he spoke harshly about white slave owners, especially those who ran plantations, referring to them as "this damnable aristocracy." He further charged slave owners with the crime of rape, noting that on their plantations "you see as many mulatto as negro children, the former bearing an unmistakable resemblance to their aristocratic owners!" Johnson now promised the Black men in the crowd that "your wives and daughters shall no longer be dragged into a concubinage, compared to which polygamy is a virtue, to satisfy the brutal lusts of slaveholders and overseers!" And he made promises to the Black women in attendance as well: "Henceforth the sanctity of God's holy law of marriage shall be respected in your persons, and the

great State of Tennessee shall no more give her sanction to your degradation and your shame!" Consistent with these sentiments, Johnson decreed that Tennessee's African Americans would have the same
right to marry as white people, an extraordinary gesture at a time
when slave states refused to recognize the legality of Black marriage.
A reporter on the scene described the wildly enthusiastic response as
the crowd took in Johnson's unprecedented promises: "'Thank God!
thank God' came from the lips of a thousand women, who in their
own persons had experienced the hellish iniquity of the man-seller's
code. 'Thank God!' fervently echoed the fathers, husbands, brothers
of those women."[21]

Johnson's speech then took an even more startling turn. Looking
to the future, he told the Blacks assembled outside his capitol residence
that they needed an exemplary leader. Drawing on the long tradition
of reading Exodus as a freedom document, he offered his hope to the
crowd that, "as in the days of old, a Moses might arise who should
lead them safely to their promised land of freedom and happiness."
Johnson's mention of Moses initiated a call and response between the
white military governor and his Black auditors: "'You are our Moses,'
shouted several voices and the exclamation was caught up and cheered
until the Capitol rung again." Hearing that adulatory response, Johnson repeated his call for a Moses and clarified that he meant a Black
Moses. With God's help, he said, "in due time your leader will come
forth; your Moses will be revealed to you." A reporter described the
response to that proposition: "'We want no Moses but you,' again
shouted the crowd." Johnson considered that plea, which seemingly
came from many voices, and (in)famously responded: "Well, then, . . .
humble and unworthy as I am, if no other better shall be found, I will
indeed be your Moses, and lead you through the Red Sea of war and
bondage, to a fairer future of liberty and peace."[22]

This was a stunning moment in Johnson's career, and he knew it.
He took great pride in the love and admiration that he apparently
elicited from the assembled Black Nashvillians. Over the next ten
years, he would refer to the speech whenever anyone questioned his

commitment to equal rights for African Americans. Having evident demagogic tendencies, he no doubt loved hearing the adulation of the multitude in response to his simultaneously paternalistic and radical speech.[23] It was paternalistic in the way he spoke from on high, as military governor, to the Blacks at the capitol; it reinforced hierarchy in the way of a master speaking to his slaves. As suggested by the Moses imagery, Johnson offered top-down beneficence and edicts, as if from Mount Pisgah. But at this particular moment in his history, the speech, with its call-and-response spontaneity, also conveyed something positive about the man that was radical for its time and place. It suggested the promise of Reconstruction. Johnson seemed genuinely to care about the Black people he was addressing and to be proposing new ways of thinking about race relations in the South.

For these very reasons, the Moses speech was not well received by the white people of Tennessee. The local newspapers vilified Johnson. The *Nashville Dispatch* wondered about the state of his mental health, while the *Nashville Daily Press* claimed that the military governor could no longer be trusted because of his abolitionism and concerns for Black people. As for the upcoming presidential election, the *Daily Press* remarked that "whoever thinks a nigger as good as a poor white man" should vote for the ticket of Lincoln and Johnson.[24]

Abolitionists responded to the widely circulating speech very differently. They took it as a sincere expression of concern for African Americans, and all the more remarkable coming from a southern leader. William Lloyd Garrison's abolitionist *The Liberator* ran an article on "Andrew Johnson's Great Speech to the Colored People," and the *National Anti-Slavery Standard* lauded the "great Tribune" who received "the blessings of the oppressed and poor." The Philadelphia-based *Christian Recorder*, the most influential and widely read African American newspaper of the time, hailed Johnson's proclamation to Nashville's Blacks as an epochal moment in Tennessee history that boded well for the nation that had just reelected Lincoln. Under the headline "Freedom! Freedom! Declared in Tennessee!," the newspaper rejoiced that "Governor Johnson, of Tennessee, who is now Vice

President elect of the United States, has declared 'That all men in Tennessee are now free! Free!' Three cheers for Governor Johnson, Vice President elect of the United States." The article went on to describe the scene of liberation in Nashville for its African American readers:

> It was one of those moments when the speaker seemed inspired, and when his audience, catching the inspiration, rises to his level and becomes one with him. . . . With breathless attention those sons of bondage hung upon each syllable; each individual seemed carved in stone until the last word of the grand climax was reached; and then the scene which followed beggars all description. One simultaneous roar of approval and delight burst from three thousand throats.

As described here, the occasion was something like an old-fashioned religious camp meeting. "Praised be God for his goodness," proclaimed another article in the same issue of the newspaper on Johnson's election as vice president.[25]

Johnson continued his efforts to reach out to the Blacks of Tennessee. Shortly after he and Lincoln won the election, he addressed four thousand festive African Americans who marched in another torchlight procession to his capitol residence. Working on the assumption that his October speech had freed all of the enslaved people of Tennessee, he now offered guidance on the challenges and pitfalls of freedom, instructing the assembled Blacks that they had "the opportunity of laboring for yourselves and families, and enjoying the wages of your honest labor." Like the many African American leaders who embraced temperance reform, Johnson urged those at the capitol to resist spending their hard-earned money on alcohol for a "drunken revel." As he had in other antislavery speeches, he addressed the issue of Black women's sexual vulnerability, asserting that slavery was "a hot bed of prostitution, polygamy and concubinage," and he concluded with impassioned words about his overall concern for Black people: "If in this world there throbs a heart inspired with the love of freedom, I claim that heart beats in this bosom. I claim the wide world as my home, and every honest man, be he white or colored, as my brother."[26] In retrospect, given his later resistance to Radical Reconstruction, Johnson's 1864 speeches to Nashville's Blacks might be taken as hypocritical. But this was 1864, with the war still on, and his words matched his strong antislavery politics of the time.

Johnson remained loyal to the antislavery cause. Addressing the Union State Convention in January 1865, he urged the group working on Tennessee's new constitution "to submit a proposition to abolish slavery, and deny the power to the Legislature to revive it in all future time." He also called for equality for all under the law, insisting that Black criminals should be punished "by the same laws that you have to punish white criminals." In a letter to Lincoln on the convention, Johnson proudly reported that the more than five hundred delegates "unanimously adopted an amendment to the Constitution forever banning Slavery in this State." He happily predicted in a speech to the convention that "five years from now the labor of the black man will be more productive than ever, for freedom simply means liberty to work and enjoy the products of one's labor." Up to the time he moved to Washington to assume the vice presidency, Johnson remained on excellent terms with Nashville's African Americans. Just before he made his move, a contingent of Black leaders gave him a gold watch, engraved with gratitude for his "*Untiring Energy in the Cause of Freedom.*"[27]

Andrew Johnson, the new vice president in attendance at Lincoln's second inauguration, was viewed as something of a southern anomaly. He had risked his life to express his antislavery and anti-secessionist views and had received the reward he was probably looking for: a path to the presidency. Ironically, given his eventual rejection of their vision of Reconstruction, Radical Republicans at the time regarded him as a more promising leader than Lincoln. And to add to the irony, for a few years during the Civil War, Johnson's ideas about antislavery, Black freedom, and the need to punish southern traitors aligned with those of the very man who would write in 1881 that Johnson's glance at the second inauguration conveyed nothing but racial hatred.

Johnson's bold political decisions and impassioned rhetoric led him to the White House for that inauguration. Douglass, whose politics of Reconstruction would dramatically depart from Johnson's, took his own risks and developed his own bold positions on race and the Civil War to earn an invitation to the celebratory event.

2

THE MISSION OF THE WAR

FREDERICK DOUGLASS'S ATTENDANCE at Lincoln's second inauguration was even more improbable than Johnson's. Born into slavery in 1818 on the Eastern Shore of Maryland, Douglass had the good fortune of being sent as a boy to Baltimore to reside with his owner's brother and family. He moved back and forth between the Eastern Shore and Baltimore during much of his time in slavery. Baltimore opened up new opportunities for the young Douglass. He taught himself to read and write, in part by tricking local white boys into helping him, and got his first glimpse of the world beyond the slave plantation. While in Baltimore, he met his future wife, the free Black Anna Murray, and plotted his escape from slavery. Disguised as a sailor, he made his way to New York City in 1838. He and Anna married there, and then the couple traveled on to New Bedford, Massachusetts, where he found work as a caulker in a shipyard and served as a lay minister.

Douglass's life took a permanent turn in August 1841 when he rose to speak at an antislavery gathering in Nantucket. The white abolitionist leader William Lloyd Garrison, who edited the antislavery newspaper *The Liberator*, famously described his response to Douglass's impromptu remarks:

> I shall never forget his first speech at the convention—the extraordinary emotion it excited in my own mind—the powerful impression it created upon a crowded auditory, completely taken by surprise—the applause which followed from the beginning to the end of his felicitous remarks. I think I never hated slavery so intensely as at that moment.[1]

Garrison was so struck by Douglass's eloquence that he signed him up as a paid speaker for his Massachusetts Anti-Slavery Society.

From 1841 to 1845, Douglass lectured throughout the Northeast and Midwest, addressing his personal experience as an enslaved person in the larger context of the debate on slavery in the United States. At a little over six feet tall, and with a voice, as one observer described, of "terrific power, of great compass, and under most admirable control," Douglass emerged as Garrison's most popular speaker.[2] In response to skeptics who said that no one as rhetorically gifted and knowledgeable as Douglass could have been enslaved for the first twenty years of his life, he wrote his autobiographical *Narrative of the Life of Frederick Douglass, An American Slave*, which Garrison published in 1845. The book became a best seller, and its success ironically made life precarious for Douglass, who was still a fugitive from slavery. In the fall of 1845 he sailed to Liverpool in order to avoid fugitive-slave hunters, and during his twenty-one months abroad in the British Isles he became an international celebrity. His British supporters purchased him out of slavery in 1846, and Douglass returned to the United States in 1847 with money from his benefactors for a printing press. Convinced that Black people needed their own antislavery newspaper, he founded the *North Star*, in Rochester, New York. At the same time, he began the process of breaking from Garrison, who was infuriated by Douglass's decision to publish a competing antislavery newspaper.

The Douglass-Garrison feud illuminates Douglass's political growth during the 1840s. When he joined Garrison's organization, Douglass signed on to the key tenets of Garrisonian antislavery: immediate abolition; nonviolent resistance, or what Garrison called moral suasion; and a belief that the U.S. Constitution was a proslavery document. Viewing the Constitution as proslavery meant that Garrisonian abolitionists had a moral duty *not* to participate in the political process, for they believed that voting was an act of complicity in a proslavery nation. But during the late 1840s, Douglass began to have second thoughts about moral suasion, arguing that the violence of slavery might demand a violent response. He also came to believe that the Constitution was in spirit an antislavery document. From such a perspective, political abolitionism—working for social change by electing antislavery politicians to office—made good sense. Around the time the Senate passed the Compromise of 1850, which included a strengthened Fugitive Slave Act, Douglass announced his break from Garrison, his own revised interpretation of the Constitution as an antislavery document, and his new association with political abolitionists such as Gerrit Smith, a New York abolitionist and philanthropist who helped to fund Douglass's newspaper, now called *Frederick Douglass' Paper*, during the 1850s.[3]

Following the Compromise of 1850, Douglass gave speeches and wrote editorials on his willingness to use violence to resist the Fugitive Slave Act, which mandated the return of escaped enslaved people to their owners. As a speaker, he continued to impress with his rhetorical skill and commanding presence. Like Andrew Johnson, Douglass was sartorially elegant, typically appearing in waistcoat, vest, and cravat. He knew how to speak to different audiences in different modes, ranging from the personal to the politically analytical to the biblically prophetic. He was also known as an excellent mimic who could do comical impressions of proslavery southerners. In 1852 the Black abolitionist William G. Allen wrote that "in versatility of oratorical power, I know of no one who can begin to approach the celebrated Frederick Douglass." Douglass, Allen said, "touches chords in

Frederick Douglass, 1852. Daguerreotype by Samuel J. Miller. (*Courtesy of the Art Institute of Chicago / Art Resource, NY.*)

the inner chambers thereof which vibrate music now sweet, now sad, now lightsome, now solemn, now startling, now grand, now majestic, now sublime."[4]

As a popular speaker and essayist, Douglass spent much time during the early to mid-1850s contesting the Fugitive Slave Act. At an August 1850 convention in Cazenovia, New York, Douglass referred to fugitive-slave hunters as "heartless pirates." Long past his moral-suasion phase, he expressed his pleasure in a June 1854 issue of his newspaper that one such hunter had been killed while attempting to capture a fugitive in Boston. He said that the man's "slaughter was as innocent, in the sight of God, as would be the slaughter of a ravenous wolf in the act of throttling an infant."[5]

When President Franklin Pierce signed into law the Kansas-Nebraska Act of 1854, which allowed the settlers themselves to decide whether the new states would be slave or free, Douglass supported the white antislavery militant John Brown's paramilitary actions in the ensuing conflict known as "Bleeding Kansas." In 1856, Brown massacred proslavery settlers and their children at Pottawatomie Creek in Kansas. Following the Supreme Court's infamous 1857 ruling in the *Dred Scott* case that people of African descent could never become U.S. citizens and, in the words of Chief Justice Roger B. Taney, "had no rights which the white man was bound to respect,"[6] Brown began to plot an armed attack on the federal arsenal at Harpers Ferry, Virginia. He hoped that such an attack would spark a widespread slave revolt. Brown met with Douglass in Chambersburg, Pennsylvania, and attempted to recruit him to the cause, but Douglass declined to participate in what he feared would be a suicidal mission. Douglass correctly anticipated the outcome: Brown led the raid in October 1859, and ten of his twenty-two compatriots, including two of his sons, were killed. Brown himself was captured and executed, a martyr to the cause whose bravery inspired further antislavery activity in the Northeast. Douglass, as his known associate, fled to England in order to avoid prosecution as a co-conspirator. For many Americans, including Douglass, Brown's assault on Harpers Ferry signaled the prospect of greater violence to come. When that violence broke out, following the election of Lincoln and the South Carolina militia's artillery shelling of Fort Sumter, Douglass embraced the Civil War as a war of emancipation that promised to bring about Black equality in the United States.

As a political abolitionist, Douglass supported Abraham Lincoln and the Republican Party, but he quickly became disillusioned with Lincoln, whom he saw as a president with no real interest in bringing about the end of slavery. In a November 1861 editorial, he referred to the "pro-slavery interference of President LINCOLN," and in a letter to antislavery leader Gerrit Smith a month later, he remarked: "I am bewildered by the spectacle of moral blindness—infatuation and helpless imbicelety [*sic*] which the Government of Lincoln presents."[7] During most of 1862, Douglass expressed little faith in Lincoln, denouncing him in September when the president met with a visiting Black delegation and appeared to support colonizing tens of thousands of African Americans to the southern Americas. Some African American leaders, most notably Martin R. Delany, had advocated Black emigration to Central America and Africa, making a distinction between white-sponsored programs to rid the nation of African Americans by shipping them to such places as Liberia, and African American–led movements in which Blacks chose their own destinations for their own reasons. Douglass throughout his career rejected emigration and colonization alike, arguing that African Americans deserved to be citizens of the nation they had helped to build.[8]

A shift in Douglass's view of Lincoln occurred when the president issued the Emancipation Proclamation on New Year's Day 1863. Delighted with the president's action, Douglass predicted that celebrations of the proclamation "shall take rank with the Fourth of July."[9] Lincoln's decision in early 1863 to recruit Black troops for the Union army also pleased Douglass. Two of his own sons, Lewis Henry and Charles Remond, joined the renowned 54th Massachusetts Volunteer Infantry Regiment, and Douglass helped to recruit hundreds, if not thousands, of African Americans into the army. He met with Lincoln at the White House for the first time in August 1863, and told the president that the Black troops should be paid the same as the white troops. Though Lincoln was unwilling to change the pay scale right away, in part because of popular prejudice against Black people, he promised that in the future the pay would be equal. Douglass was favorably impressed by the president's directness and honesty, and in a speech of December 1863 predicted, "While Abraham Lincoln will not go down to posterity as Abraham the Great, or Abraham the Wise, or Abraham the Eloquent, although he is all three, wise, great, and eloquent, he will go down to posterity, if the country is saved, as Honest Abraham."[10] Despite this praise, Douglass was a year or more away from giving Lincoln his complete support. Douglass remained concerned that Lincoln was prepared to end the war by making a deal with the Confederacy to preserve slavery, and he believed (probably correctly) that Lincoln had not yet begun to think about the process of postwar reconstruction.

As early as 1862, Douglass had begun his own thinking about how to reconstruct the nation. He imagined both the end of slavery and the achievement of equal rights for African Americans in all regions of the country. In "The Work of the Future," published in the November 1862 issue of his newspaper, he conveyed a vision of a reconstructed United States that anticipated the Radical Republicans' agenda during the Johnson presidency. He called for the federal government to help the freedpeople by legislating educational programs and protective measures in the South, and especially by ensuring that they had "equal rights before the law." Slavery might soon be abolished, but Douglass knew it would not go away quickly. He asked large and prophetic questions about the precarious situation of Black people in a defeated South, and warned that racism and the vestiges of slavery could continue to govern white-Black relations, making even liberated Blacks "the slaves of the community at large, having no rights which any body is required to respect."[11] His deliberate echo of the words of Judge Taney's ruling in the 1857 *Dred Scott* case conveyed his concerns that even with changes made on paper, whites might continue to treat the freedpeople as if they were enslaved. To prevent that, activist federal intervention and oversight would be in order.

Douglass further developed his views on the Civil War and what came to be known as Reconstruction in one of his greatest speeches, "The Mission of the War," which he first delivered in late 1863 and continued to present in revised versions at numerous venues through 1864. Speaking mainly to white audiences, he presented the war not only as a fight for abolition but also as "a great national opportunity" for social change that Lincoln so far had failed to embrace. Douglass had been enraged by Lincoln's August 1862 statement to Horace Greeley, the editor of the *New York Daily Tribune*, that "if I could save the Union without freeing *any* slave I would do it, and if I could save it by freeing *all* the slaves I would do it." Douglass was further angered by Lincoln's assertion in his December 1863 annual message to Congress that "the general government had no lawful power to effect emancipation in any state." In "The Mission of the War," Douglass lamented that "policy, everlasting policy, has robbed our statesmanship of all soul-moving utterances," and he affirmed what the mission of the war should be: "immediate and unconditional emancipation in all the States," as well as programs to "invest the black man everywhere with the right to vote and to be voted for, and remove all discriminations against his rights on account of his color, whether as a citizen or as a soldier." In a nation in which Black men were denied the vote in most states, even in the North, Midwest, and West, this was a radical agenda, the success of which, given "the national prejudice and hatred toward the colored people of the country," would depend on more than just Lincoln.[12]

The goals that Douglass set forth in his "Mission of the War" speech—emancipation and full rights of citizenship for all African Americans—had long been central to Black abolitionism. The first Black convention that Douglass attended, in Buffalo in August 1843, addressed the topic of African Americans' *"Moral and Political Condition as American Citizens."* At a Black convention held in Rochester in July 1853, which he sponsored, Douglass took up similar issues in his keynote speech. He said that the nation's Black people "are" and "ought to be *American citizens.*" The convention approved the following resolution: "Resolved, That we, as American citizens, are entitled to the right of elective franchise, in common with the white men of this country."[13]

The most important Black convention during the Civil War took place in October 1864, when over one hundred delegates from seventeen states convened in Syracuse, New York, for an extended conversation about Reconstruction and Black citizenship. As at the 1853 Rochester convention, Douglass assumed a leadership role, but from beginning to end he worked with such notable African American activists as Henry Highland Garnet, John Mercer Langston, William Howard Day, George Vashon, the novelist William Wells Brown, the caterer and Underground Railroad worker George T. Downing (who would join Douglass in visiting Andrew Johnson at the White House early in 1866), and the poet, fiction writer, essayist, and lecturer Frances Ellen Watkins Harper.

At the convention, Douglass, Langston, and Garnet took the lead in cofounding a new Black organization called the National Equal Rights League, dedicated to promoting citizenship rights for African Americans. The matter of equal rights was crucial to the convention's discussions of possible Reconstruction measures months before the end of the Civil War. Langston spoke about how "he was a believer in the Declaration of American Independence," and celebrated the principles of equality for all Americans. Garnet, who in early 1865 would become the first African American to lecture in the halls of Congress, described the horrors of the New York City draft riots of July 1863, in which white working-class men, angered about being drafted to fight in the Civil War, brutally killed over sixty African Americans in Lower Manhattan. In Garnet's view, Reconstruction necessitated working for Blacks' rights in both the North and South. Frances Harper "spoke feelingly and eloquently of our hopes and prospects in our country," envisioning the possibility of African Americans achieving legal equality. George T. Downing sharply criticized the American Colonization Society and agreed with Douglass that African Americans deserved citizenship in the United States. The delegates clashed on various points, but reached consensus, as set forth in the convention's "Declarations of Wrongs and Rights," that U.S. Blacks should be "citizens of the Republic" and have the same "immunities and privileges of all other citizens and defenders of the nation's honor."[14] They also agreed that what kept African Americans from having full rights as citizens was not the actions of a few people or of a particular section (the slaveholding South) but the racism that Blacks experienced on a daily basis in all regions of the country.

In his closing speech as the convention's elected president, Douglass addressed that racism, along with the issues, tensions, and difficulties that he imagined would accompany the grand effort to reconstruct the nation. Saluting his "FELLOW-CITIZENS," and speaking "for our race," Douglass once again called for Black citizenship, including suffrage, declaring that at the very least, the two hundred thousand Black men who fought in the Union army had earned the right to vote. "Are we good enough to use bullets, and not good enough to use ballots?" he demanded. Anticipating a Union victory, Douglass suggestively pointed to the problems the freedpeople would be facing in the South, a section that Douglass predicted would retain "a sullen hatred" toward the federal government and Black people, who would be blamed for the war. The best way to fight back against such hate, Douglass advised, was to "give the elective franchise to every colored man of the South . . . and you have at once four millions of friends who will guard with their vigilance, and, if need be, defend with their arms, the ark of Federal Liberty from the treason and pollution of her enemies."[15]

Most white southerners feared that the "four millions" would take control of southern politics. The fear on Douglass's side, which anticipated issues he would address during the Johnson presidency, was that "Jefferson Davis and his Confederate associates, either in person or by their representatives, return once more to the seats in the halls of Congress,—and you will then see your dead slavery the most living and powerful thing in the country."[16] Douglass's apprehension about Confederates retaining power in southern state legislatures would be borne out almost immediately during the first few months of the Johnson presidency.

Even as Douglass envisioned the possibilities of a reconstructed United States in which African Americans had equal rights as citizens, he continued to distrust Lincoln. He criticized the Emancipation Proclamation for failing to offer liberty to the enslaved people of the border states that remained within the Union—Missouri, Kentucky, Delaware, and Maryland—and he warned that Lincoln, the man who regularly declared that his main goal was to preserve the Union, was "not only ready to make peace with the Rebels, but to make peace with slavery also."[17]

Ten Percent Plan

Like many at the Syracuse convention, and many Radical Republicans, Douglass objected to a plan that the president had proposed
months earlier. Dubbed the Ten Percent Plan, it required just 10 percent of the number of an ex-Confederate state's 1860 voters to swear
allegiance to the Union for that state to be readmitted. Debate on the
Ten Percent Plan spanned much of 1864 and remained a point of contention between the Radical Republicans and Lincoln into the early
months of 1865. The plan also had an impact on Johnson's thinking
about Reconstruction and sheds additional light on the perspectives
of Douglass, Johnson, and Lincoln at the time of Lincoln's March
1865 inauguration.

Lincoln first proposed the Ten Percent Plan as part of his Proclamation of Amnesty and Reconstruction of December 1863. He wanted
to restore to the Union any ex-Confederate state willing to create a
new government prohibiting slavery. He was prepared to offer pardons, even to some high-ranking Confederates, as long as they took a
loyalty oath and renounced slavery. Douglass was incensed that Lincoln said nothing about helping the freed Black people of these states
and made no demands on the 10 percent to approve governments that
would allow Black suffrage. In spring 1864, a group of Louisianans
loyal to the Union, approximately 10 percent of the 1860 voting population, developed the sort of constitution that Lincoln requested and
quickly gained the president's support. The group's initiative led to a
debate in Congress about readmitting a formerly Confederate state
that basically remained as it was, except without slavery, and with up
to 90 percent of its white male electorate opposed to the new constitution. Andrew Johnson wanted firmer loyalty oaths. Congress joined
Douglass in calling for Black suffrage before there would be any consideration of readmission. As Douglass observed at the Syracuse convention and other venues into 1865, Lincoln's willingness to admit

Louisiana under these terms would have legitimized the continued disenfranchisement of Black men.

Congress responded to Lincoln's Ten Percent Plan by significantly modifying it, passing the Wade-Davis Bill on July 2, 1864. That bill, sponsored by Radical Republicans Benjamin Wade of Ohio and Henry Winter Davis of Maryland, mandated that the readmission of any ex-Confederate state to the Union should be delayed until at least 50 percent of its white male voters swore allegiance to a Union without slavery. The bill also called for a more forceful loyalty oath and rejected mass pardons of former Confederate leaders. Most important, the bill added a key element that was not part of Lincoln's plan: Black suffrage. Lincoln wanted to restore Louisiana; Congress wanted to reconstruct Louisiana.

Lincoln infuriated the Radical Republicans in Congress, and many Black activists, by pocket-vetoing the Wade-Davis Bill, refusing to sign it after Congress ended its session on July 4. This veto-by-default ensured that the bill would not become law. Using the kind of language that the Radical Republicans would eventually deploy against Johnson, Wade and Davis in early August issued a defiant manifesto on Lincoln's killing of the bill. They railed against what they termed his "dictatorial" efforts to restore Louisiana under his Ten Percent Plan, and questioned his antislavery credentials. The *New York Times* denounced the manifesto for its "arrogance and presumption," warning that it would lead to the defeat of Lincoln in the upcoming presidential election. The debate on the Ten Percent Plan, Louisiana, and the Wade-Davis Bill continued into 1865, with Wade and Davis holding firm to the principle that "the authority of Congress is paramount, and must be respected." Lincoln thought otherwise, and worked on the assumption that the executive branch should oversee policies that would restore the states to the Union.[18] Lincoln himself anticipated, and even set the groundwork for, Andrew Johnson's notion of presidential restoration.

In a letter to an English friend printed in a September 1864 issue of *The Liberator*, Douglass offered a devastating critique of the Lincoln administration as intent on keeping the United States as it always had been—a white supremacist nation that refused to give equal rights to African Americans. Douglass claimed that Lincoln was "practically re-establishing that hateful system [slavery] in Louisiana" by not including Black suffrage. He complained that the Lincoln administration continued to deny Black Union army soldiers equal pay, and wondered about Lincoln's moral vision, which he summarized as "Do evil by choice, right from necessity." He concluded the letter by deriding Lincoln for failing to propose initiatives that would "extend the elective franchise to the coloured people of the South." Lincoln, Douglass said, was prepared "to hand the negro back to the political power of his master, without a single element of strength to shield himself from the vindictive spirit sure to be roused against the whole coloured race."[19] By late 1865, Douglass would be saying the same thing about Johnson.

Publicly, Douglass began to soften his criticism of Lincoln, apprehensive that the racist and reactionary Democrat George B. McClellan might win the presidential election. But in a private letter of October 1864 to the New York abolitionist Theodore Tilton, Douglass expressed his lingering unease about the president. He informed Tilton that Lincoln wanted the enslaved people of the South to cross enemy lines and fight on the Union side, but that the president had no interest in the many who were too far south to be able to do that, which would mean *"that such only of them as succeeded in getting within our lines would be free after the war was over."*[20] The rest of the South's enslaved people, Douglass feared, would be abandoned by a president willing to cut a deal with the Confederacy in order to preserve the Union.

Douglass came to support Lincoln because of the threat posed by McClellan. But he remained concerned that what he and other African American activists regarded as a large aim of the war—to make Blacks equal citizens of the United States—was not shared by Lincoln. In prominent lectures in late 1864 and early 1865, Douglass continued to speak out against the president's seeming lack of support for Blacks' civil rights. In a speech delivered before the Massachusetts Anti-Slavery Society in January 1865, he repeated what he had said in "The Mission of the War," his Syracuse convention address, and his various critiques of Lincoln's rejection of the Wade-Davis Bill: "I am for the 'immediate, unconditional and universal' enfranchisement of the black man, in every State of the Union. . . . Without this, his liberty is a mockery; without this, you might as well almost retain the old name of slavery for his condition."[21] The "you" of the speech was implicitly directed, at least in part, at Lincoln.

As Douglass's criticism of Lincoln suggests, Lincoln and Johnson had surprisingly similar visions of Reconstruction in the early months of 1865. Both thought that the Confederate states had never actually left the Union and thus could be restored to it without the dramatic social changes—such as Black suffrage—that the Radical Republicans imagined as part of Reconstruction. They also both believed that it was the president's job, not Congress's, to oversee that restoration. Viewed in this light, the failure of the Johnson presidency could be blamed partly on Johnson's effort to continue the work of Lincoln as he understood it.

But as his second inaugural address indicated, Lincoln had come to a point where he was looking for more than simple restoration. For that reason, Douglass saw something in Lincoln that gave him hope. His warm feelings toward Lincoln in the early months of 1865 may have also been the result of his second meeting with the president in the White House, in August 1864, during which Lincoln sought advice from Douglass on how Blacks could infiltrate southern lines and encourage the enslaved people to rebel. Douglass would continue to raise questions about the president's conduct of the war, but by early 1865 he had become a gentler critic. Perhaps because of that modulation in tone, or simply because Lincoln enjoyed talking to him at the White House, Douglass got a personal invitation to attend the second inauguration.

3

"ABRAHAM LINCOLN DIES, THE REPUBLIC LIVES"

O N THE OCCASION OF Abraham Lincoln's second inauguration, Douglass wrote in his 1881 *Life and Times of Frederick Douglass*, Johnson revealed his racism in a glance, while Lincoln reached out to his Black guest as an equal. Douglass further contrasted Lincoln and Johnson on that day: "Mr. Lincoln was like one who was treading the hard and thorny path of duty and self-denial; Mr. Johnson was like one just from a drunken debauch." This characterization was not much of an exaggeration, at least with respect to March 4, 1865, for as Douglass noted, "the fact was, though it was yet early in the day, Mr. Johnson was drunk."[1] Indeed, by all accounts he was quite drunk.

Because of the rain, Johnson was sworn in as vice president in the Senate chamber. The *Congressional Globe* presented a sanitized version of Johnson's remarks that made no mention of his inebriation, and simply conveyed his thoughts on how the Confederate states had never left the Union because secession was impossible. As reported in the *Globe*, Johnson claimed that it was "the doctrine of the Federal Constitution that no State can go out of this Union; and moreover Congress cannot eject a State from this Union." This was surely a contestable point, but the *Globe* presented the pronouncement as if it had been made by a sober constitutional scholar. The *New York Times*, on the other hand, depicted Johnson as rambling, forgetful, and out of control, at one point even whispering "to a gentleman near by, sotto voce, Who is Secretary of the Navy?" After being told his name, Johnson greeted Secretary of the Navy Gideon Welles, who, in his diary entry on the inauguration, wrote that the "Vice-President elect made a rambling and strange harangue, which was listened to with pain and mortification by all his friends." As part of his harangue, Johnson claimed "that he was a plebeian—he thanked God for it." According to the *Chicago Tribune*, when Johnson took the oath of office, he boisterously elevated the Bible over his head and exclaimed: "I kiss this book before my nation of the United States."[2]

In his diary, Welles wondered whether Johnson had been drinking. Some newspaper accounts more pointedly described Johnson as intoxicated and called for his resignation. According to Secretary of the Treasury Hugh McCulloch, Johnson's speech was "the speech of a drunken man." Lincoln charitably told McCulloch a few days later, "I have known Andy Johnson for many years; he made a bad slip the other day, but you need not be scared; Andy ain't a drunkard." Other leading Republicans weren't so sure about that. Massachusetts senator Charles Sumner conveyed his outrage about Johnson's behavior at the inauguration to longtime abolitionist Wendell Phillips, stating that the Senate may have "to save the country on account of the intemperance of the Vice-Presdt." Sumner and fellow Massachusetts senator Henry Wilson even contemplated presenting a resolution requesting Johnson's resignation. But in anticipation of how quickly the Radical Republicans would embrace Johnson after Lincoln's death, Sumner four days later complained not about Johnson but about Lincoln, writing the German American jurist Francis Lieber that the second inaugural's "malice toward none" conciliatory attitude toward the South made him worry about the nation. The president's speech "& other things," Sumner told Lieber, "augur confusion & uncertainty in the future—with hot controversy. Alas! Alas!"[3] Sumner and his colleagues thought that Johnson would be much firmer about the need to punish southern traitors.

Johnson's supposedly hateful, racist glance at Douglass may have been the glance of a man who had been drinking and nothing more than that. Or Johnson, who embraced the paternalistic idea of being a white Moses to Black people, may not have appreciated a Black Moses. (Douglass had presented himself as a Moses figure in his Exodus-inspired second autobiography, *My Bondage and My Freedom* [1855].) What we know is that Johnson was drunk that day because he attempted to fortify himself during a sickness. In poor health during his trip from Nashville to Washington, and anxious about entering a new phase in his life, Johnson turned to alcohol to steady his nerves and give him strength for the journey. When he awoke the morning of the inauguration feeling debilitated, he drank some more.[4] There were moments in Johnson's presidency when he seemed out of control, which led his critics to recall this incident. But those later moments probably had more to do with the self-intoxicating nature of his long improvisatory speeches before large audiences.

In his 1881 autobiography, Douglass presented Lincoln in stark contrast to Johnson as a savior of the nation. But in the months leading up to the inauguration, Douglass, despite warm feelings toward Lincoln, remained disturbed that the president's Ten Percent Plan failed to include Black suffrage. Lincoln's desire to make Louisiana a test case for his policy also met with continued resistance from the Republicans in Congress. Sumner objected to Lincoln's apparent intention to use the Ten Percent Plan to restore, and not fundamentally reconstruct, Louisiana, sharing Douglass's view that Lincoln was at fault for not insisting on Black participation in Louisiana's government.[5] For Lincoln, the plan had the pragmatic virtue of making a start toward readmitting formerly Confederate states, but even Johnson saw it as limited. Like many of the Radical Republicans who would soon become his enemies, Johnson wanted a larger percentage of the southern male population offering more stringent oaths of allegiance to the U.S. government.

Lincoln's Ten Percent Plan was not adopted by Congress, but he made an effort to build support for its application to Louisiana in what has come to be known as his "Last Public Address." That address, which Lincoln delivered a little more than a month after the second inauguration, hinted at the kind of Reconstruction president he might have become—no doubt better than Johnson—even as it displayed some of the beliefs he shared with his vice president.

Lincoln gave the speech outside the White House on the evening of April 11, 1865, three days after Robert E. Lee surrendered to Ulysses S. Grant at Appomattox. As at the second inauguration, a festive atmosphere prevailed. At Lincoln's request, a band (incongruously enough) played "Dixie." In the speech itself, Lincoln focused mostly on his plan to readmit Louisiana to the Union by virtue of the 10 percent of its eligible voters who supported a new constitution abolishing slavery. Lincoln defined Reconstruction as "the re-inauguration of the national authority." As part of his canny, pragmatic approach to Reconstruction, he refused to weigh in on Johnson's notion, formerly his own, that the Confederate states had never truly seceded. Instead, he focused on the principal matter at hand: "We all agree that the seceded States, so called, are out of their proper practical relation with the Union; and that the sole object of the government, civil and military, in regard to those States is to again get them into that proper practical relation." Lincoln asserted that it would be easier to do this "without deciding, or even considering, whether these states have been out of the Union, than with it."[6]

Here Lincoln turned against one of Johnson's key tenets—that the states never seceded—but without offering anything specific about what he meant by "proper practical relation." That would have become clear had he served a full second term. Though Lincoln differed from Johnson in not wanting to make a constitutional issue of the meaning of secession, Lincoln shared his vision of restoration: he wanted to quickly readmit the ex-Confederate states as non-slaveholding states that would support the Thirteenth Amendment and the Union itself. That practical effort fell far short of the social and political transformation that Sumner and many other Republicans, both moderate and radical, wanted for the country, and far short of what Douglass had been calling for before and during the Civil War.

Lincoln was aware of his critics, however, and at a key moment in the speech he addressed their concerns. He conceded that it was "unsatisfactory to some that the elective franchise is not given to the colored man," and he shared for the first time his preference "that it were now conferred on the very intelligent, and on those who serve our cause as soldiers." Lincoln also remarked that though the proposed Louisiana State Constitution did not give African Americans the right to vote, Black suffrage remained a possibility, for Louisiana's was "a free state constitution, giving the benefit of public schools equally to black and white, and empowering the Legislature to confer the elective franchise upon the colored man." Lincoln may not have insisted on Black suffrage, but this final speech suggested he was considering a more serious Reconstruction policy. To some, however, Lincoln was only mouthing the right words about Black suffrage in the speech, but without addressing the difficult next step of how to make that happen. His last speech could be taken as a visionary statement on Black equality, or as a vacillation that offered little guidance for the future.[7]

But one consequential person in Lincoln's audience took all that Lincoln said about Black suffrage and Black equality at face value, and came away believing that Lincoln would push for "nigger citizenship" during his second term.[8] That person was the celebrated Maryland actor John Wilkes Booth, who had been contemplating plots to kidnap or assassinate Lincoln, and now, after hearing Lincoln talk about Black equality, felt confirmed in his mission to kill him.

Booth and his co-conspirators famously attacked Lincoln during a play at Ford's Theater the night of April 14, and Secretary of State William Seward at his home at the same time. Lincoln was fatally wounded by Booth's gunshot; Seward and several of his family members were stabbed, seriously but not fatally. Booth had hoped to kill Johnson as well, creating disarray in the government. At the time of the assassination, Johnson was at his boardinghouse. Guards quickly arrived on the scene to protect the vice president, and then took him to spend a few minutes with the mortally wounded president, who died the morning of April 15. Johnson became president a few hours later.

✴ Douglass may have gone back and forth on Lincoln, but the president's second inaugural address had persuaded him that Lincoln was the right president for the times. To be sure, he mythologized Lincoln in *Life and Times* by leaving out most of his criticism of the president's first term, but that was because he felt a closer allegiance to Lincoln after hearing the speech and conversing with him at the White House reception. When Douglass learned of the assassination, he was shattered, but he also tried to imagine that good would come of evil. While attending an impromptu public memorial service for Lincoln in Rochester on the day the president died, Douglass was noticed by one of the organizers, who called on him to speak. Douglass inspired the crowd with his soaring words: "I feel that though Abraham Lincoln dies, the Republic lives; (cheers;) though that great and good man, one of the noblest men [to] trod God's earth, (applause,) is struck down by the hand of the assassin, yet I know that the nation is saved and liberty established forever. (Loud applause.)"⁹ At this fraught moment, Douglass imagined Lincoln as a Christlike martyr whose death promised to bring renewed life and liberty to the country. Just a few months after Johnson became president, Douglass began to have second thoughts about this optimistic vision.

In his own inaugural remarks on April 15, 1865, Johnson modestly declared: "I feel incompetent to perform duties so important and responsible as those which have been so unexpectedly thrown upon me."¹⁰ Johnson had held a variety of offices in Tennessee. He had bravely stood his ground as an anti-secessionist and as Lincoln's military governor in the state, and he had displayed an unusual ability to reach out to African Americans. He was a self-taught constitutional scholar with years of experience in Congress, admired in the North and gaining regard in the South. In many ways Johnson seemed the perfect person to assume the presidency at this dark moment, as numerous Republicans attested publicly and privately. And yet Johnson, as Douglass would have been the first to avow later in 1865, could not have spoken truer words about his want of competence than when he was sworn in as the nation's seventeenth president.

PART TWO

---◆---

Reconstructions

4

"THERE IS NO SUCH THING AS RECONSTRUCTION"

SHORTLY AFTER Andrew Johnson assumed the presidency, James M. Thompson, a physician based in Virginia and a stranger to Johnson, wrote him with a radical suggestion. He advised him of "the advantages and propriety of appointing Frederick Douglass (or some other black American citizen of executive ability), the military governor of South Carolina." According to Thompson, such an appointment would provide "poetic justic [*sic*] as well as the punishment of that traitor state in such a consummation."[1] This is a striking letter for a number of reasons. To begin with, it reveals Douglass's high visibility in the United States beyond his abolitionist circle. More remarkable is how wrong Thompson was about Johnson. Based on Johnson's prior statements about his desire to punish southern traitors, Thompson assumed the president would be eager to humiliate an ex-Confederate state by putting a Black man in charge as military governor. He assumed as well that Johnson, the man who had proclaimed he could be a Moses to Black people, would seize the opportunity for such an appointment to fulfill his promise of leadership for African Americans. Thompson

proved mistaken on both counts, but he was not alone in misjudg-
ing Johnson.

Johnson turned out to be the absolutely wrong president for his
times, but that wasn't immediately clear to Thompson, Douglass, or
the Republicans who worked with him during his first few months
in office. Some Republicans thought Johnson would be bolder than
Lincoln in promoting Reconstruction programs that would genuinely
transform the southern states. After all, he had taken enormous risks
as a southern leader in remaining loyal to the Union and advocating
emancipation. Not only that, but Johnson's widely reprinted Moses
speech suggested that he genuinely cared about the freedpeople. For
many, this man seemed destined to take the United States to a new era
of freedom for Blacks and whites alike.

"Johnson, We Have Faith in You"

On April 15, 1865, the day of Lincoln's death and Johnson's inauguration, a group of Radical Republicans met in caucus. Republican
representative George W. Julian of Indiana, who sympathized with
the Radicals, joined the group, and in his daily journal described the
meeting as "intolerably disgusting." Such had been the anger of these
"radical men" at "Lincoln's policy of conciliation," Julian confided
to his journal, that they celebrated his death as "a god-send."[2] The
shocking notion, expressed by members of Lincoln's own party, that
the assassination was God's gift to America spoke to these Radicals'
frustrations with what they regarded as Lincoln's willingness to make
peace between the North and South by simply restoring the former
Confederate states to the Union, only without slavery. In the view of
the Radicals, who reviled Lincoln's Ten Percent Plan, that was not why
the war had been fought. They wanted a genuine Reconstruction of
the South that swept former Confederate leaders from power, confiscated property from the plantation owners, and brought political and
social equality to the freedpeople. For the Radicals who met in cau-

cus on April 15, Andrew Johnson, the man sometimes disparagingly called "the Accidental President," seemed a happy accident indeed.

Over the next few weeks, various Radicals visited Johnson at the White House and got assurances from the new president that he shared their views. Johnson could be boisterous as a speaker, but he was also known as a quiet listener who, for a while at least, kept his opinions to himself. The New York lawyer and diarist George Templeton Strong described the impeccably dressed and groomed Johnson at the time he assumed the presidency as "dignified, urbane, and self-possessed."[3] That self-possession, along with his reserve when he wasn't speaking to large groups, served his purposes, as he got people to reveal themselves. Johnson had a poker face, and it wouldn't be too much of a stretch to extend the metaphor to say that when the Radicals met with him, they showed their hands while never getting a look at his. Either that, or they fell for his bluffs. They saw and heard what they wanted, and they attended to their losses later.

One of the first visitors to Johnson was Radical Republican senator Benjamin Wade of Ohio. After talking about his hopes for Reconstruction, Wade said to the president, "Johnson, we have faith in you. By the Gods, there will be no trouble now in running the government." Impressed by Johnson's cordiality, Wade had only one concern: that the new president would favor mass executions of the former Confederates. After all, Johnson recently told District of Columbia ministers, "The time has come when you and I must understand and must teach that *treason is a crime.*"[4] At this early point in Johnson's presidency, Wade hoped that he could keep his compatriot in Reconstruction from taking a bloody vengeance on the South.

Massachusetts senator Charles Sumner met with Johnson in mid-April. A friend of Douglass's who in 1856 had nearly died from a caning on the Senate floor by proslavery South Carolina congressman Preston Brooks, Sumner had had his own troubles with Lincoln. In the summer of 1864 he wrote a friend that he hoped Lincoln *"patriotically & kindly"* would choose not to run for a second term. Following Lincoln's assassination, Sumner thought that Johnson would prove to

Charles Sumner, c. 1865.
Photograph by Matthew
B. Brady. (*Courtesy of the
Library of Congress, Prints
and Photographs Division.*)

be a good alternative to a president whose Louisiana plan suggested a
lack of interest in Black suffrage.[5]

Sumner's letters to colleagues during Johnson's first few weeks in
office conveyed his enthusiasm. Reflecting on his meeting with Johnson shortly after Lincoln's death, Sumner wrote that he "found the
new Presdt. discreet, properly reserved, but firm & determined."
Sumner made another visit to Johnson with Supreme Court Chief
Justice Salmon P. Chase, a longtime abolitionist from Ohio. They
both encouraged Johnson to voice his support for equal rights for African Americans. According to Sumner, Johnson was "sympathetic in
manner" and seemingly on their side. Sumner visited the president a
few days after this meeting, and Johnson, the politician who sought
to please in the moment, told the senator that as far as Black suffrage was concerned, "there is no difference between us; you and I are
alike." Sumner felt "joy and gratitude that the President had taken
this position," and as he later confided, "felt that the battle of his own

life was ended." Sumner subsequently wrote the Duchess of Argyll, a long-standing abolitionist, about his great admiration for the new president; and in a letter to the British radical John Bright he passed along the most hopeful news of all: "I am satisfied that he is the sincere friend of the negro, & ready to act for him decisively."[6]

Sumner's confidence in Johnson extended into May, for everything that Johnson said to Sumner, along with his calculated silences, suggested they were fellow travelers on the road to Reconstruction. As Sumner reported to the German American jurist Francis Lieber, Johnson made several large claims during their meeting: that "colored persons have to have the right of suffrage; that no state can be *precipitated* into the Union; that rebel States must go through a term of *probation*."[7] Sumner wanted to hear precisely these words. From his perspective, Johnson could now be compared favorably to Lincoln in terms of his concerns for African Americans. At this early point in the Johnson presidency, Sumner viewed Johnson as the radical and Lincoln as the conservative.

Other Republican and abolitionist leaders likewise embraced the Johnson presidency. The Wisconsin-based Republican statesman and journalist Carl Schurz, who had earlier praised Johnson's willingness to fight for "the death of slavery," met with the president in May. Like Sumner, he came away thinking that he and Johnson were in complete agreement. He conveyed the happy news to Sumner that the objects the president aimed at were "all the most progressive friends of human liberty can desire."[8]

Even those Radical Republicans and abolitionists who didn't meet personally with Johnson thought he was one of their own. His strong antislavery views and uncompromising attacks on southern "traitors" had consolidated that reputation. Gerrit Smith, one of the "Secret Six" who financed John Brown's 1859 attack on Harpers Ferry, wrote Johnson just days after he became president: "I know your history— and I honor & love you. I know your sufferings & perils at the hand of the rebels." Wendell Phillips, a contributing editor of the influential *National Anti-Slavery Standard*, proclaimed in a late April speech that

Johnson was abolitionists' "natural leader" because Johnson's life history revealed his hatred of slavery. Johnson, Phillips asserted, understood that the time was right to confiscate land from the aristocratic plantation owners and place it "in the hands of the *masses*."[9]

William Lloyd Garrison, the nation's most influential abolitionist, offered equally admiring words on Johnson, making him sound like the greatest abolitionist of them all. In an April 28 editorial titled "Andrew Johnson, President of the United States," he celebrated Johnson's October 1864 Moses speech for arraigning "the 'master' class for their long career of lust, tyranny and crime." Presenting him as African Americans' great advocate, Garrison also predicted that Johnson would offer "no *pardon* for the rebel leaders," for the president had regularly expressed his views that those guilty of "the enormity of the crime of *treason* . . . must suffer the pains and penalties thereof."[10]

Amnesty

On May 29, 1865, just a month after Garrison's celebratory editorial, Johnson issued an Amnesty Proclamation that caught his admirers, and many others, by surprise. His dramatic about-face appeared to go against everything he had been preaching on the subject for the past five years, along with everything he had said to Radical Republicans and abolitionists for the prior six weeks. The man who had been so firm in his contempt for southern secessionists, so intent on punishing the ex-Confederates, now abruptly announced that he would pardon most rebel leaders and just about all male citizens of the ex-Confederate states. He spelled out the terms in his proclamation, declaring that he would forgive all who had, "directly or indirectly, participated in the existing rebellion," if they were willing to pledge loyalty to "the Constitution of the United States, and the union of the States thereunder." There were a few exceptions, such as ex-Confederates with more than $20,000 in property and former Confederate officers. But even those people could achieve amnesty, he explained, by applying directly to him.[11]

Within days of his Amnesty Proclamation, Johnson offered pardons to hundreds of ex-Confederates. He soon set up a staffed office to deal with the thousands of additional requests for pardons that came to the White House. Few such requests were refused. During that same time, Johnson approved a new state government in North Carolina led by ex-Confederate officers, and in the other ex-Confederate states he appointed provisional governors who had clear ties to the leadership of the former Confederacy. The freedpeople had no role in these new governments.

In late May and June of 1865, Johnson's vison of Reconstruction became clear: it would be guided by the president and not Congress, and its main goal would be to *restore* the ex-Confederate states to the Union without making any significant demands for change beyond abolishing slavery.[12] This was restoration without a plan for reconstruction. Encouraged by Johnson, Republicans had hoped for a fundamental transformation of southern society that would bring equal rights to the freedpeople. But that was not part of Johnson's vision. He wanted the former Confederate states to be quickly readmitted to the Union after setting up new state governments, and he had no problem with former Confederate leaders being part of those governments. All he asked was that the states ratify the Thirteenth Amendment, offer some sort of statement about their regret for seceding (even though he believed no state truly had seceded), and repudiate their war debts. But Johnson could not formally readmit the states; that was the role of Congress, which was on break until December.

Had Johnson been contemplating such a betrayal of the Radical Republicans' ideas about Reconstruction when he was meeting with their leaders? If so, he turned out to be quite a confidence man. A newspaper profile from the days when Johnson was an up-and-coming congressman praised him for being "well conned," by which the writer meant that Johnson was a persuasive speaker.[13] But in those early meetings there must have been some conning going on, for in the first week of May 1865 Johnson had already shown himself to be sympathetic to the ex-rebels by approving a provisional government in Virginia that included a number of former Confederate leaders.

What drove Johnson's deceit? Beyond political shrewdness, several possibilities present themselves. Racism was an obvious motivation: Johnson may have conceived of himself as a leader for African Americans, but that did not mean he regarded Blacks as equal to whites in the way of people like Sumner and Stevens. As a southerner, he also resented northerners' desires to impose racial equality on the South when it was lacking in the North. But there remains the question of why he was willing to pardon the very southerners he had been attacking since 1861. The simplest answer is that the war was over and he wanted quick closure. A more intriguing possibility is that Johnson liked wielding the power of pardon over the wealthy southerners he had formerly reviled. The very men who, he imagined, held him in contempt when he was a working-class young man now needed his assistance in order to retain their property. The wheel had turned and he was on top.

Perhaps the most important factor inspiring Johnson's Amnesty Proclamation was his particular way of interpreting the U.S. Constitution. Guiding his actions during the crucial first few months of his presidency, and in the months and years to follow, was a well-nigh mystical reading of the Constitution in which the states were always and forever part of the Union. People could secede, bad leaders could secede, but not the actual states. There was something ludicrous about this notion, but it's worth recalling that Lincoln shared a similarly mystical vision of the Union, though he never took a position on whether the states had seceded. Johnson clung to his belief in the impossibility of secession, and two days after his May 29 proclamation he explained himself in a newspaper interview with General John A. Logan of Illinois, a lawyer who had been a Democratic congressman before the war and had become a Republican. Johnson told Logan that slavery had caused the war, but now that slavery had been abolished, he wanted "to see the Union restored as it was previously to the war." When Logan asked about Reconstruction, Johnson responded: "General, there is no such thing as reconstruction. These States have not gone out of the Union, therefore reconstruction is unnecessary."[14] What was necessary, as Johnson would state repeatedly, was a quick restoration of the eleven ex-Confederate states as overseen by the president.

Though his Amnesty Proclamation and his views on presidential restoration surprised many Republicans, disillusionment with Johnson came relatively slowly and not uniformly among members of his party. For most of 1865, he was a popular president whose vision of white reconciliation across the sectional divides appealed to many Americans.[15] He also received praise for championing the Thirteenth Amendment, which ended slavery. Approved by Congress in January 1865 and ratified by year's end, that amendment, he could (and did) boast, was a signal achievement of his early presidency. Johnson, like Lincoln, believed that the states should have the final say on providing the franchise to African Americans, which put him at odds with former abolitionists and Radical Republicans. But this position hardly lost him support in the North and Midwest, where most states had provisions barring African Americans from voting. Given the choice on the ballot, most whites voted to uphold such provisions. In 1865, for instance, the white male electorate in Connecticut, Wisconsin, and Minnesota handily defeated Black suffrage initiatives.

In the wake of Johnson's May 29 Amnesty Proclamation, those Radical Republicans who had initially supported him, and had believed he shared their desire for equal rights for African Americans, began to wonder if they had been tricked, or even if Johnson was mentally sound. How else explain the president's sudden change of mind except as evidence of lunacy? Sumner, who had been charmed by Johnson to the point of thinking the struggle for Black rights was over, complained to a colleague about Johnson's "madness" in recognizing a North Carolina state government led by former Confederates. Sumner used the same language of madness when he described

Johnson and his Reconstruction policies to Chief Justice Chase. By late July Sumner concluded that Johnson had duped him, pretending to be as passionate about rights for Blacks as the Radical Republicans were. As summer turned to fall, Sumner could see the impact of Johnson's resistance to Reconstruction. Mississippi became the first of several ex-Confederate states to adopt Black Codes, laws that disempowered African Americans by sharply restricting their mobility and legal rights. In Mississippi in particular, Blacks were forbidden to own or rent land, they had no right to bear arms, and they could not meet in groups after sunset. Authorities had almost unlimited power to arrest Blacks as vagrants and place them in chain gangs or force them to do uncompensated work on the former slave plantations. Even with these new laws specific to Black people, which to some extent served to extend the life of slavery, Johnson was prepared to argue for Mississippi's readmission to the Union. Sumner was appalled, and by late 1865 he was furious. As he wrote John Bright in November of that year: "What could you expect from an old slave-master & an old democrat?"[16]

Still, Sumner hadn't given up hope, and he refrained from making angry public speeches about Johnson until early 1866. Like many of the Radicals who initially believed Johnson was one of their own, he continued to work behind the scenes, writing letters to Johnson suggestive of his support, even as he tried to modify the president's views on Reconstruction. "As a faithful friend and supporter of your administration," he wrote to the president in November 1865, "I most respectfully petition you to suspend for the present your policy towards the Rebel States." That policy, he said, "abandons the freedmen to the control of the ancient Masters."[17] Sumner would not remain a faithful friend or supporter much longer.

Like Sumner, Thaddeus Stevens, the Radical Republican congressman from Pennsylvania, continued to operate as if he could influence Johnson. Arguably Johnson's most pugnacious critic, Stevens wrote the president in July 1865 as a Republican Party man, urging him to wait on making decisions about the new southern state

Thaddeus Stevens, c. 1865. (*Brady-Handy Collection. Courtesy of the Library of Congress, Prints and Photographs Division.*)

governments until Congress reconvened in December. "Among all the leading Union men of the North with whom I have had intercourse I do not find one who approves of your policy," Stevens said bluntly. "They believe that 'Restoration' as announced by you will destroy our party . . . and will greatly injure the country." He added a further caution that additional pardoning of Confederate leaders would "greatly embarrass Congress."[18]

Stevens's view of Reconstruction, as elaborated in a number of his speeches, was that southerners were "a conquered people" and the South "a conquered territory."[19] Accordingly, he maintained, without directly attacking Johnson in public, that Congress had a moral imperative to impose its own set of policies on this conquered territory.

Stevens quickly emerged as the most forceful exponent of the idea that Congress, and not the president, should oversee and direct a more far-reaching Reconstruction of the ex-Confederate states. With

Congress in recess until early December, Stevens aired his views in widely reported speeches during the summer and fall that put Johnson and southern leaders on edge. In a September 1865 speech titled "Reconstruction," for instance, Stevens called for legislation that would radically change how southerners treated Black people, while urging Congress to confiscate the property "of every rebel belligerent whose estate was worth $10,000, or whose land exceeded two hundred acres in quantity."[20] Johnson's Amnesty Proclamation set the limit at $20,000, but excluded landowners who personally petitioned Johnson for a pardon. Johnson was fine with southern landowners holding on to their property; Stevens wanted confiscated lands going to the freedpeople. But even as his views diverged sharply from Johnson's, Stevens persisted in trying to work with the president through early 1866.

Carl Schurz also tried to collaborate with Johnson. Concerned about the situation of the freedpeople, Schurz developed a plan, approved by Johnson, to spend several months in the South and file reports on conditions there. In a series of respectful letters written to Johnson between July and October of 1865, Schurz described the racism and violence that Blacks faced in the South, presumably believing that Johnson would take his reportage seriously and find ways to help the freedpeople. In a July letter from Hilton Head, South Carolina, he informed Johnson that "the planters were but lately endeavoring to hold the negro in a state of slavery." In August he wrote from Macon, Georgia, that plantation owners seemed "to have combined to keep the negroes in their former state of subjection, and to kill those that refused to submit." Later that same month he reported from Vicksburg, Mississippi, that the violence against Blacks made it "absolutely indispensable that the country should be garnished with troops as thickly as possible."[21]

Johnson never responded to Schurz's letters. They were buried in the *Congressional Record* as Executive Document No. 11, House of Representatives, 39th Congress, 1st session. Given all that Schurz put himself through, we might describe him as another victim of a Johnson con job. But some Republicans did read Schurz's reports. In December, Sumner remarked to the Duchess of Argyll that Schurz had shown that the freedpeople were "worse off than when slaves; being exposed to the brutality & vindictiveness of their old masters." Johnson's efforts to cast these reports aside, Sumner said, suggested that he was "hide-bound in prejudice" and determined to remain oblivious to "the real condition of things." At year's end Sumner concluded that the man he initially regarded as "the sincere friend of the negro" had "no sentiment or heart for the poor freedmen."[22]

Like many of the Radical Republicans, Frederick Douglass also hoped for a smooth transition from Lincoln to Johnson. He did not turn against Johnson right away, even as the president's policies increasingly indicated that he wanted to restore, not reconstruct, the ex-Confederate states. Douglass saw nothing requiring public complaint during the first few months of Johnson's presidency. Hitting the lecture circuit in the immediate wake of the Civil War, Douglass principally remained engaged with the issue of equal citizenship for African Americans, which he had been advocating since the 1840s and regarded as the most important initiative of the postwar moment. He evocatively explained his commitment to Black citizenship in May 1865: "Till we get this, we shall be a crippled people, and shall be thankful for crutches to hobble along with."[23]

Citizenship was a vexed issue at this time. Before the principle of "birthright citizenship" was codified in 1868 in the Fourteenth Amendment, there was no substantive federal definition of citizenship. The states had the main role in defining it through laws about who was eligible to vote, serve on juries, and make contracts. Black citizenship itself was highly contested, and laws governing Black suffrage were something of a patchwork. Most of the New England states allowed African Americans to vote; some, such as New York, had stringent property-qualification requirements; and still others, such as New Jersey and Pennsylvania, had once allowed Blacks to vote and then rescinded the right (New Jersey in 1807 and Pennsylvania in 1838). Like all of the states of the former Confederacy, the majority of the states that fought for the Union did not allow Black people to vote. The Supreme Court's ruling in the 1857 *Dred Scott* case that Blacks could never become U.S. citizens inevitably dimmed prospects for expanding that right. But as Douglass and other African American activists asked just a few years later, if Black men could fight for the country during the Civil War, shouldn't they have the right to vote? Douglass sought "universal" or "impartial" suffrage for Black men, by which he meant voting rights without the constraints of property qualifications, literacy tests, or any other sort of hurdle. He had been advocating women's suffrage since the 1840s, but he saw that as a separate, if related, reform. First he wanted Black men to have what white men had, impartial suffrage, which he contrasted with the limited suffrage that Lincoln, Johnson, and other white leaders sometimes seemed willing to concede. Citizenship brought many privileges, but for Douglass the most crucial at the postwar moment would be the right to vote. Without that right, he repeatedly argued, the war was not really over and not completely won.[24]

Douglass's quest for citizenship rights for African American men equal to those of white men placed him in direct conflict with William Lloyd Garrison and some of his supporters, who admired Johnson and thought that the abolitionist struggle had achieved a triumphal end with Congress's adoption of the Thirteenth Amendment. Black citizenship would come, Garrison believed, but in its own good time. The conflict between Douglass and Garrison became even more contentious at the May 10, 1865, meeting of the American Anti-Slavery Society in New York City, when a split opened between those who thought the group had done its job and those, like Douglass, who regarded Black citizenship as equal in importance to abolition. Garrison, the founder of the society, called for a celebratory dissolution. In response, Douglass offered these bold, blunt words: "Slavery is not abolished until the black man has the ballot." Douglass had a large majority with him. By a count of 118–48, the delegates voted to keep the society going until Black male suffrage was the law of the land, and then, in a pro forma move intended to honor the founder of the society, reelected Garrison president.[25] Garrison graciously resigned, leaving the presidency to Wendell Phillips, who would work for Black civil rights with Douglass, Sumner, and many others over the next several years.

After this meeting, Douglass continued his push for Black civil rights, frustrated that change didn't come more quickly. He had not yet turned against Johnson, but in June he implicitly raised questions about the president's policy of restoration in a speech about Lincoln at New York's Cooper Institute. Douglass stated that under Lincoln's rule, Americans "saw the Confederate states, that boldest of all conspiracies against the just rights of human nature, broken to pieces, overpowered, conquered, shattered to fragments—ground to powder and swept from the face of existence." Like Thaddeus Stevens, Douglass thought of the South as a conquered territory in need of reconstruction. But somewhat surprisingly, in this particular speech he suggested that Johnson was doing his job: "Already a strong hand is felt upon the helm of state. Already the key note of justice has been sounded." But was that "strong hand" Johnson's or that of the Radical Republicans? Douglass implied it was both. He went on to make optimistic claims based on what he wanted to believe about Johnson. Drawing on Johnson's earlier speeches, he reminded his auditors that Johnson had promised that traitors would be punished. News of Johnson's May 29 Amnesty Proclamation, which changed all that, had not yet reached Douglass. His source for another claim in this speech isn't clear, and that was his assertion "that the Emancipated Negro, so long outraged and degraded," would soon be "enfranchised and clothed with the dignity of American citizenship."[26] Perhaps Douglass believed that saying such a thing would make it so.

By late summer 1865, with Black citizenship and suffrage nowhere in sight, Douglass, like Sumner, Stevens, and other Radical Republicans, began privately expressing his dismay at the Johnson presidency, writing critical letters about Johnson to such friends as the Quaker abolitionist and suffragist Martha Greene. Reluctant to give up hope herself, Greene urged Douglass not to turn on Johnson too quickly. She asked him in a letter of August 1865: "Did you not once have as little faith in Pres. Lincoln, when you said he was 'wrong from choice, & right from necessity,' as you have now in Johnson?"[27] Perhaps, Greene suggested, her friend would prove to be as wrong about Johnson as he was about Lincoln.

Douglass took Greene's comments to heart, for he held off awhile longer from publicly criticizing the president, even as he continued to urge Congress to do the legislative work to bring equal rights to African Americans. One of the reasons he may have gone easy on Johnson in the early months of his presidency was that Johnson, however troubling his policies, had been reaching out to African Americans as their Moses.

5

A MOSES IN THE
WHITE HOUSE

ANDREW JOHNSON WAS a racist, like most white Americans of
the time. But he was a racist who believed strongly that he
cared about Black people. He regularly asserted in his speeches that
he was the rare southern leader who had taken a stand against slavery,
most emphatically in his October 1864 Moses speech, which supposedly liberated all of the enslaved people of Tennessee. Though that
speech lacked the force of law, it helped to bring about changes in the
state and made Johnson into a kind of folk hero among Nashville's
African American population. Such was the fame of the speech that
the image of the new president as a potential leader of Black people
came up again and again, often at Johnson's instigation, whenever he
addressed the issue of Blacks' civil rights.

Johnson took pride in his relationship to African Americans. But
the Blacks he had reached out to in Nashville had been former slaves,
or enslaved people themselves, and he spoke to them from the pedes-
tal of a military governorship with a clear sense of racial hierarchy.
He relished the power that he had over his audience, and he enjoyed
the adulation he received from those he regarded as his inferiors. His

Moses speech was sincere, idealistic, incisive, and paternalistic. His repeated invocations of that speech suggest that it made him feel good about himself, and part of what he liked about the memory was his conviction that he had received so much love from Black people.

The situation was different in Washington, D.C., where African Americans pressed their claims for the full rights of citizenship. In February 1865, when Johnson was vice president, Henry Highland Garnet, pastor of the 15th Street Presbyterian Church in Washington, became the first Black to speak in Congress, addressing an overflow audience of Blacks and whites. A generation earlier, in a famous 1843 address at the African American convention in Buffalo, Garnet had encouraged enslaved Black people to use all possible methods, including violence, to resist the slave masters. In his 1865 lecture at the Capitol, in the waning days of the war, Garnet condemned slavery, hailed the Thirteenth Amendment, and made the case for Black citizenship. He called on Congress to *"Emancipate, Enfranchise, Educate, and give the blessings of the gospel to every American citizen."* [1] Douglass and Garnet attended Black conventions together and were sometimes at odds, but in this speech, delivered in the halls of Congress, perhaps with Johnson in attendance, Garnet evoked their shared goals—and the goals of nearly all African American activists of the period.

"Your Moses"

When Johnson assumed the presidency, he immediately reached out to such activists. He began by accepting a visit from a Black delegation led by John Mercer Langston. Langston was Johnson's best-known African American supporter. Born free in Virginia in 1829, he was educated at Oberlin College and in 1854 became the first Black admitted to the Ohio bar. During his Oberlin years and beyond, Langston regularly attended Black conventions with Douglass and participated in the Underground Railroad. Like Douglass, he helped to recruit Black troops for the Union army. He met Johnson for the first time

John Mercer Langston,
c. 1873. Photograph
by C. M. Bell Studio.
(*Courtesy of the Library
of Congress, Prints and
Photographs Division.*)

in 1864 and instantly regarded him as an inspirational leader. When Langston looked back on that meeting in his 1894 autobiography, he referred to Johnson as "the distinguished military governor of Tennessee" and called it "entirely natural" that he had supported him for the vice presidency.[2]

The two men bonded in Nashville shortly after Johnson gave his Moses speech. Langston described the speech glowingly in his autobiography, remarking on how Johnson gained the respect of the Blacks in attendance. Just a few months later, in December 1864, a group of Nashville's Black leaders invited Langston to give a speech there. Johnson sent a letter, too, assuring the visiting Black abolitionist that he would be safe and protected in the southern city. According to Langston's account, when he arrived in Nashville, Johnson invited him to the statehouse and urged him "to exercise in his address the largest freedom of sentiment and expression." Johnson attended the lecture, titled "The War, Our National Emancipator," making Langston feel appreciated and given due dignity. Afterward, Johnson congratulated Langston on the address and asked him to visit his office the next day.[3]

As it turned out, Johnson had a plan for Langston: he wanted him to meet with injured Black Union troops in an open-air hospital near Nashville and convey the military governor's gratitude for their service. Johnson gave this seemingly moving confidence to the visiting speaker: "Tell them that I do not come myself because I could not face them without such feelings as would render me wholly incapable of addressing them."[4] Langston was pleased to do what Johnson asked, and their friendship carried over into 1865 and beyond.

Shortly after Johnson became president, Langston brought a delegation of Black men to meet with Johnson in the Treasury Building. The group represented the National Equal Rights League, the recently created African American organization promoting Black suffrage and other forms of legal equality central to citizenship, such as the right to own property. Langston and his fellow delegates told Johnson that they hoped he "would see to it that every law which concerned their welfare was duly executed." Langston, who chaired the delegation, reported that he and his associates came away satisfied that "the president was earnest and positive in the promise that his colored fellow-citizens should find in him a friend mindful always of their welfare."[5]

The April meeting with Langston and his committee provided Johnson with good publicity. Langston wrote it up for the *Philadelphia Press*, and he sympathetically conveyed Johnson's view of the risks he had taken as a southerner in adopting an antislavery position. "It may be a very easy thing, indeed popular, to be an emancipationist north of the line," Johnson told Langston, "but a very different thing to be such south of it. South of it costs a man effort, property, and perhaps life." Langston responded sympathetically and saw no reason to be concerned about Johnson's future actions toward African Americans. Johnson's "past history," Langston said, offers "full assurance" that "our liberty and rights will be fully protected and sustained."[6]

Johnson made time for other such meetings with Black groups. In May 1865 he spoke to a delegation from the National Theological Institute for Colored Ministers, presenting himself as the ideal leader for African Americans. He told them about his Moses speech and how he had emancipated the enslaved people of Tennessee. A Moses to Tennessee's Black people, he now aspired to be a Moses to all of the nation's Black people. In this new role, he promised his visitors, "I shall continue to do all that I can for the elevation and amelioration of your condition." He also offered the advice that he gave at Nashville and would continue to give over the years, "that freedom simply means liberty to work and enjoy the product of your own hands."[7] He never mentioned the franchise.

Here and afterward, Johnson also consistently failed to say anything about the racism that made it difficult, and often impossible, for African Americans to rise in the United States. But during this meeting he floated an ominous idea that he would return to in some of his subsequent meetings with Black people, namely that if hostility persisted between Blacks and whites, Blacks might have to leave the country. As the meeting came to an end, Johnson offered an eerie blessing to the ministers that seemed to anticipate the failure of race relations in the United States: "I trust in God the time may soon come when you shall be gathered together, in a clime and country suited to you, should it be found that the two races cannot get along together."[8]

Colonization remained a live possibility for Johnson, as it had for Lincoln well into his first term as president. Transporting over four million African Americans to such places as Liberia and Central and South America would surely have been impossible, even with the support of such organizations as the American Colonization Society, but Johnson's political imagination was expansive on the subject. He would refer to colonization periodically during his presidency, including when he met with Douglass in February 1866, but without addressing how he would engineer or pay for such an initiative. More often, though, Johnson claimed to support African Americans' efforts to improve their situation in the United States.

As an avowed champion of Black people, Johnson continued to meet with various African American groups in the early months of his presidency. In June 1865, he welcomed Black delegations from Kentucky and Virginia to the White House. Both groups sought added police protection for the freedpeople. The spokesperson for the Kentucky delegation worried over Blacks' vulnerability to mob violence, reporting, as just one example, that white men "carry bull whips and upon Meeting colored Men, women or children in the Public high ways any time after dark . . . surround them and flay them alive in the public Streets." The delegates from Virginia shared similar accounts of whites' anti-Black violence. The problem, as the spokesperson for the Virginia group put it, was that Blacks had "nowhere to go for protection." Johnson assured both delegations that the freedpeople "need have no apprehension," though he failed to explain why this should be so. Would they be protected by state police? Federal troops? Johnson observed that conflicts between the races would inevitably arise while the freedpeople were in "transition," but in that way he seemed to be blaming the victims.[9] Nevertheless, both groups expressed their gratitude to a president willing to set aside time to listen to their concerns.

Johnson's amiable relations with African Americans continued after these meetings. He gave permission to the Colored People's Educational Monument Association to hold a celebration in memory of Abraham Lincoln on White House lawns during Johnson's first Independence Day in office. Permitting the celebration at his official residence further burnished the president's reputation as the friend of Black people. The gathering also allowed Black and white supporters of Black suffrage to make their case in a public forum. Unable to attend because he was in Rochester, Frederick Douglass sent a letter that was read to the crowd, calling for "the immediate, complete, and universal enfranchisement of the colored people of the whole country." Sumner also missed the event. His public letter echoed Douglass's in demanding suffrage for African Americans. Though Sumner had begun to turn on the president by this point, Johnson's decision to allow the gathering may have softened him, leading him, probably in earnest, to draw on one of Johnson's favorite conceptions of himself. "I counsel patience," Sumner wrote, "and confidence in the President, who has told you that he will be 'Your Moses.'"[10]

On this festive Independence Day event in 1865, people like Massachusetts Radical Republican senator Henry Wilson expressed admiration for the president, reminding the hundreds of Blacks on the White House grounds that Johnson had promised to be a Moses to them. Given that history, Wilson assured the crowd that Johnson would "be to you what Abraham Lincoln would have been, had he been spared to complete the great work of emancipation and enfranchisement."[11] Wilson placed Lincoln and Johnson together in harmonious succession.

In his last public speech Lincoln had said, with respect to his Louisiana plan, that he could imagine giving the vote to literate Blacks, Black property holders, and Black soldiers. Historians have celebrated that speech and predicted that Lincoln as a Reconstruction president would have eventually championed impartial Black suffrage. But perhaps it's just as likely that, in the pragmatic interest of sectional reconciliation, he would have continued to advocate limited Black suffrage, at least for a while. We'll never know. What we do know is that four months after Lincoln's death, Johnson proposed limited Black suffrage, and he did so in the pragmatic way of Lincoln. But there was one major difference: Lincoln went public with his plan, while Johnson temporarily kept his private.

Johnson made his proposal in an August 15, 1865, letter to William L. Sharkey, a lawyer, state politician, and former Whig who had been a staunch Unionist during the war. Johnson must have found Sharkey's Unionism appealing, for he had appointed him provisional governor of Mississippi and charged him with developing a new state constitution. In the letter, Johnson shared an idea about that constitution; he told Sharkey that there were good strategic reasons for including a provision offering limited Black suffrage. "If you could extend the elective franchise to all persons of color who can read the constitution of the United States in English and write their names," he advised, as well as to those "who own real estate valued at not less than two-hundred and fifty dollars and pay taxes thereon," there would be a significant payoff: "You would completely disarm the adversary and set an example the other States will follow." By "the adversary," Johnson meant the Radical Republicans of his own party, who were "wild upon negro franchise" but in most instances did not allow Blacks to vote in their home states.[12] From Johnson's perspective, offering southern Blacks limited suffrage would foil the Republicans' efforts to keep the ex-Confederate states from rejoining the Union when, after a long summer recess, Congress took up the matter in December.

✳ Johnson wanted to outmaneuver the Radicals, whose advocacy of Black suffrage in the South he correctly perceived as gaining traction among northern voters. Still, his letter to Sharkey represents a striking moment in his early presidency in which history could have moved in a considerably different direction. Had Sharkey followed Johnson's advice, and had other southern leaders followed Sharkey's lead, the South would have witnessed the beginnings of a process that was significantly different from the simple restoration that Johnson had defined as Reconstruction. But Sharkey rejected Johnson's proposal, writing that Louisiana's constitutional convention would accept the end of slavery, but would leave the question of suffrage for future discussion. Sharkey also made clear that he had no immediate intention of pursuing the matter because, like many southern whites, he believed free Blacks posed a danger to whites. Ignoring the violence and terror that the freedpeople faced on a daily basis, Sharkey in a brazen reversal said: "The negroes are bold in their threats and the people are afraid. I have called for volunteer companies of militia in each county to suppress crime which is becoming alarming."[13] Militia companies like those formed by Sharkey further contributed to the anti-Black violence that Schurz observed in the South during the summer of 1865.

Despite the rebuff from Sharkey, Johnson continued to entertain the possibility of Black suffrage, and in October 1865 he decided to go public with the idea during an interview with George L. Stearns, a wealthy white Massachusetts-based radical abolitionist.

Stearns had achieved notoriety as a member of the so-called Secret Six who helped to fund John Brown's 1859 attack on Harpers Ferry. During the Civil War, Stearns worked with Douglass and other African Americans to recruit over ten thousand Black soldiers for the Union army, and as the war approached its end, he threw himself into the campaign for Black civil rights. Early in 1865 he published with his own money thousands of copies of *The Equality of All Men before the Law*, a collection of three speeches advocating Black citizenship, including Douglass's "What the Black Man Wants." In May of that year, Stearns urged Johnson to "secure to all men without distinction of Race or Color, equal rights, and privileges," and now during their interview, published in the *New York Times*, he asked Johnson to offer his support for Black suffrage. Sounding a bit like Lincoln, Johnson responded somewhat agreeably that the states should "try to intro- duce negro suffrage gradually; first those who had served in the army; those who could read and write, and perhaps a property qualification for others, say $200 or $250." The Radical Republicans and Douglass wanted a more comprehensive plan for impartial Black suffrage— voting rights for Black men that would not be restricted by property ownership—but at the time Johnson's statement of support for limited Black suffrage was surprising coming from a southern president who knew that leaders like Sharkey, and his constituents, would be resis- tant. For that reason, Johnson continued to insist that unrestricted suf- frage for Black men risked setting off "a war of the races," especially if working-class whites regarded Blacks as taking their jobs and gaining political power at their expense. Perhaps sensing Stearns's disapproval of his efforts to stoke white working-class resentment, Johnson made a cutting point clearly intended for readers of the *New York Times*. He observed that while northern Republicans called for Black suffrage in the South, Blacks were not allowed to vote in many of these same pol- iticians' home states. Cannily and sarcastically, probably with Penn- sylvania congressman Thaddeus Stevens in mind, he told Stearns: "If I interfered with the vote in the rebel States, to dictate that the negro shall vote, I might do the same thing for my own purposes in Pennsylvania."[14]

Even with Johnson's warnings about a race war and his mocking of northern hypocrisy, Henry Ward Beecher, the popular New York minister, brother of the best-selling antislavery novelist Harriet Beecher Stowe, and advocate of Black citizenship, found Johnson to be appealing in this interview. Beecher wrote Johnson to "express the great satisfaction which I have felt in reading your remarks to Mr. Stearns." He added: "The religious men of the north and west are rapidly growing into confidence in your patriotism, and wisdom, second only to that which they felt for Mr. Lincoln; a confidence which I am sure will increase."[15]

Johnson received praise from the African American press as well. Shortly after the interview with Stearns, an admiring squib titled "President Johnson" in the October 14 issue of the Philadelphia-based *Christian Recorder* called attention to a speech that "our worthy Chief Magistrate" delivered to the 1st District of Columbia Colored Volunteers and urged all of its subscribers to read it. Clearly, the editors of this popular newspaper continued to believe that Johnson worked in the interest of African Americans. In that speech, which was published in the *New York Times* and elsewhere, Johnson told the Black military men who had fought for the nation that the time was right for them to "give evidence to the world that you are capable and competent to govern yourselves." Working industriously in a nation that Johnson implied offered no barriers to their success was the way to make "black men white." When the veterans responded to this odd (and insulting) formulation with cheers, the president followed up with another assertion that was intended to speak to possibilities of human equality but continued to ignore the wildly differing situations of white and Black people in the post–Civil War United States: "He that is most meritorious and virtuous and intellectual and well-informed, must stand highest without regard to color."[16]

Johnson's seeming racial inclusivity and his willingness to meet with African Americans were no doubt what led the editors of the

Christian Recorder to praise him throughout most of 1865. The praise sometimes bordered on the reverential. A person whose initials were P. V. G. wrote in a "Letter from Washington" around the time of Johnson's speech to Black veterans: "Brethren, we are grateful . . . to President Johnson for his kindness to us." The *Christian Recorder* printed a few articles that raised questions about Johnson's approach to Reconstruction, but overall the editors of this influential African American journal held out hope that Johnson would follow in what they imagined would have been the progressive footsteps of Lincoln. Here was a president, they wanted to believe, committed to achieving a democratic nation for all, regardless of race.[17]

Douglass and "Associate Effort"

While the *Christian Recorder* was keeping its faith in Johnson, Douglass was losing his. He was seething with resentment at the president's policies during the fall of 1865, concerned about the amnesty for Confederate leaders, the attempt to bring the ex-Confederate states back into the Union with virtually no changes at all (beyond the acceptance of the Thirteenth Amendment), and the failure to address the issue of Blacks' civil rights. At Boston's Music Hall, he lambasted Johnson for pardoning so many ex-Confederates, and he sardonically predicted that Jefferson Davis would be next on his list. Warning that the gains of the Civil War were "on the verge of being lost," Douglass placed much of the blame on the "imbecility or the treachery of President Johnson."[18]

Douglass voiced similar dissatisfaction with Johnson in a late September 1865 address at Baltimore's newly created Douglass Institute, named after him. Earlier in his career, Douglass had objected to the self-segregating tendencies of all-Black institutions and organizations, especially those championing Black emigration. But at this precarious moment of possibly lost opportunity, he acknowledged the value of what he called "colored associations and institutions of all kinds."

Situated at the site of a former university, the Douglass Institute was founded by a group of Baltimore African Americans with the goal of educating Black youth in a venue relatively sheltered from the city's pervasive anti-Black racism. During the antebellum period, Blacks in Philadelphia and New York had created their own schools and reading societies for similar reasons and with similar goals. As Douglass explained in his speech to an audience numbering close to one thousand, African Americans needed to stand together to demand their rights. The challenges presented by Johnson's policies and a racist white citizenry made all-Black institutions and groups "eminently necessary." Blacks could best meet the challenges of the time, Douglass suggested, by embracing the collective unity exemplified by the new Douglass Institute and the Black convention movement that he had supported since the 1840s.[19]

Douglass engaged in such collective work over the next several months. He traveled to Cleveland in October to attend a meeting of the National Equal Rights League, the organization promoting full citizenship for African Americans that he had cofounded with John Langston and Henry Highland Garnet at the 1864 Black convention in Syracuse. Langston, the friend and admirer of Johnson, served as president of the meeting; Douglass was one of ten vice presidents. Perhaps because of Langston's influence, there were no direct attacks on Johnson at this convention. But the participants unanimously demanded "that the Elective franchise be extended to men of color." In the closing lecture, the Philadelphia-based Black activist and businessman William D. Forten called on African Americans to work together to contest the notion "*that this is a white man's country.*" In order to do that successfully, Forten advised, "we must be a unit."[20]

African American leaders did indeed form a "unit" in Boston for another Black convention just a few days before Congress returned to session in December 1865. As he did at the National Equal Rights League meeting, Douglass took a relatively subordinate role at this convention, giving a short speech while leaving the leadership to others. But in that speech he presented an idea that soon had significant consequences: he proposed sending a Black lobbying group to Washington, D.C., "to influence the legislation of Congress."[21] The convention's delegates enthusiastically supported the proposal, approving as their first resolution that such a contingent take up residence in the capital city in the very near future. Specifically, they wanted the group to make the case for what they regarded as the most essential component of Reconstruction: Black citizenship. The concern at the Boston convention was that the Radical Republicans might not have this goal at the very top of their list. Most Black activists also believed that it was important to make their own case for citizenship and not be overly dependent on the Republicans.

The convention's participants approved other resolutions as well. They declared that Blacks, who were not allowed to testify in some northern or any southern courts, should have "equality before the law." They condemned the recent election results in Connecticut, Wisconsin, and Minnesota that continued to deny "colored American citizens the right to vote." They also called on Congress, "either by general law or through the agency of the Freedmen's Bureau," to give the freedpeople greater protection "from the hatred of their former owners." Johnson wasn't mentioned, but these resolutions implicitly criticized the president for failing to take action to protect the rights—and bodies—of Blacks in the North and South. The proceedings closed with the convention's president, the seasoned Black abolitionist Charles L. Remond, declaring that "this nation would have no peace until the suffrage question was settled."[22]

Because Black suffrage remained a central component of the Radical Republicans' plan for Reconstruction, Remond's remarks spoke to the larger political debate between Congress and the president that broke out publicly when the Thirty-Ninth Congress convened on December 4, 1865. Just before that formal opening of the legislative session, while African Americans were meeting in Boston, Senator Charles Sumner visited the White House on December 1, pressing his desire for Black suffrage on George Bancroft, the celebrated Boston historian who, somewhat improbably, worked as one of Johnson's principal advisers and speechwriters. Bancroft sent Johnson a memo about his meeting with Sumner, saying that he had spent hours trying "to calm him down on the suffrage question, & he admitted fully that *the President* could not have granted suffrage." One wonders how or whether Bancroft managed to calm his fellow Bostonian, or if he truly gained that concession. Bancroft concluded his memo by asserting, correctly, in light of recent votes against Black suffrage across the country: *"Public opinion is all with you."*[23]

Three days after Sumner's visit with Bancroft, Johnson addressed Black suffrage head-on in his first annual message to a Congress that was overwhelmingly Republican (136 of the 193 representatives) and still did not have a House representative or senator from the ex-Confederate states. In a document that was partly written by Bancroft, Johnson continued to sound as if he cared about the freedpeople. He avowed his commitment to "the security of the freedmen in their liberty and their property, their right to labor, and their right to claim the just return of their labor." Sumner couldn't have put the matter any better than that. Johnson now counseled white Americans to "avoid hasty assumptions of any natural impossibility for the two races to live side by side, in a state of mutual benefit and good will." Instead of advocating African Americans' "forced removal and colonization," as he had on occasion, he said it made better sense to encourage the freedpeople "to honorable and useful industry, where it may be beneficial to themselves and to their country." Acknowledging slavery as an "evil," Johnson insisted that (white) Americans had an obligation to help the freedpeople by ensuring that the hurdles they faced "not be attributable to any denial of justice."[24]

As for the prospect of Black suffrage, Johnson offered some support for the idea, but insisted that it was not for him or Congress to impose suffrage on the ex-Confederate states. Such federal action, he argued, would be an assumption of power "which nothing in the Constitution or laws of the United States would have warranted." With respect to the four million freedpeople, he recommended a gradual approach to suffrage developed at the state level, in which Blacks would "show patience and manly virtues" and in due course would be rewarded with the franchise.[25] Johnson insisted that such an approach, in which being "manly" meant being quietly patient, would eventually bring about the social change desired by the Radical Republicans and Black activists. Johnson said nothing in this message that was explicitly opposed to Black suffrage. Instead, he displayed a willful naïveté about the possibility of African Americans obtaining rights in any state where they were denied suffrage—northern, midwestern, western, and, especially, southern—without federal intervention.

Had Johnson simply offered remarks on limited Black suffrage at the state level, his presidential message might have been well received by moderate Republicans and some Democrats. But much to the annoyance of the Radical Republicans in Congress, the message also elaborated his understanding of Reconstruction as principally the work of the president, and mainly about restoration.

Johnson used various forms of "restore" in his message, refusing to use the word "Reconstruction." He contested Thaddeus Stevens's notion that the South was a conquered territory to be overseen by Congress, maintaining once again that secession was constitutionally impossible because "all pretended acts of secession were, from the beginning, null and void." Because he believed that secession had never happened, Johnson called for no meaningful action from the federal government and no substantive changes in the laws and practices of the southern states. "It would remain for the States," Johnson said, to "complete the work of restoration,"[26] and that, he counseled, could happen quickly, in a matter of days. So much for Black rights and Reconstruction.

Even with his remarks on gradual Black suffrage, most congressional Republicans regarded Johnson's message as a provocation. They remained concerned about how people like Georgia's Alexander Stephens, formerly vice president of the Confederate States, had ended up in leadership roles in the provisional state governments approved by Johnson. Shortly after Johnson sent his message to lawmakers, congressional Republicans flexed their legislative muscle and made their most aggressive move to date: they refused to seat representatives from any of the "restored" state governments. The Republican majority objected to the large number of ex-Confederate military and political leaders in these proposed governments, as well as to the lack of Black representation or suffrage. The Radical Republicans wanted change. Thaddeus Stevens and his colleagues continued to believe that the South was a conquered territory in need of reconstruction.

Johnson's support for these provisional governments led Stevens and other Republican leaders in mid-December 1865 to create a Joint Congressional Committee on Reconstruction. This proved to be a momentous step with far-reaching consequences. The committee consisted of fifteen members, twelve of whom were Republicans, and was charged to hold hearings on the anti-Black violence in the ex-Confederate states and set the terms for readmitting them. The formation of this oversight committee brought the battle between Congress and the president out into the open. Congressional Reconstruction now overruled presidential restoration, as the Republican-majority members of Stevens's committee decreed that the ex-Confederate states seeking readmission to the Union would have to meet their requirements, which were far more stringent than Johnson's.

Douglass and other African Americans kept their eyes on this emerging conflict between Congress and the president. In the immediate wake of Johnson's message to Congress, Douglass once again addressed one of his largest priorities for Reconstruction—Black suffrage—in a year-end speech on Abraham Lincoln, probably delivered in the Rochester area. He presented Johnson as no Lincoln, or at least not the Lincoln that Douglass had begun to mythologize. Lincoln, he said, was "a progressive man" committed to "Liberty and Equal Rights," a man who would have evolved with the times. "Had Mr. Lincoln lived," he proclaimed, "we might have looked for still more progress." After all, just before the assassination Lincoln had favored extending the franchise "to two classes of colored men, first to the brave Colored Soldiers who had fought under the flag, and second to the very intelligent part of the Colored population [in the]

South." Douglass would not have known of Johnson's private letter to Mississippi's provisional governor, Sharkey, and he may not have known about Johnson's October 1865 remarks on Black suffrage to the District of Columbia Colored Volunteers. But he had observed enough to cast judgment. In Johnson's actions of the fall and winter of 1865, and in his message to Congress, Douglass saw a president with no interest in working at the federal level for impartial Black suffrage and Black civil rights. The assassination of Lincoln was a tragedy for all Americans, he said, but, given where Johnson was taking the nation, he concluded that it was "an unspeakable Calamity" for African Americans.[27]

By late 1865, Douglass had come to believe that Blacks faced an unimaginable crisis: a continued refusal by the very nation they fought for during the Civil War to grant them their basic rights as citizens. But he also saw promise in the bold resistance and actions of the Republican Congress, and he may have even seen a glimmer of hope in Johnson's willingness, in his first annual message, to allow for the possibility of suffrage for some African Americans. Congress was preparing aggressive action to reconstruct the South, and even the resistant President Johnson showed on occasion that he was willing to listen to Black people. The time was right to send a Black lobbying group to Washington to meet with congressional leaders and the president.

6

THE BLACK DELEGATION
VISITS A MOSES
OF THEIR PEOPLE

FREDERICK DOUGLASS and the other members of the Black delegation began to arrive in Washington, D.C., in late January
1866. They carried the charge of the December 1865 Boston convention, along with the support of the National Equal Rights League,
to make the case that Blacks' civil rights should be absolutely central to Reconstruction. The lobbying group consisted of George T.
Downing of Washington, D.C., who was the nominal leader and took
the delegation's major organizational role. He was an African American caterer and abolitionist who was born in New York and worked
as a restaurateur in Newport and Providence, Rhode Island, while
contributing to the efforts of the Underground Railroad. During the
Civil War he recruited Black troops in Massachusetts and then moved
to Washington, D.C., where he became friends with Senator Charles
Sumner. That friendship paid dividends, for Sumner got him the job
of running the U.S. House of Representatives' dining room. In mid-
1860s Washington, Downing had perhaps as much clout as Douglass.

George Thomas Downing, c. 1880s. Photographer unknown. (*Courtesy of the Schomburg Center for Research in Black Culture, Photographs and Prints Division, The New York Public Library.*)

Historian Stephen Kantrowitz describes Downing as "the ambassador of black America to official Washington."[1]

The others in the party were Frederick Douglass, his son Lewis Henry, and six other activists, one of whom was an unidentified white man. The best known of the delegates, besides Douglass, were the wealthy abolitionist businessmen William Whipper of Philadelphia, who had cofounded the Black self-help group the American Moral Reform Society in 1835, and John Jones of Chicago, who had been active in Chicago's Underground Railroad and in 1865 had helped to repeal Illinois's "Black Laws" limiting Blacks' legal rights. Downing, as the local contact, knew Republican politicians and helped out with lodgings and other logistical matters. The Boston convention had passed a resolution granting members of the lobbying group $10,000 for their expenses; it's not clear how much of that was actually raised, but the delegates did have some funding to begin their work.

Lewis Henry Douglass, Frederick Douglass's oldest son, had learned much from his father about typesetting, printing, and editing, and would work during the early 1870s on his father's newspaper the *New National Era*. At this point, at age twenty-five, several years after serving as a sergeant major in the renowned 54th Massachusetts Volunteer Infantry Regiment, he was well equipped to handle the secretarial responsibilities for the group, and he took the initiative in representing the delegation. In a letter to Sumner, Lewis set forth the group's goals, telling him that the lobbyists came to Washington to "urge that the actions of the government be based on the principle of Equality before the Law for all American Citizens, without regard to color." That principle was clearly not at work in Washington, D.C., for he also complained about how the delegates were denied access to the Senate gallery, despite being "decently attired." Instead, they were shunted off to a segregated area that made it difficult for them to hear the debates. Lewis expressed their anger at being "colonized" in this way, and asked Sumner "as a friend of justice and impartial liberty to do what in your judgment the case may demand." It was, Lewis said, a matter of self-respect. Sumner quickly arranged for the group to attend the Senate's daily sessions in the main gallery.[2]

From their enhanced place in the Senate chamber, the Black delegation witnessed one of Sumner's most famous speeches, "The Equal Rights of All," which he began on February 5 and concluded on February 6, the day before the group would meet with Johnson in the White House. In this two-hour speech, Sumner offered support for Illinois senator Lyman Trumbull's recently proposed Civil Rights Bill, which laid the groundwork for the principles of equality and birthright citizenship that would become central to the Fourteenth Amendment. Sumner specifically called for Black suffrage in the ex-Confederate states. Conceding that African Americans in some of the northern states were also not allowed to vote, Sumner said that northern Blacks could wait awhile longer, but that southern Blacks needed the vote as soon as possible in order to protect themselves from anti-Black violence. The franchise, he said, would help southern Blacks influence policy, elect Republicans, and ultimately "save the Republic." Near

Lewis Henry Douglass, c. 1865. Photographer
unknown. (*Courtesy of the Moorland-Spingarn
Research Center, Prints and Photographs Division.*)

the end of the speech, Sumner initiated a chant: "The ballot is *peace-
maker* . . . The ballot is *reconciler* . . . The ballot is *schoolmaster*. . . . The
ballot is *protector*." He concluded with a pointed and actually quite
visionary reminder that whites constituted only around one-fourth
of the world's population, which led him to remark to the whites in
attendance that "in claiming exclusive rights for 'white,' you degrade
nearly three quarters of the human family."[3]

On behalf of the Black delegation, Lewis Henry wrote Sumner that
the group appreciated his "able, masterly and exhaustive argument."[4]

Meeting with President Johnson

Sumner's speech energized and inspired the delegation for their meeting with President Andrew Johnson on February 7, 1866. Sumner and other Republicans had helped to schedule the session, but not much help was needed, for Johnson had a history of talking with Black people, preferably in large groups, and preferably with those who would listen quietly to what he had to say.

When Douglass met with Lincoln in the White House in 1863 and 1864, the two men spoke in private. No one took notes on their conversations. Douglass himself told stories about their get-togethers in his 1860s lectures, and then retrospectively in his 1881 autobiography. By contrast, when the delegates entered Johnson's office, they were greeted by the young white stenographer James O. Clephane, who was renowned for his ability to record speeches and conversations through a shorthand system he had invented. Lincoln had admired Clephane and named him secretary to the U.S. secretary of state William H. Seward, a position that Clephane continued to hold during the Johnson administration.[5] Johnson must have thought his hosting of the Black delegation would go well and provide him with good publicity. He would put on a show for the stenographer, who would pass along a transcript to a Washington newspaper. Despite his recent controversies with the Radical Republicans, he could demonstrate to the Blacks in attendance, and to those reading about the gathering, that he really did care about Black people and could be trusted to oversee his own version of Reconstruction.

Clephane described Johnson greeting the delegates as they entered the Executive Office and shaking each man's hand.[6] Those friendly handshakes constituted act one, scene one, of Johnson's calculated performance. But the show wouldn't go as anticipated, for Johnson had come face-to-face with another master performer.

Johnson's plan was to deliver something like his stock speech on Black self-help and the benefits of African Americans gradually gaining their full rights as citizens. But he held off on the speech in order to allow Downing to announce the contingent's reasons for visiting. Speaking cordially and with respect, Downing opened the conversation by saying that the group had come as "friends meeting a friend." Perhaps the friendliness was a rhetorical ploy, or perhaps Downing was responding positively to Johnson's past efforts to reach out to African Americans. Downing then announced the main reason for the meeting. Representing the formerly enslaved Blacks of the South and the free Blacks of the North, they had come to ask the president for his help in ensuring "equality before the law" for all African Americans.[7]

Downing knew that Johnson had claimed to be a Moses to Black people, and he spoke directly to the Moses conceit as part of his initial rhetorical gambit by saying that Blacks sought "a passage to equality" through the "Red Sea." It is difficult to know whether he was being ironic or canny in working with an image that he hoped Johnson would find flattering. Downing subsequently set forth the demands for citizenship that had become central to Black activism of the period. African Americans, he told the president, "should be protected in their rights as citizens, and be equal before the law." And perhaps in another effort to flatter the president, he stated: "We are citizens, we are glad to have it known to the world that you bear no doubtful record on this point." With his reference to "the world," he signaled his awareness that this was not a private meeting and that many would experience it through the stenographer's transcript. Downing went on to say that he continued to "cherish the hope" that Blacks would be enfranchised in the District of Columbia and throughout the nation, and that Johnson should consider deploying federal forces to make that happen.[8]

Johnson may have planned to deliver his own speech then and there, but Douglass took the opportunity to step forward and address the president. Normally a man of many words, Douglass succinctly told Johnson that he and the group came "to show our respect, and to present in brief the claims of our race to your favorable consideration." Like Downing, he was deferential. He asked Johnson to place "in our hands the ballot with which to save ourselves," and he reminded the president that Black men had served in the Union army during the Civil War.[9] He also noted the unfairness of African Americans being subject to taxation without representation. As suggested by his brief remarks, Douglass appeared willing to subordinate himself to the larger delegation as represented by Downing, at least at the outset of the meeting.

Johnson then launched into what Douglass later termed a "set speech," with the seeming expectation that, as with his recent speech to the Black volunteers of the District of Columbia, he would be listened to in silent admiration or with occasional applause. Douglass reported in his 1881 autobiography that the speech went on for "at least three-quarters of an hour," but based on the transcripts in February 1866 newspapers, it is safe to say that it was considerably shorter, in part because the delegates refused to listen for that long. They wanted a conversation.[10]

Before Johnson was interrupted, he rehearsed some of his main points about African Americans and Reconstruction. He asserted, as he regularly did, that he was "a friend of humanity, and especially the friend of the colored man." He supported his claim to friendship in ways that would have brought bemused looks from the group, for he proudly asserted: "I have owned slaves and bought slaves, but I never sold one." Perhaps sensing some skepticism or surprise, Johnson became more aggressive, stating that he did not like "to be arraigned by some who can get up handsomely rounded periods and deal in rhetoric." That remark, with its reference to the stylistic device of the periodic sentence (a long sentence that is not completed grammatically or semantically before the final clause or word), was probably aimed at Douglass, the most rhetorically gifted of the group. Douglass and others in the delegation, Johnson maintained, failed to understand that the immediate adoption of universal Black suffrage would "end in a contest between the races, which if persisted in will result in the extermination of one or the other," but probably the Blacks. As someone who prided himself on caring about African Americans,

Johnson said to the lobbyists: "God forbid that I should be engaged in such a work!"[11]

Not too long after this meeting, violence against African Americans would erupt in Memphis and New Orleans, and Johnson would blame the Radical Republicans, Douglass, and the Black delegation. For now, though he was becoming defensive and hostile, Johnson was probably thinking about the stenographer. He still wanted to project generosity to those who would be reading about the meeting. In response to Downing's reference to the Red Sea, he turned to one of his favorite images of himself. "Yes, I have said, and I repeat here," Johnson remarked, "that if the colored man in the United States could find no other Moses, or any Moses that would be more able and efficient than myself, I would be his Moses to lead him from bondage to freedom." Going further, he proclaimed: "Yes, I would be willing to pass with him through the Red Sea to the Land of Promise—to the land of liberty." But there were limits to his Mosaic leadership, and he went on to tell the group that he was unwilling to support policies that risked triggering white violence against Blacks. In that respect, Johnson was unlike Moses, for the biblical Moses readily assumed risks in order to bring liberty to his people.[12]

The tension between Johnson and his Black auditors became increasingly evident as Johnson tried to carry on with his speech. The stenographer's report allows us to picture the scene. After offering his opening general statement and comparing himself to Moses, he stated to the group: "Now, let us get closer up to this subject, and talk about it." According to the stenographer, as Johnson spoke about getting closer to the subject, "the President here approached very near to Mr. Douglass." Why did Johnson approach Douglass? Because he noticed the skepticism or dissent clearly marked on his face? Because he thought that, as president, he could overwhelm and crush the spirit of the renowned African American leader? Because he harbored anger at the man he had seen from a distance at Lincoln's second inauguration and now resented as Sumner's friend and spokesperson for the race? Clephane did not supply visual details, but the sight of the dapper president and equally well-dressed Black abolitionist just an arm's distance apart must have been arresting, especially with the height difference: Douglass would have been looking down at the considerably shorter Johnson. Looking up at Douglass, the president launched into an argument about how he had opposed slavery both as a monopoly that gave power to an aristocracy and as an immoral and unethical "abstract principle." Johnson no doubt expected an approving quiet assent when he made those claims, but Douglass, the man Johnson thought he had under control, interrupted him. To describe what happened next, the stenographer adopted theatrical form to capture the back-and-forth between them:

> **Mr. Douglass.** Mr. President, do you wish—
> **The President.** I am not quite through yet.[13]

In his June 1865 lecture at New York's Cooper Institute, Douglass declared that Lincoln "was one of the very few white Americans who could converse with a negro without any thing like condescension, and without in anywise reminding him of the unpopularity of his color." Douglass would not be able to say the same of Johnson, and in his account of this meeting in his 1881 autobiography, he wrote that Johnson "refused to listen to any reply on our part."[14]

That didn't mean Douglass gave up trying to be heard or noticed. When Johnson, after interrupting the interrupting Douglass, returned to his speech to maintain that the Blacks of Tennessee were themselves corrupted by slavery, to the extent that they supposedly respected slave owners more than working-class whites, Douglass must have indicated his skepticism, for Johnson stopped his speech to address Douglass, whose history he apparently did not know. Amazingly, he asked Douglass, "Have you ever lived upon a plantation?"—which set off another exchange between the two:

> **Mr. Douglass.** I have, your Excellency.
> **The President.** When you would look over and see a man

who had a large family, struggling hard upon a poor piece of land, you thought a great deal less of him than you did of your own master's negro, didn't you?

Mr. Douglass. Not I!

The President. Well, I know such was the case with a large number of you in those sections.

Johnson, whose use of "you" linked Douglass with the slaves of Tennessee (as if all Black people were one and the same), now informed Douglass yet again that "the colored man appreciated the slave owner more highly than he did the man who didn't own slaves."[15] Douglass regarded such sentiments as nonsensical and condescending, and the back-and-forth between "Mr. Douglass" and "The President" soon came to dominate the stenographer's account of the meeting.

With his questions and remarks, and even his facial gestures (which the stenographer recorded), Douglass clearly sought to manipulate the proceedings in an effort to take control from Johnson. He wanted to put on display Johnson's intransigence and racial condescension, along with his resistance to Reconstruction programs that would advance the rights of African Americans. Perhaps aware that he was losing control of the meeting, Johnson tried to instruct Douglass and his associates about "the hate that existed between the two races," as well as the probability (so he regularly argued) that if whites and Blacks were "thrown together at the ballot-box" there would "commence a war of races." His position was essentially a repetition of what he had said in an interview in the *Washington Morning Chronicle* several weeks earlier, when he warned that "the agitation" to give the vote to all African Americans in the District, and not just to a literate and propertied elite, "would engender enmity, contention, and strife between the two races, and lead to a war between them . . . and the certain extermination of the negro population." In this disingenuous way, Johnson could frame his opposition to impartial Black suffrage as a concern about Black people. Douglass, who may well have read that *Chronicle* interview, had a crisp response at the ready: "That was said before the war." By contrast, Douglass suggested, the post–Civil War moment offered opportunities for a new interracial democracy.[16]

From Johnson's perspective, however, democracy was about majority rule. He told Douglass and the delegation that if whites voted against giving the ballot to African Americans, as they recently had in northern and midwestern states, then those decisions should be respected. "Is there anything wrong or unfair in that?" he asked rhetorically. The stenographer reported Douglass's quick response: "Mr. Douglass (smiling). A great deal that is wrong, Mr. President, with all respect."[17]

The smile is intriguing. Why did the stenographer choose to include that detail? Did he mean to signal Douglass's disrespect or his own sympathy for Douglass's position? That smile, which to some who read the newspaper report made Douglass appear condescending, evidently unsettled Johnson, who continued to talk about his fears of a race war.

But as the interview appeared to be coming to an end, Johnson returned to his more gracious, paternalistic voice, and the parties offered conventional blandishments to each other. Johnson even promised his guests: "Anything I can do to elevate the races, to soften and ameliorate their condition, I will do, and to be able to do so is the sincere desire of my heart." Douglass thanked Johnson "for so kindly granting us this interview." Downing also thanked the president, saying that he and his associates appreciated Johnson sharing his views, even if "we certainly do not concur, and I say this with all due respect."[18]

At this point the meeting was over, at least from Johnson's point of view. Then Douglass cannily reopened the conversation as the others were heading for the door. "If the president will allow me," he said, "I would like to say one or two words in reply. You enfranchise your enemies and disfranchise your friends."[19]

Douglass's accusation, which meant to remind Johnson that he had once regarded southern secessionists as treasonous enemies, set off another several minutes of exchanges between Douglass and Johnson that increasingly exasperated the president. Douglass's main point was precisely what Carl Schurz had argued in his reports to Johnson on his travels in the South. Slavery may have ended on paper, but white southerners sought to perpetuate something like slavery through violence, Black Codes, and the practice of peonage. Douglass at this late moment in the meeting now attempted to instruct Johnson, informing him that Blacks "have not the single right of locomotion through the Southern States now." He went on to explain: "There are six days in the year that the negro is free in the South now, and his master then decides for him where he shall go, where he shall work, how much he shall work." Douglass was referring to the six days between Christmas and New Year's Day, when, before the abolition of slavery, the masters permitted revelry (which Douglass saw as degrading debauchery); these were rare days of rest for the enslaved people on the plantation. Douglass's allusion to those six days meant to suggest that nothing much had changed since slavery.[20]

The back-and-forth between Douglass and Johnson led to a defiant final exchange on Black suffrage itself:

> **Mr. Douglass.** Let the negro once understand that he has an organic right to vote, and he will raise up a party in the Southern States among the poor, who will rally with him. There is this conflict that you speak of between the wealthy slaveholder and the poor man.
> **The President.** You touch right upon the point there. There is this conflict, and hence I suggest emigration. If he [the freedman] cannot get employment in the South, he has it in his power to go where he can get it.[21]

Douglass imagined a political coming together of the white working classes and formerly enslaved people, while Johnson thought it just fine for the freedpeople to leave the South even though (as Douglass had mentioned) their mobility was severely limited by lack of funds and the local white patrols watching over them. They would need financial resources and even federal police protection to make such a move.

Johnson's repeated references during the meeting to "slaves" and "the wealthy slaveowner" showed that he still mentally inhabited antebellum Tennessee. In a way he was conceding that the peonage system—in which the formerly enslaved worked on plantations in order to pay back the excessive rents they were charged for living there—was not so different from slavery. But Johnson's reference to emigration shocked Douglass and his fellow delegates. It came close to affirming a position that, even after the abolition of slavery, nothing could be done for Black people in the South. Johnson's mention of emigration also evoked the controversial subject of colonization: the idea that such was the historical enmity between Blacks and whites that the two races could not peaceably live together, and for that reason African Americans should be sent to the southern Americas or Africa. Colonizationists and emigrationists essentially believed that Blacks could never become U.S. citizens.[22] Was that what Johnson was telling the Black delegation?

As the contingent finally prepared to depart, Douglass remarked to his compatriots: "The President sends us to the people, and we go to the people." Johnson picked up on Douglass's words, declaring to those in the room and to those who would soon read Clephane's transcription in newspapers: "Yes, sir; I have great faith in the people. I believe they will do what is right."[23]

The discussion had ended, but the conflict between Johnson and activist African Americans, especially Douglass, had entered a new phase, in which both sides better understood each other. Johnson no doubt thought he had properly instructed this particular group. And though the Black delegates failed to get what they wanted—Johnson's endorsement of equal rights and impartial suffrage for African Americans—they may have gotten something just as valuable with the help of Douglass's performative genius: a widely publicized meeting in which Douglass and his associates forcefully articulated their views while making a mockery of Johnson's claim to be a Moses to their people.

Aftermath

Just hours after the meeting, Clephane's skillful transcription of what Johnson probably thought was an overall favorable interview with the Black delegation appeared in the same day's *Washington Evening Star*. A lightly revised version appeared the next day in the *Washington Morning Chronicle*. The account was subsequently reprinted in newspapers across the country, including the *Illinois State Register*, the *Salt Lake Daily Telegraph*, and the *San Francisco Evening Bulletin*.[24]

Aware that the meeting was not following his script, Johnson at various points came close to losing his temper. To his credit, he stuck with the interview. He remained composed before the challenges to his beliefs and judgment, but his anger was building. Shortly after the Black delegation left his office, he exploded to his personal secretary: "Those d—d sons of b—s thought they had me in a trap! I know that d—d Douglass; he's just like any nigger, & he would sooner cut a white man's throat than not." Historian Paul Bergeron maintains that "the absolute reliability of the quotation can be questioned," at least word for word, but it is probably close to what Johnson said, for we can discern the submerged rage in his exchanges with the smiling Douglass. Johnson's secretary, who was not the most loyal civil servant, and whose name is unknown, confided the comment within twenty-four hours of the meeting to Philip Ripley, a reporter for the *New York World*, a newspaper generally supportive of Johnson, and Ripley included it in a letter of February 8 to his editor, Manton Marble. Reluctant to embarrass Johnson, Marble chose not to print what Johnson had said about Douglass, but he did report on the meeting in his newspaper, concluding that "on the whole, the negro mission to the White House was a failure."[25]

Looking back on the Black delegation's meeting with Johnson in his 1881 *Life and Times,* Douglass predicted that the interview would "take its place in history as one of the first steps" to the achievement of equal rights for African Americans. It had such an impact, he argued, because of the role of publicity. To be sure, he wrote retrospectively and shaped his account for readers in 1881. But he was correct in saying that the meeting accomplished a good deal by making the president state his position on Reconstruction without the help of his speechwriters. "What was said on that occasion," Douglass wrote, "brought the whole question virtually before the American people. Until that interview the country was not fully aware of the intentions and policy of President Johnson on the subject of reconstruction, especially in respect of the newly emancipated class of the South."[26] By December 1865, and even earlier, most Radical Republicans were aware of Johnson's views on the freedpeople. The achievement of the Black delegation, with the help of Douglass's skillful goading of Johnson, was to get those views to U.S. newspaper readers in such baldly explicit terms.

Douglass and his associates, in other words, showed true media savvy, and they continued to do so after the meeting by looking for a way to spin their version of it to the press. Concerned that Johnson's opening speech to the Black delegation would dominate newspaper reports, the group attempted to preempt the president. Douglass recounted how "the members of the delegation met on the evening of that day, and instructed me to prepare a brief reply, which should go out to the country simultaneously with the President's speech to us."[27] Though Douglass took credit for the group reply, he consulted with his colleagues, and the actual text was recorded (and perhaps partly written and edited) by his son Lewis. Their media strategy worked, as their reply appeared before Johnson's own response to the meeting and subsequently gained wide circulation. It was printed in numerous newspapers side by side with the stenographer's account of the meeting, starting with the February 8, 1866, issue of the *Washington Morning Chronicle,* the same issue that printed the stenographer's revised account of the February 7 meeting. In this and other newspapers, the response guided readers to understand the meeting from the perspective of the Black delegation.

The bold response showed little respect for Johnson's conception of Reconstruction. Published under the title "Reply of the Black Delegates to the President," the lobbyists charged that the president's views were "entirely unsound and prejudicial to the highest interests of our race as well as our country at large." They then refuted all of Johnson's key ideas, starting with his claim of "an existing hostility on the part of the former slaves toward the poor white people of the South." They allowed that some tension existed—its "root and sap" lay "in the relation of slavery, and was incited on both sides by the cunning of the slave masters"—but they asserted that a Reconstruction policy that enfranchised the freedpeople would ease such tension. The abolition of slavery brought promising opportunities for Blacks and whites alike, they explained, and offered the best possible hope for creating a new era of interracial friendship. But Johnson, the delegates asserted, wanted just the opposite, and so he incited white people to resent Black people, with predictable results. They asked Johnson: "How can you, in view of your professed desire to promote the welfare of the black man, deprive him of all means of defence, and clothe him whom you regard as his enemy [the former slaveholders] in the panoply of political power?" They instructed the president that "peace between the races" would not be achieved "by degrading one race and exalting another, by giving power to one race and withholding it from another, but by maintaining a state of equal justice between all classes." Finally, they responded to Johnson's implied support for colonization, construing his advice that southern Blacks should consider emigrating to the North as a broader recommendation to leave the country. That would be shortsighted, they said, for African Americans helped to build the nation as laborers and soldiers. To remove them from the country would provide "a terrible shock to its prosperity and peace."[28]

Despite their efforts, the editorial commentaries on the meeting in major newspapers often skewed against Douglass and his colleagues.

A February 9 article in the *New York Times* criticized members of the Black delegation for failing to express "gratitude for the vast sacrifices which their emancipation has entailed on present and future generations of Northern freemen." Negative responses in the press produced critical and sometimes threatening letters to Douglass and his associates. In an anonymous, ungrammatical letter sent to Douglass on February 16, the writer warned: "You old son of a Bitch we give you twenty four hours from Date to leave the D.C. if You Donot You must take the consequence." An unfriendly letter of February 19 addressed to the entire delegation, and signed "Your Friends," castigated the Black men for their disrespect toward Johnson, calling them "impertinent" and saying that Johnson would have been "justified in having you ejected from his mansion." The "Friends" also advised the delegates to "stop your babble" on the topic of Black suffrage.[29]

The group received a much friendlier letter from the Black nationalist Martin R. Delany. A major in the United States Colored Troops and based at the Freedmen's Bureau in Port Royal Island, South Carolina, he praised the delegates for their "*manner*": "Your position before the saged president, and reply after you left him, challenges the admiration of the world. At least it challenges mine, and as a brother you have it." Delany continued to put some faith in Johnson, however, so he advised the group not to "misjudge the president," but to "believe, as I do, that he means to do right; that his intentions are good; that he is interested . . . in the welfare of the black man."[30]

Responses to the meeting from abolitionists and other African Americans were more critical of Johnson. In an article titled "Our 'Poor White' President," the *National Anti-Slavery Standard* contrasted the "Anglo-Saxon" president to his main interlocutor, Frederick Douglass, "a negro, with nothing to back him but his own manhood and talent." In this gendered celebration of Black manhood, the verdict was clear. "If we are compelled to accept Andrew Johnson as our representative," the *Standard* reported, "we blush for the white race."[31]

An equally critical assessment of Johnson began to take shape in the prominent African American newspaper the *Christian Recorder*, which had previously printed mostly positive pieces on the president. Ten days after Johnson's meeting with the Black delegation, and the same day that the article in the *National Anti-Slavery Standard* appeared, the *Recorder* reprinted the widely circulating newspaper account based on Clephane's transcription, along with the "Reply of the Colored Delegation to the President" and an editorial commentary. If the paper had been unsure of Johnson in 1865, that uncertainty had vanished by early 1866. As the editorial made clear: "We are no longer in doubt as to the views of the President in relation to Negro Suffrage. He has spoken plainly and declared his opposition to it." The editorial praised the Black delegates for successfully controverting Johnson's arguments in their reply, and singled out the "well-tempered boldness of George Downing and the dignified, sagacious, and statesmanlike manner of Frederick Douglass." These two men, the editorial concluded, "certainly make us feel quite proud of our race."[32]

In a follow-up article in the *Christian Recorder*, a contributor named "Occasional the Second" captured the ingenuity of Douglass and his associates during their dramatic visit to the president: they had "induced him to declare his pro-slavery proclivities." That is precisely what Douglass had been up to: *inducing* Johnson to unveil his views. "Occasional the Second" explained that by bringing Johnson's positions into the open, the delegation had accomplished something important that promised to produce positive social change. "Do not feel gloomy" about the revelation of Johnson's "pro-slavery proclivities," the writer urged. "Good will grow out of his apostasy."[33]

Johnson's own effort to frame the interview, "Further Remarks in Response to Black Delegates," appeared in the February 11 *New York Times* four days after the initial Black reply. Johnson delivered his dilatory, roundabout response in the form of a reporter's summary of a conversation between the president and Henry J. Raymond, a founder of the *New York Times* and now a Republican congressman who, like Johnson, rejected the Radical Republicans' vision of Reconstruction. After Raymond expressed his concern that the president might be accused of not caring about Black people, Johnson responded that if his past actions "were not a sufficient guarantee that he meant well toward the colored people, and would endeavor to secure to them a fair chance, nothing he could say or do now would give any such guarantee." Johnson then spoke directly about "Mr. DOUGLASS and his friends," maintaining that their demands for immediate Black suffrage "tended to embitter feelings," while the president's administration sought "to cultivate calmness and confidence." Johnson insisted that he was, "if he knew his own heart, the colored man's friend" (though the president's private remarks would suggest that he marked Douglass an exception), and he vowed that he would persist in his efforts to "restore the Union."[34] The word "reconstruction" or its variants never came up in this interview.

Starting shortly before and continuing after the publication of his response, Johnson received letters from friends and admirers praising him for the way he stood up to the Black delegation. A number of the letter writers singled out Douglass as the principal provocateur and enemy to Johnson, and were bothered by a Black man talking back to the white president. In a letter of February 8, William L. Hodge, the former assistant secretary of the Treasury in Franklin Pierce's administration, accused "Douglass & his fellows" of "impudence" and congratulated Johnson for giving them "a just and stinging reproof." Another Johnson cheerleader remarked that "you was more than a mactch [sic] for the great Fred Douglass." The writer decried the "many fanatics" who "think their Pet Douglass is far a head of your Exellency [sic] in profound wisdom." From this writer's point of view, Johnson's "truth . . . closed Mr. D's fine arguments and will open the eyes of many thousands of the blinded in the country." Another Johnson partisan, Charles Dement, a farmer and land manager in Illinois, was milder. He commended Johnson for the "policy indicated in your reply to Fred Douglas [sic] and other colored men," calling it "one of conciliation, a policy that appeals at once to the better impulses of human nature."[35]

The most interesting of these extant letters came from James H. Embry, a white Nashville lawyer and Union Democrat who had befriended Johnson during the Civil War. Embry praised Johnson's performance and insisted that the Supreme Court's *Dred Scott* ruling of 1857 had already "decided that the Negro is not a citizen." Douglass and his allies pressing for citizenship risked triggering what Embry called "the *Second Rebellion*—a Rebellion against the peace and quiet of the people and the unity of the nation." Embry also set forth a conspiratorial vision that had the Black delegation in cahoots with Radical Republican politicians and doing their bidding. He claimed that "Fred. Douglas had been sent for by Sumner, Stevens, . . . & Co to go to Washington" as part of a larger Radical Republican plan to pressure "the Administration to force Negro Suffrage upon the South."[36]

But Embry commented on more than Johnson's meeting with the Black delegation. He had been tracking Douglass, reading his speeches, and paying special attention to his comments on Johnson. Embry's concerns, he confided to the president, led him to go hear Douglass in person.

Embry chose to attend a Douglass lecture on February 9, 1866, titled "Abraham Lincoln and His Administration." He reported to Johnson that Douglass's remarks were insulting and abusive throughout, and that he was especially bothered by the way Douglass mocked Johnson's advice that Blacks needed to prove they were capable of living in freedom. Embry told of how Douglass falsely presented Lincoln as trying "to elevate the Negro to a civil and political equality with the white man," while Johnson had supposedly "surrendered to the Rebellion and was using the power of the Government to deprive the negro of his rights as a freed man." Embry closed his letter to Johnson on an ominous note. "This same Fred. Douglass," he warned, sought "to inculcate through the South the doctrine that the negro ought not to labor for any whites where the Elective Franchise is denied."[37]

How many other letters did Johnson receive about Douglass? We know that someone calling himself "Administration Friend" wrote Johnson in early March to report that Douglass had been invited by office clerks in Washington to speak negatively about the president and to "excite the negroes to rebel." That correspondent even sent along a broadside announcing a recent Douglass talk on the president's policies. But did anyone report to Johnson on the controversy surrounding Douglass's lecture on Lincoln at the First Presbyterian Church in Washington, D.C.? Prior to Douglass's scheduled lecture on February 13, a few days after the speech Embry attended, the church trustees publicly announced that they did not want Douglass speaking there because of his rudeness to Johnson during the Black delegation's visit. The trustees' outrage provided good publicity for the talk, which was well attended, including by someone who "sprinkled the aisles with capsicum [pepper] which caused much suffering and constant coughing." Embry, Johnson, and friends may have also heard that Douglass in his lecture at the church mocked the idea that Johnson was the Black people's Moses. Comparing Johnson to Lincoln, as he regularly did in his Lincoln speeches, Douglass extolled Lincoln as "a progressive man—one who did not begin as a Moses and end as a Pharaoh."[38]

The Black delegation had stripped the mask from Johnson, revealing the racism and southern sympathies guiding his notion that Reconstruction should be about presidential restoration. That racism began to show itself more clearly as he became angrier about the opposition he faced from within his own party, which had very different ideas about Reconstruction. Without that opposition, a more benign and pragmatic Johnson might have emerged to push a gradualist program of Black suffrage in the spirit of Lincoln. Even so, Johnson would have clung to his notion of restoration as a constitutional imperative. Distrustful of the Republicans—and viewing the moderates and Radicals as one and the same—Johnson not too long after his meeting with the Black delegation decided to try to form his own political party.[39] Douglass regarded such a move as an effort to create a presidency that would be above the law and wouldn't have to pay heed to Congress. Douglass and Johnson would not meet again in person, but they continued to track each other and respond to each other as the nation moved closer to an impeachment crisis.

PART THREE

---•---

Chaos and Resistance

7

THE PRESIDENT'S RIOTS

O N FEBRUARY 19, 1866, the man who had recently told the Black delegation that he was a Moses to Black people vetoed Congress's extension of the Bureau of Refugees, Freedmen, and Abandoned Lands, also known as the Freedmen's Bureau. Based in Washington, D.C., and with offices scattered throughout the ex-Confederate states, the Freedmen's Bureau offered essential services to the approximately four million freedpeople in the South. With nine hundred agents, many of whom were former soldiers, and volunteers from the North and South, the bureau helped to distribute much-needed food and clothing to the impoverished people emerging from slavery. And it did much more: the bureau provided medical assistance in newly built clinics; it offered legal protection and guidance on contracts; it tried to ensure that Blacks were properly paid for their work; and it had a crucial role in education, setting up schools and training institutes that were often staffed by volunteers from missionary societies. In its first few months, the bureau confiscated land from a number of southern plantation owners for redistribution to thousands of formerly enslaved people. The bureau also offered some police protection for the freedpeople. It was, in many respects, a radical agency that challenged the racial hierarchies and exclusions that had been central to slave culture. Though it was resented by most white southerners, Republicans viewed the bureau as doing the essential work of Reconstruction.[1]

Johnson accepted the need for the Freedmen's Bureau when it was formed in March 1865 as a war measure, but by May 1865, the month of his Amnesty Proclamation, he had turned against it because of his sympathies for southern whites and his commitment to restoration over Reconstruction. During the summer and fall of 1865, he sought to undo the work of the bureau, issuing executive orders that returned property to the original white owners, even though Blacks had already set up farms on some of these lands. The bureau had been established with funding in place for only one year. Johnson vetoed the Republicans' extension of that funding on the grounds that, with the war over, the southern states should be allowed to develop their own policies toward the freedpeople. He said that the bureau had no right to dictate procedures to the South and that Congress had no right to establish military or any other authority over states that, from his perspective, had never left the Union. He also insisted that no major bills should be passed while the ex-Confederate states lacked congressional representation.

Johnson's continued belief in southern restoration over Reconstruction was no doubt crucial to his veto of the Freedmen's Bureau Bill. His contentious meeting with the Black delegation may have had an impact as well, for in the weeks following the meeting he seemed more adversarial and just a bit unhinged. He had lost control of the meeting, and that made him want to lash out at those he considered his enemies. But even as Johnson regarded the Freedmen's Bureau Bill and other initiatives to help the freedpeople as unconstitutional impositions of federal power over the states, he avowed, "I share with Congress the strongest desire to secure the freedmen the full enjoyment of their freedom and property."[2] He either didn't care about or was willfully blind to the harm done by the southern Black Codes and various forms of anti-Black violence. Congress failed by two votes to override Johnson's veto, but tried again later in 1866 and mustered the votes to extend the life of the agency.

Johnson's Freedmen's Bureau veto message was relatively measured. He was less temperate in his "Washington's Birthday Address," delivered impromptu two weeks after his meeting with the Black delegation and against the advice of his advisers. On February 22, 1866, supporters of the Democratic Party met at Grover's Theatre in Washington, D.C., to voice their objections to federal legislation promoting Black equality. After the meeting, with their emotions still running high, the men assembled outside the White House to cheer on the president they believed shared their views. Johnson, who had been a Unionist Democrat before joining Lincoln's ticket, increasingly came to seem a nominal Republican, displaying his greatest sympathies for the sort of Democrats who had come to celebrate him at the White House. Pleased with the attention, he vented his anger to this sympathetic audience, delivering a speech that celebrated his leadership for "vindicating the union of the States." He emphasized his love for the Constitution, and voiced his fear that he would one day be "beheaded" by the Radicals. But if that were to happen, he said, there was every possibility that his blood, like Christ's, would "seed" a "Church." As the crowd of rowdy Democrats cheered him on, he identified their common enemies as those opposed to restoring the ex-Confederate states to the Union, specifically "THADDEUS STEVENS, of Pennsylvania, . . . Mr. SUMNER, of the Senate, . . . and WENDELL PHILLIPS." These Radical Republicans, he said rather threateningly, were "dead ducks" not worthy of his "ammunition."[3]

According to the *New York Times,* Johnson received "a storm of applause" for this vituperative performance. The African American newspaper the *Christian Recorder* described the speech as "incoherent, abusive, and unsystematic" from a man "more to be pitied than feared."[4]

One month after speaking to this group, Johnson vetoed Congress's Civil Rights Act, which affirmed that all native-born people (with the exception of Native Americans) were citizens of the United

States, and all had equal rights as citizens. He could have signed the bill and made peace with Congress, but he chose to do otherwise. In an effort to assert his executive authority, Johnson in his veto message complained about Congress passing new bills while lacking southern representation. But he also played on white resentment when he said that "the distinction of race and color" in the Civil Rights Bill worked "in favor of the colored and against the white race." Returning to the theme sounded in his White House meeting with Douglass and his associates, he warned: "The tendency of the bill must be to resuscitate the spirit of rebellion."[5] Convinced of the increasing possibility of a war between the races that Blacks would inevitably lose, he presented his veto as a friendly effort to protect Blacks from white working-class wrath. Congress was not convinced and quickly overrode the veto.

The *Christian Recorder* was also not convinced of Johnson's benefecence. In a piece on the Civil Rights Bill titled "The Veto.—The Nation Aroused," the editors wrote that "the colored people . . . had prepared their minds for this action of the President, because his *animus* was exhibited in the interview with Douglass, Downing, Brown, and others."[6]

Meanwhile, Douglass in his lectures had been making clear that Johnson belied the Moses comparison, especially after he saw him at the White House. In the wake of the February 7 meeting, Douglass had gone after the president with a new aggressiveness, maintaining a rhetorical drumbeat of attacks as Johnson began vetoing virtually every Reconstruction bill that Congress sent his way. Douglass was especially cutting in a speech delivered in Washington, D.C., to an interracial Black-suffrage group headed by Pennsylvania congressman William D. Kelley. George T. Downing and Freedmen's Bureau commissioner Oliver O. Howard also attended the meeting and offered brief comments. Perhaps because Downing was in attendance, much of Douglass's speech focused on the Black delegation's visit to Johnson, with Douglass, in a sense, continuing his conversation with Johnson.

And so Douglass, in this March 1866 speech, repeated the story of that visit, telling the group how Johnson, the self-proclaimed Moses to Black people, insisted that "the Government had already done enough for the negro." For those who hadn't read reports of the meeting, Douglass remarked on how "Mr. Johnson assured the colored delegation that if he had not already given them sufficient proof of his interest in the welfare of their race by his past course, there was nothing he could say to convince them of it." Douglass mocked the man who claimed to be interested in the welfare of Black people, using what a reporter called "considerable humor, and a good deal of sarcasm, as well as sound reasoning." Douglass expressed his faux concern for a president who supposedly "feared assassination by colored men." Dismissing rumors of such plots, he concluded that "Johnson was only in danger from moral assassination." Douglass built to a resounding series of questions about the president as he neared the end of his first full year in office: "But what . . . shall be said of Andrew Johnson? . . . But what . . . shall be said of him who told us that traitors must take a back seat in the work of restoration, if he now invests those same traitors with the supreme control of the States in which they live? What shall be said of him who promised to be the Moses of the colored race, if he becomes their Pharaoh instead?"[7]

Douglass paused, and then offered a short and simple response: "Why this must be said of him: that he had better never have been born."[8] The reporter on scene failed to note the audience's reaction, but one imagines that Douglass received exuberant cheers.

Johnson desperately clung to the mantle of Moses by continuing his attempts to demonstrate his leadership to African Americans. In an April speech to Blacks celebrating the fourth anniversary of the abolition of slavery in Washington, D.C., Johnson acknowledged the existence of whites' "prejudice and unkindness" but, as he had many times before, put the burden on African Americans to challenge such attitudes by giving "evidence to the world, and the people of the United States whether you are . . . worthy of being freemen." According to Johnson, Blacks must prove themselves in a culture that he once again claimed offered few barriers to their upward mobility. Convey-

ing that message in the context of what he believed were years of offering his support for Black people, Johnson promised those attending his
speech that "the time will come, and that not far distant, when it will
be proved who is practically your best friend."9

But that was not to happen. Blacks' distrust of Johnson only intensified over the next several months, following two widely reported
anti-Black riots, indeed massacres, in major southern cities.

Memphis and New Orleans

The Memphis Riot of 1866, also known as the Memphis Massacre,
took place over the first three days of May. Tension had been building
between Memphis's Black soldiers, who had served during the war
as part of the United States Colored Troops, and the city's predominantly Irish American police officers, who had strongly supported the
Confederacy. The state itself had been divided in its loyalties, and was
the last southern state to secede. Those who had aligned themselves
with the Confederacy continued to harbor anger against Black people. That anger exploded into violence after a false rumor began to
circulate that a Black soldier had killed a white policeman. A group
of police officers confronted the Black soldiers and shot several dead.
The remaining soldiers managed to take refuge in Fort Pickering,
but that did not stop the violence from escalating into a rampaging
attack on the city's Black people. The police, joined by a white mob,
burned Black schools, churches, and dozens of residences. The police
and their accomplices shot indiscriminately at Blacks, and reportedly
raped numerous Black women. An investigator described a series of
atrocities, including murders of "defenceless old men and women" and
of a younger woman who was "thrown into the flames of a burning
house and consumed." Over forty-five Black people were killed and
hundreds more were injured. Two or three whites were killed, but not
by the Black soldiers. (One white was killed by another for talking to
a Black man; one or two others by their own weapons.) Federal troops

eventually declared martial law and managed to bring a semblance of order to the city.[10]

For Black activists, Radical Republicans, and even many moderate Republicans, the massacre pointed to the racist intransigence of southern whites, the need for additional federal action to protect the freedpeople, and the bloody consequences of Johnson's resistance to Reconstruction. For those sharing Johnson's views on restoration over Reconstruction, the riot, as they termed it, revealed the dangers of the Radical Republicans' efforts to empower African Americans.

In a May 17 letter from Memphis, James B. Bingham, a Unionist Democrat and journalist who had supported Johnson when he was military governor of Tennessee, told the president exactly what he wanted to hear: that the Blacks were responsible for the violence in the city, and that the riot was "a literal verification of your prophecy to Fred. Douglas [*sic*], when he waited on you for universal suffrage for the negro." Bingham informed Johnson that he made the same case to Brigadier General Clinton B. Fisk, a major at Nashville's Freedmen's Bureau, after he arrived in Memphis to investigate the situation for Congress, telling him that the riot verified the president's "Douglass argument—all of which he admitted." (This was a mendacious mischaracterization. In fact, Fisk was appalled by the white violence and thought the government should make reparations to Memphis's African American community.) Viewing the violence through the lens of Johnson's "Douglass argument," Bingham falsely claimed that after a collision between a Black soldier and "white driver," the soldier killed the driver, and that this cold-blooded murder infuriated the Irish police, who were already upset by what they regarded as Black incivility and insubordination. Bingham said that "when the negro soldier no longer had an officer *to obey*, he was betrayed into unusual violence."[11]

Northern newspapers initially shared Bingham's views. The headlines in the May 3 and May 5 issues of the *New York Herald*—"Negro Riot in Memphis" and "The Memphis Negro Riots"—tell that story. An article in the May 12 *New York Times* promising to provide "the facts" about Memphis blamed drunken Black soldiers for being "guilty of excesses and disorderly conduct," while conceding that the police were out of control. "In all parts of the city, wherever they could be seen," the *Times* reported, "negroes were fired upon by policemen as well as citizens."[12] Overall, however, the article suggested that the Blacks must take the main responsibility for instigating the violence.

Newspapers and journals supportive of the Radical Republicans cast the blame on the white policemen, but even more on the Johnson administration. "The Moral of the Memphis Riots," an extensive work of reportage published in the May 15 issue of the *Nation*, best captured the Radical Republican and even African American perspective on the horrific events in Memphis. The anonymous writer warned that the violence in Memphis was "but a fair sample of scenes which we may often expect to witness at the South as soon as the federal troops cease to do police duty." Though Johnson was not mentioned by name, the *Nation* contested his notion that the South was equipped to protect the freedpeople without the help of the federal government. "What was peculiar about the Memphis riot," the writer said, "was that the officers of the law, the very persons on whom the colored population will have to rely for protection as soon as the troops are withdrawn, took a leading part in it." The *Nation* predicted that if similar outbreaks of anti-Black violence were to occur anywhere in the South, "the local police, if they interfered at all, would interfere in the same way." Convinced of the vulnerability of southern Blacks because of "the hatred, and malice towards the colored population," the journal championed the Republicans' Reconstruction policies as the best possible hope for the freedpeople.[13]

The Republican-dominated Congress initiated an investigation of the massacre, and in mid-June approved the Fourteenth Amendment to the Constitution. That amendment, which took up some of the main provisions of the Civil Rights Act, offered birthright citizenship to African Americans, thereby nullifying the Supreme Court's 1857 *Dred Scott* ruling that Blacks could never become citizens of the United States. The amendment, which Congress would soon mandate had to be ratified by any ex-Confederate state seeking readmission to the Union, was particularly tough on the southern economy because it relieved the federal and state governments from paying debts incurred by the former Confederate states. It also refused to compensate southern slave owners for the loss of their slave property and prohibited former Confederate leaders from serving in the new state governments (that would prove to be difficult to enforce). The amendment did not provide voting rights for African Americans, which disturbed Douglass and other African American leaders, but the insistence on Black citizenship was an important first step. The amendment additionally offered an incentive to the ex-Confederate states to adopt Black suffrage by partly keying congressional representation to the number of a state's Black voters. Johnson opposed every provision of the Fourteenth Amendment, but it was quickly and overwhelmingly approved in Congress, almost as if in direct response to what senators and representatives had learned about the horrors of Memphis.

Johnson was not completely obtuse about the damage done to his conception of presidential restoration by what he persisted in calling the "riot" in Memphis. In an effort to restore his reputation among African Americans, he agreed to a July 1866 interview with Paschal B. Randolph, a Black doctor and spiritualist working to help the freedpeople in Louisiana. As he did at the meeting with the Black delegation, Johnson staged the interview in an effort to display his concern for African Americans, inviting a reporter from the moderate (and generally sympathetic) *New York Times* to be in attendance. Randolph had requested the interview in order to solicit Johnson's support for establishing schools for African Americans in a state where whites' hostility posed a challenge to Black education. Performing for the *Times* reporter, Johnson throughout the interview responded graciously to Randolph. He called Randolph's educational goal "a laudable object, and a one which I entirely and heartily approve of," and paternalistically added that if "the colored people would devote more attention to the work of education, and less to politics, it would be greatly to the benefit of your race."[14]

Johnson's patronizing efforts went even further, as he repeated his awkward boasting to the Black delegation that he had owned people as slaves but never sold them. That remark received a better reception from Randolph, who informed the president: "I have just seen a man who was once one of your slaves, and he tells me of your kind treatment to him and his fellows." Still, Johnson seemed unaware that there was something odd in presenting himself as a friend to Black people by claiming to have been a good slave master. He then turned to one of his favorite topics, informing Randolph that he had promised to be "the Moses of your people and lead them to liberty—liberty which they now have."[15] If Randolph saw anything incongruous about that comment in the current circumstances, he kept it to himself. Blacks had just been killed in great numbers in Johnson's home state, and their liberty remained compromised at best throughout the South, in considerable part because of the president's resistance to Reconstruction. All of which is to say that this was an odd time for Johnson to declare himself a Moses to Black people, and it's odder still for the way he linked his behavior as a slave owner to his status as a Moses. His references to himself as Moses were coming to resemble a rhetorical nervous tic.

In the spirit of his Mosaic self-conception, Johnson during his interview with Randolph offered something of an apology to Black people for the violence in Memphis and elsewhere in the South: "I am aware that great abuses have existed in the Southern States since the close of the war, and that in some instances violence has been used toward the recently emancipated slaves. I earnestly regret and deprecate this state of things." This was a remarkable concession for Johnson. Even so, he defended his opposition to federally mandated Black suffrage, assuring Randolph and readers of the *New York Times* that "the difficult question would be eventually solved justly and satisfactorily." A "long desultory conversation" followed, the *Times* reporter wrote, in which "the President frequently remarked that the colored man would eventually learn that he was their best friend; he seemed desirous that he should be thus esteemed."[16] Here the reporter offered a penetrating insight into Johnson's psychology: the man really did want to be esteemed by as many people as possible. Shortly after the publication of the interview, Johnson donated $1,000 of his own money toward the Black schools that Randolph had championed. The donation was reported in the August 1 issue of the *National Intelligencer*, the most widely read political newspaper in Washington.

The interview may have cast Johnson in a better light, but Black suffrage remained the desideratum and demand of politically engaged African Americans. Martin R. Delany, who had applauded Douglass and the Black delegation but was not yet disillusioned with Johnson, made precisely that request in a letter to Johnson of July 25, 1866, which he penned shortly after Johnson's interview with Randolph. Still an officer at the Freedmen's Bureau in Port Royal, South Carolina, Delany had witnessed anti-Black violence in the state and, like many African Americans, was deeply disturbed by the violence in Memphis. He wrote Johnson, "as a black man," to urge him at this fraught time to support "the *enfranchisement* . . . and recognition of the *political equality* of the blacks with the whites in all of their relations as American citizens." There were racial problems in Memphis and other southern towns and cities, but Delany offered a more urgent global rationale for Johnson to support Black suffrage. If the president were to do that, he counseled, there would be "no earthly power able to cope with the United States as a military power; consequently nothing to endanger the national integrity." Reminding Johnson of the role of African Americans in the Civil War, Delany signed his letter "M. R. DELANY, *Major 104th U. S. C. T.*" (United States Colored Troops).[17]

As events quickly revealed, the divide between Blacks and whites in the South continued to pose a distinct threat to what Delany termed the "national integrity." The same day that the *National Intelligencer* posted news of Johnson's donation to Black schools in Louisiana, the nation learned of another incident of mass violence against African Americans in the very state where Randolph was attempting to build those schools.

Lincoln had viewed Louisiana as a test case for placing Union loyalists in power, but under Johnson former Confederates held sway.

Blacks could not vote, and the Black Codes, which allowed authorities to arrest Blacks for so-called vagrancy, were used to intimidate
the freedpeople into taking peonage jobs on the former slave plantations. With Lincoln's visionary plan in mind, African Americans and
their relatively small number of white supporters organized a convention, scheduled for July 30, 1866, at the Mechanics' Institute in New
Orleans, with the hope of making the state's constitution more racially
inclusive. But when the predominantly Black delegates marched to the
institute on the day of the convention, hostile white police officers and
other aggressive whites surrounded them. Insults were shouted back
and forth, and then the police commenced shooting.

As in Memphis, the police action sparked widespread violence
against African Americans. Over the next few hours the police and
other whites pursued the Black delegates, who took refuge in the
Mechanics' Institute and waved white flags of surrender. That didn't
stop the police and their accomplices from entering the building and
shooting the unarmed men. The result was another bloody massacre. The violence continued outside the institute and throughout New
Orleans, as the mayor and other city officials refused to intervene. By
day's end, before federal troops arrived to restore order, at least forty-
eight Blacks were dead and over two hundred wounded. A number of
the Blacks' white supporters were also killed. Some of the surviving
Black delegates, including those who were wounded, were arrested
for their allegedly criminal actions. A hastily produced grand jury
report blamed the Black convention delegates for inciting the riot and
charged not a single white person with murder.[18]

Johnson received a report on the massacre from U.S. military
commander Major General Philip H. Sheridan. Unlike James Bingham, who blamed the Memphis riot on Douglass and the Radical
Republicans, Sheridan identified the racist white police force as the
major instigator. He informed Johnson of how the police began "an
indiscriminate firing on the building" where the Black delegates had
retreated, and subsequently stormed the building and "opened an
indiscriminate fire upon the audience until they had emptied their

revolvers." Sheridan did not hold back on the brutality of the attack, describing how "the wounded were stabbed while lying on the ground, and their heads beaten with brickbats." The responsibility for all this, he said, rested with the mayor of New Orleans, John T. Monroe, for encouraging the violence and hiring "known murderers" for his police force. Sheridan was outraged that civil authorities failed "to arrest citizens who were engaged in this massacre."[19]

With Memphis still on the minds of many, there was even greater outrage about the anti-Black violence in New Orleans.[20] Once again the Republicans sought to investigate what happened, and newspapers throughout the North wondered about the ability of southern states to protect the freedpeople. Wendell Phillips, in an article in the *National Anti-Slavery Standard*, termed the massacre "the President's Riot at New Orleans." He wondered if Johnson might be planning "a *coup d'etat* at Washington . . . by trying the effect of a riot in the commercial capital of the Confederacy." He warned that "what New Orleans is to-day, Washington will be in December, ruled by the President and his mob,—unless the people prevent."[21]

The African American press had been slow to respond to Memphis, but was quick to New Orleans. The *Christian Recorder*'s reporters focused on the police violence directed against Blacks in a state that, as Johnson had recently assured Randolph, supposedly watched out for its freedpeople. One correspondent raised the question of culpability: "Who are the responsible parties? President Johnson, or the Mayor of the city, or the vassals that perpetrated the deed? We answer, all are guilty; but those who had the power to restrain and refused, or sanctioned, are doubly guilty." The *New Orleans Tribune*, the first daily African American newspaper, claimed that the massacre "had its origins in the turbulent and vindictive spirit of Slavery and Rebellion, and received its strength and encouragement from the Administration of Andrew Johnson."[22]

As the *Christian Recorder*, the *New Orleans Tribune*, the *National Anti-Slavery Standard*, and most Republicans presented the situation, Johnson himself bore principal responsibility for what happened. He stood

Thomas Nast, *The Massacre at New Orleans*, 1867, oil on canvas.
(*Courtesy of the Library of Congress, Prints and Photographs Division.*)

at the head of the nation's chain of command. His refusal to support legislation to restrain white violence arguably made him the most responsible of all. Thomas Nast, in one of his nationally famous editorial cartoons, scathingly depicted Johnson as a man with blood on his hands. In *The Massacre at New Orleans*, Nast portrays Johnson watching the violence from a shed whose front wall is inscribed with his oft-repeated phrases on race relations, including "Our Moses."

Douglass, in turn, linked the two highly publicized massacres to the initiative that Johnson refused to support: impartial Black suffrage. Blacks needed the vote before more lives were lost: "With us disenfranchisement means New-Orleans; it means Memphis."[23] At the Southern Loyalists' Convention in September, Douglass would have even more pointed things to say about Johnson's responsibility for anti-Black violence and the abysmal failure of his presidential policies.

8

SHADOWING JOHNSON, DEFYING THE LOYALISTS

W ITH HIS VETOES of the Freedmen's Bureau Bill and the Civil Rights Bill, Johnson had essentially lost the support of his own party in Congress. The Republicans' alienation was clear from their speedy overrides of both vetoes. The violence in Memphis and New Orleans further eroded the president's Republican support. Johnson, who had always felt an affinity with the South, found himself increasingly aligned with the Democratic Party, especially on the issue of southern "restoration." During the summer of 1866, in the wake of the violence in Memphis, the president had a vision: Why not create a new political party, with himself at its helm, consisting of the many Democrats and few Republicans who backed his views on presidential restoration over congressional Reconstruction? To that end, he worked behind the scenes with his advisers to schedule a National Union Convention in Philadelphia in mid-August.

Republican leaders responded to Johnson's machinations with their own meeting in Philadelphia, the Southern Loyalists' Convention, scheduled to begin just two weeks after Johnson's convention ended. The plan was to bring together northern and southern Republicans, but with a particular emphasis on those southerners (like Johnson) who had remained loyal to the Union during the Civil War and now (unlike Johnson) supported the Reconstruction policies of the Republicans. Given its location, timing, and constituency, the Southern Loyalists' Convention shadowed Johnson's. And if the Loyalists' convention was meant to shadow Johnson's convention, then it would make sense to include Frederick Douglass, a former Marylander who had long been shadowing Johnson as his most prominent African American critic. At Philadelphia, Douglass would have the opportunity to showcase his opposition to Johnson and advocate his own priorities for Reconstruction before an influential audience at a highly publicized political event. But would it make sense to have a Black participant at such a convention? That became a matter of debate among the Loyalist delegates, especially those from the northern and border states.

Douglass was not the only person shadowing his opposition. Johnson and his associates had long been shadowing Douglass. The president's associates kept him informed of Douglass's activities. James B. Bingham's letter to Johnson from Memphis about the "Douglass argument" suggested that Douglass to some extent haunted Johnson and his supporters.[1] Oddly enough, the president's men would eventually reach out to Douglass during the summer of 1867 to invite him to become part of the Johnson administration. But that was a move of desperation, which had its sources in the events of the summer and fall of 1866 when Douglass's star went up and Johnson's was sinking.

Swing around the Circle

The National Union Convention, which Johnson hoped would lead to the creation of his new party, took place in Philadelphia over three days in August 1866. Perhaps because he wanted to appear presidential, Johnson chose not to attend the convention. Instead, he was represented by his ardent supporter James R. Doolittle, a Republican senator from Wisconsin who had been a Democrat before the war and would return to the Democratic Party not too long after this convention.

Doolittle served as president of a gathering that did little more than offer resolutions in support of Johnson's efforts to protect the South from the Radical Republicans. For good reason, the *New York Herald* described the Philadelphia meeting as "the Johnson Convention," and went on to say that the delegates mainly sought to make sure "the loyal blacks . . . have no rights whatever but such as the late rebels choose to concede them." Abolitionist Wendell Phillips similarly called the meeting "the Great Rebel Convention." Nothing much came of the convention, but after it concluded Doolittle traveled to the White House to brief Johnson on its proceedings. The next day Senator Reverdy Johnson of Maryland spoke publicly at the White House on the achievements of the convention. In his public response to the senator's remarks, the president underscored the need for a new political party that would take on the Radical Republicans. While Johnson and his advisers worked to restore the Union, he said, the Republican Congress's "every step and act tended to perpetuate disunion and make a disruption of the States inevitable." Johnson didn't mention Memphis or New Orleans, but his position was clear: the Republicans' policies of "penalties, retaliation, and revenge" had produced the violence in the South that the same Republicans now decried.[2] Something needed to be done.

To spread the news about his new political movement, Johnson undertook a speaking tour that became known as his "Swing around the Circle." The avowed aim of the tour was a trip to Chicago to honor the unveiling of a monument to Stephen A. Douglas, the Democratic leader who had been Lincoln's rival in Illinois. Paying homage to a man who had supported states' rights and slavery, as Johnson had at the time of the 1860 presidential election, was Johnson's way of further distinguishing himself from the Republicans, even if his views had changed on slavery. The tour provided the president with an opportunity to publicize his case against the Republicans while promoting the possibility of his new party, so he made numerous stops along the way, circling from New York to Illinois and then over to Missouri and back again to Washington, D.C. The popular general Ulysses S. Grant—who would later break with Johnson—was among those whom Johnson asked to accompany him. Grant would have preferred to stay in Washington, and he expressed his displeasure through excessive drinking. Nevertheless, the presence of Grant, a national hero even in the South for his gentlemanly treatment of the defeated Confederate army, added stature to a tour in which Johnson seemed increasingly agitated and unruly, repeatedly getting into verbal confrontations with his audiences while delivering his speeches.[3]

Johnson delivered one of his more rambunctious speeches from the balcony of a hotel in Cleveland on September 3, 1866. Grant was not able to join him on the balcony, possibly because he was drunk. Johnson himself may have been drunk, or he simply got into a fighting mood when people in the audience dared to interrupt him. The speech was punctuated by a number of wild exchanges with hostile questioners. When an audience member shouted a remark critical of the president, Johnson lashed back: "Where is the person that can place their finger upon one single hair breadth of deviation from one single pledge I have made, or one single violation of the Constitution of the country? What tongue does he speak? What religion does he profess?" Someone yelled, "Hang Jeff. Davis," with the implication that Johnson, the man who had pardoned so many ex-Confederates, was responsible for the greatest traitor of them all escaping a deserved punishment. (The former Confederate president was at the time imprisoned in Virginia.) But was Davis the greatest traitor of them all? In response to this heckler, Johnson, to the cheers of his supporters, named the true enemies of the republic deserving of punishment: "Hang Jeff. Davis? . . . Why don't you hang Thad. Stevens and Wendell Phillips? . . . I am prepared to fight traitors at the North, God being willing, with your help." To which another audience member bellowed, "You can't have it," which set off "prolonged confusion."[4]

Then yet another voice called out: "What about New Orleans?" That question, which implied that Johnson bore some responsibility for the horrific violence, set him off, and he flew into a rage. In the home state of Radical Republican Benjamin Wade, Johnson proceeded to thrust a dagger at the hypocrisy of those northerners calling for suffrage and protections for the freedpeople. "Take the beam out of your own eye," Johnson told his hecklers, "before you see the mote in your neighbor's eye. You are very much disturbed about New Orleans—but you will not allow the negro to vote in Ohio."[5]

The next day's *Cleveland Plain Dealer* captured the back-and-forth between Johnson and his audience, and the report was widely reprinted in northern newspapers, to the further detriment of Johnson's reputation. Many Americans still believed in the idea of presidential decorum, and they now read about a president who picked fights with his own constituents.

Johnson's clashes with members of his audiences continued at other venues. The president thought he had the crowd on his side during a September 8 speech in St. Louis near the end of his Swing around the Circle. That led him to make a number of questionable and bombastic claims, including about the massacre in New Orleans. He once again blamed the deaths in New Orleans on the Radical Republicans, maintaining that the violence was "substantially planned" by those whose "incendiary" speeches excited "that portion of the population, the black population, to arm themselves and prepare for the shedding of blood." The Republicans, Johnson maintained, bore responsibility for "every drop of blood that was shed." He continued to play to the racism of the crowd when he complained that the Freedmen's Bureau gave advantages to Black people over white people, and he even suggested that the bureau's policies made slaves of white people. "There is a set amongst you that have got shackles on their limbs," he said, "and are as much under the heel and control of their masters, as the colored man that was emancipated." For that assertion he was cheered.[6]

Those cheers led Johnson to bring up the topic of impeachment. The Republicans, he told the mostly friendly crowd, believed he had "committed a high offence" with his vetoes of the Freedmen's Bureau. He had heard vague rumors that some thought he "ought to be impeached," and the very idea of impeachment put him in a frenzy. Referring to himself in the third person, he blustered, "*Y-e-s, y-e-s*; they are ready to impeach him." He portrayed himself as a martyr at the hands of the Radical Republicans. "I have been traduced, I have been slandered, I have been maligned, I have been called Judas," he said. That alleged charge led him to ask a series of rhetorical questions: "If I had played the Judas, who has been my Christ that I have played the Judas with? Was it Thad. Stevens? Was it Wendell Phillips? Was it Charles Sumner?" The mention of figures who were admired by some in the crowd elicited a mix of "hisses and cheers." When a skeptic yelled that the apostles had a Moses, too, Johnson reflexively leaped at the opportunity to assert his own Mosaic character. "Yes, there was a Moses," he shouted back. "And I know sometimes it has been said that I have said that I would be the Moses of the colored man." That led to a call of "Never," but also to cheering. "Why, I have labored as much in the cause of emancipation as any mortal man living," Johnson continued. "But while I have strived to emancipate the colored man, I have felt, and now feel, that we have a great many white men that want emancipation." The crowd responded to that claim with "laughter and cheers."[7]

Near the end of the St. Louis speech, in an echo of the earlier moment in Cleveland, Johnson responded to a call from the crowd to hang Jefferson Davis. As in Cleveland, he turned that request on its head: "Why don't you hang Thad. Stevens and Wendell Phillips?" According to a reporter on the scene, that query was met with "great cheering."[8]

When Johnson returned to Washington in mid-September, he had lost much of his support from major newspapers in the North and Midwest. Both the press and Republican politicians criticized the violent rhetoric of his attacks on Stevens and Phillips, as well as Johnson's lack of presidential decorum. The *Chicago Tribune* called the St. Louis speech "the crowning disgrace of a disreputable series. It is the longest and worst of his harangues. Its wickedness cannot be exaggerated. It out Johnsons Johnson." Even Gideon Welles, Johnson's sympathetic secretary of the navy, confided to his diary on September 17 that the president "may have injured his cause by his many speeches."[9]

"You Might as Well Ask Me to Put a Loaded Pistol to My Head and Blow My Brains Out"

Johnson's speeches from his Swing around the Circle were very much on the minds of the Republican delegates to the Southern Loyalists' Convention, which took place in Philadelphia the first week of September 1866 and overlapped with the final few days of Johnson's speaking tour. The participants at the convention responded to the recently concluded National Union Convention and to Johnson himself. Douglass remarked in his 1881 autobiography that Johnson's retrograde policies "gave importance to this convention, more than anything which was then occurring at the South; for through the treachery of this bold, bad man, we seemed then about to lose nearly all that had been gained by the war."[10]

Douglass's retrospective accounts of events in his autobiographies can sometimes be misleading, but he tells a striking story in *Life and Times* about his participation at the Southern Loyalists' Convention that can be corroborated by speeches and newspaper articles of the time. Douglass gave several speeches at the convention that took direct aim at Johnson, but his later account, written when he sensed Reconstruction had failed, suggested that the failure of Reconstruction had as much to do with the North as the South—exemplified by the desire of some participants of the Southern Loyalists' Convention to make the event for white people only.

As the name of the Southern Loyalists' Convention suggests, the goal was to challenge Johnson's policy of restoration by emphasizing the perspective of those in the South who had remained loyal to the Union. The original idea for the convention came from southerners themselves, with the main organizers based in Texas, Alabama, and Louisiana. One of the original organizers was Anthony Paul Dostie, a white dentist and civil rights advocate from New Orleans who had been killed, along with many Blacks, on the day of that city's massacre. The convention had over three hundred representatives from both the South and North, but only one "loyal" Black person.[11] Born in Maryland and at the time living in Rochester, Douglass was the exception, and to many of the white participants, he was a problematic exception at that. Douglass shared the goal of the convention to condemn Johnson and his policies, but he nonetheless found himself at the center of a controversy that revealed the difficulties of creating a new era for African Americans in the United States, with or without Johnson.

The controversy, as Douglass described it, began with a meeting of Republicans in Rochester, "a city of over sixty thousand white citizens and only about two hundred colored residents," where the predominantly white Republican group chose him to be Rochester's delegate at the convention. Rather than cheering this decision, some of the convention's other delegates regarded Douglass's election as bad news, fearing that "the clamor of social equality and amalgamation" would trouble their meeting, which, paradoxically, was in support of Reconstruction policies intended to bring about social equality. According to Douglass, those concerned about "amalgamation"—a term used at the time to arouse whites' racial anxieties—were mainly northern and border-state Republicans, who "found it much more agreeable to talk of the principles of liberty as glittering generalities, than to reduce those principles to practice."[12] Such was his damning critique of his own political party.

The situation got worse before it got better. On the train from Harrisburg to Philadelphia, several delegates approached Douglass, urging him not to attend the convention because northerners and southerners disliked people of his race. Again, paradoxically, they believed they could more readily accomplish their egalitarian goals through a racially exclusive convention. These delegates insisted that "it was a time for the sacrifice of [Douglass's] own personal feeling for the good of the Republican cause." Douglass dramatically responded to their request for his self-sacrifice: "Gentlemen, with all respect, you might as well ask me to put a loaded pistol to my head and blow my brains out, as to ask me to keep out of this convention, to which I have been duly elected."[13] He also warned that the delegates risked being branded cowards and hypocrites by those who truly cared about equal rights.

Cowards and hypocrites they were. Once the participants arrived in Philadelphia, they chose to ignore the Black delegate. Douglass found their behavior especially hurtful during the formal public march to the convention site. He walked alone, recognizing, as he bitingly phrased it in his autobiography, that he "was the ugly and deformed child of the family, and to be kept out of sight as much as possible while there was company in the house."[14] But then everything changed because of Theodore Tilton, the brash young editor of the New York–based *Independent*, one of the nation's leading progressive weeklies.

Tilton had recently assumed the editorial responsibilities from the renowned preacher Henry Ward Beecher, the brother of Harriet Beecher Stowe, who herself regularly published essays in the *Independent*. During the mid-1870s, Tilton would publicly accuse Beecher of committing adultery with his wife, the suffragist Elizabeth Richards Tilton, and take him to trial; in the aftermath of a libel trial that failed to produce a decision, Tilton abandoned his wife and relocated to Paris. But that was in the future. On the day that the delegates marched, Tilton, a "man of the purest Caucasian type," as Douglass put it, approached Douglass and created a spectacle by walking arm in arm with the Black man. But rather than inciting mob violence, Tilton's bold act warmed the onlookers. Douglass recalled being "utterly surprised by the heartiness and unanimity of the public approval," even in a city once known "for the depth and bitterness of its hatred for the abolition movement." In a heartfelt testimonial to Tilton, Douglass proclaimed years later: "I never appreciated an act of courage and generous sentiment more highly than I did that of this brave young man when we marched through the streets of Philadelphia on this memorable day."[15]

Even with Tilton's intervention, Douglass continued to face racism from the Republican delegates themselves. A week before the convention, the Pennsylvania lawyer and banker Samuel Shoch, who planned to attend the convention, had written his congressman, Thaddeus Stevens, about his and others' objections to Douglass's involvement. He asked Stevens to use his "influence with Mr. Douglas [*sic*] to induce him to remain at home or decline the appointment." Phrasing the request so that it spoke to political pragmatism and not his own racism, Shoch warned that the participation of a Black man threatened to "injure our cause," perhaps leading to the loss of "some Congressmen in the doubtful districts." Stevens, for all of his idealism and commitment to Blacks' rights, shared Shoch's concerns. It was too late for him to talk Douglass out of attending, but in a tortured letter to Republican William D. Kelley, who attended the convention (Stevens did not), he characterized Tilton's generous act of reaching out to Douglass as moral preening. "A good many people here are disturbed by the practical exhibition of Social equality in the Arm-in-arm performance of Douglas [*sic*] and Tilton," he informed Kelley. "Why it was done I cannot see except as foolish bravado." Stevens was sensitive enough to know that his objections to Tilton's actions "did not become radicals like us." Still, aware of the pervasiveness of racism in all sections of the country, the man who worked so tirelessly to improve the lot of the freedpeople worried that the cause would be undermined by public expressions of friendship toward African Americans, even in the North. Like Shoch, he had pragmatic concerns that "the old prejudice, now revived will lose us some votes."[16]

Stevens's letter to Kelley, dated September 6, 1866, ended up in the same day's issue of the *New York Times*, which suggests that Stevens himself leaked it, with the hope that an attack on Tilton's "foolish bravado" would offer reassurances to moderate voters that the Republican Party had not become "Black." Stevens was both an idealist and a pragmatist; he didn't want to lose votes to the Democrats. As it turned out, Tilton's bold act of friendship, with all of its bravado, helped to make Douglass a key figure at the convention. Douglass was not scheduled to speak, but delegates now demanded that he do so. In his four days at the convention, he gave three speeches, all centered on Johnson, and all greeted enthusiastically. As he had in some of his speeches earlier that year, Douglass in effect continued the conversation that he had with the president at the White House seven months earlier.

Johnson had warned Douglass and the Black delegation that suffrage for all African American men could lead to a war between the races. In his first speech to the convention, the biracial Douglass remarked that he contained "the black and the white race combined" in his very body. "So far as my own experience goes to show it," he went on to say, "from the peaceable manner in which the blood of the two races have lived together for the last fifty years in this organism— (Laughter)—I have not the slightest fear of a war of the races." In response to Johnson's suggestion at the February meeting that Blacks might want to leave the South or even the country, Douglass in the same speech affirmed that the Black man was "a permanent part of the American people," and would remain so: "No scheme of colonization or no mode of extirpation can be adopted by which he shall be entirely eradicated from this land." At the end of his meeting with the Black delegation, Johnson had voiced his faith in the American people to make the right decisions about Reconstruction. In his second speech to the convention, Douglass reminded his audience that Andrew Johnson expressed his belief "in the American people—in their good sense, in their patriotism and their honor." To which Douglass replied, as he had in February, "I believe in this more than he, for he is appealing to anything else but their good sense and their honor."[17]

Douglass in his third and final speech turned to the recent massacre of African Americans in New Orleans. Black people had attempted to meet in a convention in New Orleans, just as the nearly all-white Loyalists now met in Philadelphia, "animated by the same spirit that was murdered down in New Orleans." The murderer, he maintained, was "Andy Johnson," the man who aspired "to be our Moses" but so far had "taken the back track." Douglass then alluded to Johnson's ongoing Swing around the Circle, especially those moments when Johnson appeared to be drunk. "A negro sober knows as much as a white man drunk," Douglass joked, and "a negro knows as much sober as Andy Johnson in any condition you may name."[18]

Douglass did more than indict Johnson while at the convention; he sought to persuade the delegates, many of whom were from the South, of the wisdom of supporting Black suffrage in the North and South. He called for the federal government, not the states, to determine voting policy. "The negro is a man," Douglass asserted in his opening speech, "and we have recently become aware that a great revolution is going on—a great political revolution in the United States. It is for manhood suffrage." That statement met with "great applause." Two days later he made a similar plea: "I ask you to enfranchise the negro. The honor of the nation demands it."[19] Tilton joined Douglass in the call for federal action on Black suffrage, as did the charismatic Anna Dickinson, still in her early twenties and already one of the nation's most popular (and well remunerated) speakers on a range of reform issues, including Black and women's suffrage. Douglass supported both causes, but in the immediate postwar years he had narrowed his attention to first extending the vote to all men regardless of color. Dickinson supported Douglass's cause at this convention and beyond; other women's rights advocates challenged him later in the decade.

The convention's organizers had not intended to produce a resolution endorsing Black suffrage. One of their main goals was to produce a resolution backing the Fourteenth Amendment, which they succeeded in doing. But Douglass, who was dissatisfied with the amendment for its failure to address Black voting rights, pushed on his favorite issue. Despite the objections of representatives from the border states, some of whom withdrew, Douglass, with the help of Tilton and Dickinson, got the remaining loyalists of the North and South to agree on a resolution affirming their support for impartial Black suffrage. That was the outcome he celebrated at the convention and later in *Life and Times*.

Douglass got good press for the role he played at the convention. According to a reporter for the *Christian Recorder*, the group was "enraptured with the eloquence of Frederick Douglass . . . as the principles of truth and justice fell from his lips." Another article in the same African American newspaper gave a fuller account of how Douglass, with Tilton's help, surmounted the racism he faced from supposedly progressive politicians. "The treatment which Frederick Douglass has received will astonish the world," the *Christian Recorder* announced, and "the manner in which Mr. Douglass has borne himself has won for him a respect not exceeded by that accorded to any member of the Northern delegation." The newspaper also rhapsodized about his unmatched oratorical skill. The *New York Herald*, then New York's most widely read newspaper, also exclaimed over his speeches, describing how they were met with "deafening applause and cheering."[20]

Douglass had many triumphs in his career. Facing down racism from northern Republicans at the Southern Loyalists' Convention stood high among them.

9

SOURCES OF DANGER TO
THE REPUBLIC

OUGLASS REACHED greater national prominence after the
Southern Loyalists' Convention. He capitalized on it by submitting an essay to the *Atlantic Monthly* on Johnson, Reconstruction,
and Black suffrage. He also worked up a speech called "Sources of
Danger to the Republic," which he gave repeatedly over a ten-month
period, starting December 1866 and continuing in a wide range of
venues through October 1867. "Sources of Danger" is one of Douglass's greatest speeches, offering shrewd insights into the limits of the
U.S. Constitution at a time of crisis. Addressing his audiences as a
social critic, political theorist, and prophet, he also confronted the
problem of what to do about a dangerous president—an issue that
would confound Americans long after Johnson departed office.

"Your Justly Celebrated Magazine"

Almost immediately after returning to Rochester from the Southern
Loyalists' Convention, Douglass got to work on a long essay on Recon-

struction. He sent it off unsolicited to the firm of Ticknor and Fields, the publishers of the *Atlantic Monthly*, telling the editors that if the essay was too long for publication in the *Atlantic*, they could "print it in pamphlet." He also told the editors that submitting to the *Atlantic* fulfilled a cultural aspiration "about appearing, once in my life, in your justly celebrated magazine."[1]

Founded in 1857 by the poet James Russell Lowell, and at the time edited by James Fields of the prestigious Boston publishing house Ticknor and Fields, the *Atlantic* had emerged as the leading journal of "white highbrow literary culture," with a circulation of around fifty thousand.[2] The journal sympathized with the Republicans' position on Reconstruction, and it also made an effort to publish African American writers, such as Charlotte Forten, William Parker, and Nicholas Said. Fields must have been thrilled to receive the manuscript from Douglass. Using his editorial prerogative, he carved two sharp and punchy essays from the manuscript—"Reconstruction" and "An Appeal to Congress for Impartial Suffrage"—which he published in the December 1866 and January 1867 issues, respectively.[3]

In both essays, Douglass presented the nation as at a crossroads. More than a year after the South's surrender at Appomattox, the war risked becoming "a miserable failure, barren of permanent results." Johnson had pardoned former Confederates and then allowed them to construct their own "sham governments" that continued to exclude Blacks. With Memphis and New Orleans in mind, Douglass asserted that Johnson's advocacy of presidential restoration over congressional Reconstruction led to "the present anarchical state of things in the late rebellious States,—where frightful murders and wholesale massacres are perpetrated in the very presence of Federal soldiers." As Douglass and other African American activists emphasized, Johnson's policy decisions contributed to the deaths of Black people. To some extent, the man was a murderer. But Johnson had committed other crimes as well, and in the December essay titled "Reconstruction" Douglass did not hold back on his judgment. The president, he declared, "stands

to-day before the country as a convicted usurper, a political criminal, guilty of a bold and persistent attempt to possess himself of the
legislative powers solemnly secured to Congress by the Constitution."
Johnson in his Swing around the Circle lecture tour had embarrassed
himself with what Douglass called "the most disgraceful exhibition
ever made by any President."[4] But it was a useful exhibition, Douglass
observed, because it turned the people against Johnson. In the recent
fall elections, Republicans had made considerable gains and now had
a veto-proof two-thirds majority in both houses of Congress. After
more than a year of chafing, Congress at long last had the opportunity
to set in place its own policies to reconstruct the nation.

Writing in late 1866, before the new Congress began its session,
Douglass called on Republicans to adopt "a radical policy of reconstruction" that would make a "clean slate" of the defeated ex-Confederate
states. Congress had two options for doing this, he said. It could take
the extreme and virtually impossible step of exerting control over the
southern states by positioning "a Federal officer at every cross-road,"
or it could take the easier and more attractive step of granting Black
men "the elective franchise," a "right and power," as he termed it,
which would "form a wall of fire for his protection." Black suffrage
would do the work of a federal occupying force by allowing the freedpeople to elect their state representatives and in this way shape policy.
Johnson may have been treacherous for supporting restored southern
governments that disenfranchised African Americans, but the new
Congress could undertake the "grand work of national regeneration
and entire purification" by ensuring Blacks' equal rights as citizens.[5]
Douglass's concern at this point was that Congress would not rise to
the occasion, as evidenced by its failure to include Black suffrage as
part of its recently passed Fourteenth Amendment.

While the Fourteenth Amendment conferred birthright citizenship and equal rights on African Americans, it left the matter of voting
to the individual states. In Douglass's view, that equivocation created
a hollow citizenship. "To tell me that I am an equal American citizen,
and, in the same breath, tell me that my right to vote may be consti-

tutionally taken from me by some other equal citizen or citizens," he had written in the *National Anti-Slavery Standard*, "is to tell me that my citizenship is but an empty name." In the *Atlantic*, Douglass called the Fourteenth Amendment an "unfortunate blunder" that created an "emasculated citizenship" for African Americans. He maintained that true Reconstruction could not occur without the empowerment of Black people through the franchise, and that the Republican Congress needed to recognize that. In an aggressive rhetorical phrasing that came close to an ultimatum, and which may have baffled even the *Atlantic*'s most progressive readers, he insisted that "the nation must fall or flourish with the negro."[6]

Douglass continued to confront Congress and the *Atlantic*'s white readership in his January 1867 essay, "An Appeal to Congress for Impartial Suffrage." He warned of the possibility of "a war of races," not from expanding Blacks' rights (as Johnson regularly claimed) but by denying those rights. Withholding the vote from the Black man, he said, constituted "a crime against the manhood of a man," and Congress was implicated in that crime.[7]

Douglass's perspective on the moral urgency of Black suffrage diverged from the way some Radical Republicans presented the case. Massachusetts congressman George Sewall Boutwell, for instance, who would become one of the House managers of Johnson's impeachment trial, made the more politically pragmatic claim that the lack of Black suffrage in the South harmed white men in the North. Boutwell was known for championing Blacks' rights, but in a convoluted argument published in the *Atlantic* a few months earlier, he pointed out that the practice of counting nonvoting Blacks toward a southern state's congressional representation (as Johnson and other white southerners wanted) ultimately degraded "the white race of the North by depriving every man of his due share in the government of the country." In such a scheme of representation, he said, "two white men in the South would possess the political power of three white men in the North," with the imbalance allowing the South to reemerge as "the controlling force in the government of the country."[8] Like all of the Radical Republicans, Boutwell believed that Black suffrage would help the Republican Party in both sections; and like many of these Republicans he had a genuine interest in improving the situation of Blacks in the South. But in this particular *Atlantic* piece the freedpeople themselves seemed not to matter.

Douglass may have been responding to Boutwell, or to similar arguments set forth by other northern Republicans. In his *Atlantic* essay "Impartial Suffrage," Douglass made a more disinterested—and trenchant—moral argument for Black suffrage by ignoring party politics and insisting on Blacks' humanity. A policy of impartial Black suffrage in all sections of the country, he asserted, would be good for the nation, helping to create "a common liberty and a common civilization." With this more idealistic approach, Douglass suggested his distance from the argumentative strategy informing Boutwell's essay. Douglass pleaded with Republican congressmen to think more broadly and boldly about the future of the nation, and to act before the window of opportunity on Reconstruction closed. "The destiny of unborn and unnumbered generations is in your hands," he stated. "As you members of the Thirty-ninth Congress decide, will the country be peaceful, united, and happy, or troubled, divided, and miserable?"[9] He continued to ask this question of Congress, his readers, and his auditors over the next three decades.

Douglass's *Atlantic* essays appeared at a time when Johnson sought to tone down his rhetoric and express his own desire for a peaceful and united country. In his annual message to Congress of December 3, 1866, Johnson did not call for the hanging of his political enemies, as he had during his road trip. Instead, he invited "an entire restoration of fraternal feeling." But he offered his olive branch with conditions. He clung to his belief that fraternal feeling across the country depended on restoring the ex-Confederate states to the Union with virtually no requirements beyond their support of the Thirteenth Amendment. He also continued to believe that legislation passed by Congress without the participation of those states lacked constitutional authority. In order to present the southern states as ready for restoration, he had to ignore the anti-Black violence of Memphis, New Orleans, and elsewhere. As stubbornly obtuse as ever about the vulnerability of the freedpeople in the ex-Confederate states, he assured Congress that all of the southern states had enacted "measures for the protection and amelioration of the condition of the colored race."[10]

On January 5, 1867, around the time that Douglass's article on Black voting rights appeared in the *Atlantic*, Johnson vetoed the District of Columbia Franchise Law, which granted voting rights to African American men. The man who had supported limited forms of Black suffrage persisted in arguing for moving gradually. The ballot, Johnson explained, was "a privilege and a trust," which required "of some classes a time suitable for probation and preparation." He continued to resent Congress's refusal to seat representatives from the ex-Confederate states, and he continued to insist, fruitlessly, that bills coming out of Congress lacked constitutional authority because of these vacancies. But the most cutting (and troubling) remarks in Johnson's veto of the Franchise Law centered on his vision of democracy. He insisted that Congress, by passing a law to introduce impartial Black suffrage for Washington, D.C., had "disregard[ed] the wishes of the people of the District of Columbia." By "people," Johnson meant white male voters. In a December 1865 vote on Black suffrage, he pointed out, only 35 of 6,556 whites approved of Black suffrage. In Georgetown, that number was just 1 of 833.[11] Johnson's argument was limited in obvious ways. The writers of the Constitution favored not the power of majorities over minorities but rather the protection of minorities, as indicated by the ten Constitutional Amendments of the 1791 Bill of Rights. Yet Johnson saw no need to extend such protections to Black people.

Congress quickly overrode Johnson's veto, marking the first time that it used its legislative power to legalize Blacks' voting rights. That action pleased Douglass. But much still needed to be done to bring forth the reconstructed nation that Douglass and other African Americans envisioned, and so Douglass hit the lecture circuit with his stirring "Sources of Danger to the Republic."

The National Hall Lectures

The same month that Douglass published "Reconstruction," he delivered the first version of "Sources of Danger to the Republic" to a
white audience in New Jersey. He revised "Sources of Danger" continually, presenting it upwards of twenty times in less than a year to
white and Black audiences in every region of the country except the
Deep South. He gave one of the earliest full iterations of the speech
in an African American–sponsored lecture series in Philadelphia on
January 3, 1867, two days before Johnson vetoed Black suffrage in the
District. That version shows Douglass building community with Black
activists by sharing his anger at Johnson's and other white leaders'
recalcitrance on Black rights.[12] The series also featured the acclaimed
African American poet, essayist, and orator Frances Ellen Watkins
Harper, who offered a blistering lecture titled "National Salvation."

Organized by the Social, Civil, and Statistical Association of the
Colored People of Pennsylvania and chaired by the Black abolitionist William Still, who was best known for his work as a leader of the
Underground Railroad, the Philadelphia lecture series of 1866–1867
was conceived for predominantly African American audiences. The
series kicked off on November 30, 1866, at National Hall, then a popular venue for civic gatherings, with a lecture by Boutwell, who overall was seen as supportive of Black people. Douglass, William Wells
Brown, Frances Harper, and other notable African American leaders
took the stage in 1867.[13] Unlike the halls of Congress, here was a place
to critique Johnson and the course of Reconstruction without the concerns that sometimes worried the Radical Republicans about alienat-
ing white voters.

Douglass's "Sources of Danger to the Republic" and Harper's
"National Salvation" stand out as highlights of the series. "Sources of
Danger" is one of Douglass's best speeches about the past, present, and
future of the U.S. nation. Harper's "National Salvation" is one of the
great speeches about the interconnected dangers posed to Black people

Frances Ellen Watkins Harper. Illustration in William Still, *The Underground Railroad* (1872). (*Courtesy of the Library of Congress, Prints and Photographs Division.*)

by Johnson and white racist culture. Douglass and Harper admired each other and spoke together in several lecture series, even on the same stage on occasion.[14] They overlapped in their thinking about Reconstruction, but they took their arguments in somewhat different directions. Their lectures formed a diptych as Johnson approached his third year in office.

Remembered chiefly as a poet and fiction writer, Frances Harper had also gained acclaim as a charismatic public speaker at a time when many thought it inappropriate for women to speak before mixed (male and female) audiences. A writer for the *Christian Recorder* offered the highest possible encomium to her talent as a speaker: "We have heard Frederick Douglass, and hesitate not to say that for beauty of expression, richness of illustration, and, in a word, rhetorical finish, she is his superior."[15]

During 1866 and 1867, Harper denounced the president in a number of speeches, always as part of a larger vision of the problem of racism in northern culture. In a celebrated speech of May 1866, which she delivered at the Eleventh National Women's Rights Convention in New York City, she reminded Susan B. Anthony, Elizabeth Cady Stanton, and the other influential women's rights advocates in attendance that Black women faced the distinct problem of racism even in cosmopolitan cities like New York and Philadelphia. For Harper, the country had greater troubles than Andrew Johnson, whom she saw as a metonym for racism in its local and national forms. Nevertheless, speaking before the country's leading women's rights advocates, Harper turned her sights on the president, whom she called "the incarnation of meanness." Offering a psychological explanation that anticipated modern interpretations of Johnson, she opined that because he was once discriminated against by "the rich slaveholders" for being a poor white, he now needed to discriminate against those whom he regarded as his inferiors. That explanation led to a punning joke about the president as "a poor white man" who kept "poor whits."[16]

In her "National Salvation" lecture at Philadelphia's National Hall, delivered on January 31, 1867, Harper suggested that Johnson's "poor whits" had continued to deteriorate. A dynamic speaker with a talent for metaphor and ironic humor, Harper was at times wildly, exuberantly critical of Johnson, but as she had done in her May 1866 speech at the women's rights convention, she also addressed the problem of racism in northern cities that were particularly vexed by it.

A transcript of Harper's speech appeared in an adulatory article in the *Philadelphia Daily Evening Telegraph*, a relatively new addition to Philadelphia's white press with a good city circulation. Though some whites attended the speech, African Americans made up the majority of the audience. They were regular lecture-series attendees who shared Harper's hopes that "legislation and jurisprudence" at both the local and federal levels could help to erase the "distinctions between man and man, on account of his race, color, or descent." Harper was capable of soaring optimism, as when she described Reconstruction as "still . . . one of the greatest opportunities, one of the sublimest chances that God ever put into the hands of a nation or people."[17] And that was true, she said, despite Andrew Johnson.

Harper strategically framed her attack on the president by positioning him in relation to the Blacks of Tennessee. She told her audience that she had recently visited Johnson's home state, spending time with the rural Blacks who, she said, had not yet been helped by Reconstruction. Attesting that she learned "some of the most beautiful lessons of faith and trust" from the Black people living "amid the cabins and humble homes of Tennessee," she spoke scornfully of the man who continued to pride himself on supposedly emancipating Tennessee's enslaved Blacks in October 1864 and accepting their mantle as leader. "There may be some people," she said, "who think within themselves that it is a little strange Andrew Johnson, after having promised the colored people that he would be their Moses, should turn around, and instead of helping them to freedom, should clasp hands with the Rebels and traitors of the country." To the cheering crowd, Harper contrasted the honest Blacks of Tennessee with the duplicitous white president: "When I have gone among some of the people of Tennessee, who have breathed their words of faith and trust, I see in Andrew Johnson a man whose hands are not clean enough to touch the hems of their garments."[18]

Harper then turned to the other pillar of her speeches of this period: northern racism. Stating that she refused to "bathe my lips in honey," she excoriated those clasping "hands with Rebels in the city of Philadelphia." Philadelphia's "Rebels" included white workers on the public streetcar who literally "kicked off" a Black woman who tried to board. For Harper, that moment showed how aspects of slavery remained alive and well in a city, and state, where Blacks could not vote. It was a single incident, but one that ramified because of its representativeness. "Friends," she said to the crowd, "when that man kicked that woman, he kicked me. He kicked my child, and he kicked the wife and child of every colored man in Philadelphia." She linked the racism in Philadelphia to the larger national situation in which Blacks, even those men who fought for the country during the Civil

War, were regularly attacked in the North and South. Like many African American commentators, she evoked the recent reminders of Black vulnerability on "the streets of New Orleans and Memphis red with the blood of unexpiated murders."[19]

According to Harper, Johnson should take some of the blame for the racism and hate that continued to pervade the country, but not all. He was a symptom, she explained, but such was his obvious evil that he could paradoxically serve as a cure as well. In a wonderful use of metaphor at the most rousing moment of the speech, Harper compared the president to a curative dressing that could bring good health to the diseased national body. She told her rapt audience: "We have needed Andrew Johnson in this country as a great national mustard-plaster, to spread himself all over this nation, so that he might bring to the surface the poison of slavery which still lingers in the body politic." Johnson's racist leadership had certainly done that. But, Harper asked, "when you have done with the mustard-plaster, what do you do with it? Do you hug it to your bosom, and say it is such a precious thing that you cannot put it away? Rather, when you have done with it, you throw it aside."[20]

One could imagine Thomas Nast creating an image derived from Harper's conceit. Johnson would be lying facedown, arms and legs akimbo, over the map of the nation, absorbing into his body the racism of Memphis, New Orleans, Philadelphia, and elsewhere, leaving the nation cured. If he could actually do such a thing, metaphorically or otherwise, Harper suggested, Johnson would have served his purpose.

She went on to mock Johnson, the man who had gone on a widely publicized lecture "swing," as a drunk: "I have lived to see the time when the President, though he don't swing upon the gates, does swing around the circle, and though he does not lick molasses candy, takes something that is a great deal stronger." The *Philadelphia Daily Evening Telegraph* described the "sensation" set off by that charge. The Philadelphia-based *Christian Recorder* reported that Harper overall gave a "unique, logical, and superbly delivered lecture."[21]

In "National Salvation," Harper commented on the present moment in Philadelphia and the South. Douglass in "Sources of Danger to the Republic" also addressed the present, but he looked to the past and future as well. In a May 1866 essay, "The Future of the Colored Race," Douglass called himself "not a propagandist but a prophet."[22] Over the decades and centuries, he has continued to speak prophetically to Americans, as if he anticipated the various ways the nation could go wrong. In all versions of "Sources of Danger," Douglass asked: What happens when a "bad man" occupies the White House? What kind of power can he assume under the U.S. Constitution? What are the dangers to watch out for, and how might they be forestalled? Viewing Johnson in this larger temporal context, Douglass made the escalating conflict between Johnson and Congress into an occasion to rethink the nation's Constitution. He knew all too well that Johnson wasn't the first bad man to assume the office of the presidency, and he would not be the last. From Douglass's perspective, at least during late 1866 and 1867, constitutional reform, not impeachment, remained a primary imperative.

By all accounts, Douglass's "Sources of Danger" lecture on January 3, 1867, like Frances Harper's "National Salvation" lecture, was something of a spectacle at Philadelphia's National Hall. According to the next day's edition of the *Philadelphia Daily Evening Telegraph*, the hall was "literally packed last night with people to hear Mr. Douglass' address." The *National Anti-Slavery Standard* reported that "there was no unoccupied seat in the body of the vast hall, the capacious platform was thronged, and during the entire evening many persons stood in the aisles." According to the *Evening Telegraph* (a newspaper not known for progressive views on the subject of race), Douglass "was frequently interrupted with applause, and he evidently made the best effort of his life," taking "some of his warmest admirers by surprise." The more sympathetic *National Anti-Slavery Standard* described how the audience listened "with reflective attention to this eloquent champion of liberty. Words of encomium were freely uttered in behalf of his noble speech." Throughout the lecture of "about two hours," Douglass received "enthusiastic demonstrations of accord." Shaped for a Black audience, the lecture showed Douglass thinking with other African Americans about Reconstruction and the problem of Johnson, who in this iteration of the speech (and not in those directed at white audiences) he called at one point "Massa Johnson."[23] (For a complete transcription of the Philadelphia version of "Sources of Danger to the Republic," reprinted for the first time, see the appendix to this volume.)

Unsurprisingly, Douglass in much of the opening of the lecture focused on the importance of Black suffrage. As in his *Atlantic* essays and many of his speeches of the time, he argued that Reconstruction was failing because the "loyal"—African Americans who supported the war effort—were not allowed to vote and thus remained subordinate to white power. Douglass spoke eloquently of the vulnerability of southern Blacks to racist violence. "Loyal men by the score—by the hundred," he charged, "have been deliberately slaughtered in the presence of the Star-Spangled Banner in New Orleans; and . . . at this hour the murderers are still at large, unquestioned by the law, unpunished by justice, unrebuked by the public opinion of the neighborhood where they lived." Federal intervention was clearly needed to protect the Blacks of the South—more troops, a commitment to the Freedmen's Bureau, an effort to protect Black civil rights—but ultimately Douglass came back to the transformative power of Black suffrage. "The ballot-box," he said, "upon which we have relied as a protection from the passions of the multitude, has failed us, broken down under us." To his auditors at Philadelphia's National Hall who were not allowed to vote, he advised that white racists would continue to impose their will on the nation as long as Blacks of both sections of the country were denied the right to elect their own representatives.[24]

Given that Black suffrage was as much about Congress as Johnson, Douglass kept Johnson out of the speech, at least for a while. But he changed tactics when he arrived at the importance of having had

Lincoln as the nation's Civil War president. In a move for rhetorical effect, Douglass refused to use Johnson's name. It was only because Lincoln had been killed, Douglass said, that the "vilest embodiment of ingratitude and baseness, who shall be nameless now, occupied the Presidential chair." His reference to Johnson as the "nameless" elicited "laughter and cheers." In a further sarcastic move, he suggested that if Lincoln had lived, "the Government of which we are so proud to-day, might have been only a matter of history."[25]

But the Philadelphia lecture addressed much more than Black suffrage and the still unnamed Johnson. Douglass soon moved to what he called "the subject of the evening, the Sources of Danger to our Republic."[26] One of the main dangers, he asserted, was the Constitution itself.

Like Johnson, Douglass had long been engaged by the Constitution. During the 1841–1845 period, when he worked for William Lloyd Garrison as an abolitionist lecturer, he championed Garrison's notion that the Constitution was a proslavery document and that principled people should therefore not participate in elections because when they did, they implicitly sanctioned slavery. Like Garrison, Douglass had even thought it might make sense for the North to break from the South to form a more moral nation with a different constitution. Douglass ended his association with Garrison by the late 1840s, and in 1850 announced that he had come to regard the Constitution as an antislavery document in spirit. From that new perspective, he could justify his political abolitionism—his efforts to bring about social change through the electoral process. The election of Lincoln and the successful outcome of the Civil War would have vindicated that position. But then came the accidental presidency of Andrew Johnson.

Douglass admired much about the Constitution. In the spirit of his post-Garrisonian reading, he continued to believe that it was a freedom document, "free from bigotry, free from sectarianism, free from complexional distinctions." Still, people created the Constitution, and like anything created by people, it had "its defects," which had become more apparent because of "a bad and wicked President."

Standing before the crowd as a champion of "democracy in its purity,"
he instructed his auditors that they had a choice between either "a
purely republican Government" or "a monarchical government." In
the authoritarian president, Douglass, like many of Johnson's critics,
saw a man who wanted to be king. With the help of the Constitution,
Douglass charged, Johnson had managed to assume "kingly powers."[27]

As Douglass elaborated in his lecture, the Founders who wrote the
Constitution had a blind spot. Even though they led a rebellion against
monarchical England, they remained nostalgic for monarchy. For

"King Andy." Illustration by Thomas Nast. *Harper's
Weekly*, November 3, 1866. (*Courtesy of The Ohio State
University Billy Ireland Cartoon Library & Museum.*)

that reason, they failed to build proper checks on presidential authority into the Constitution. This omission allowed presidents to consolidate what Douglass termed "the one-man power." Turning his
attention to Johnson, whom he now called by name, Douglass accused
"Andy Johnson" of "fostering in our form of Government the one-
man power." Douglass assailed the authoritarian president, mock-
ingly noting that Johnson had a habit of "mistaking himself for the
United States instead of the President of the United States." Playing to
his Black audience, he said, to much laughter, "It is Massa Johnson
now." The Constitution may be flawed in allowing Johnson so much
power, but Douglass took comfort in its mandate for regular elections
so that "our king cannot reign [for] life." Still, Douglass's historical
and prophetic point, relevant to past ineffective presidents like James
Buchanan (who immediately preceded Lincoln), as well as to Johnson,
was that the Constitution, because of the Founders' miscalculations,
gave more power to the president than that possessed by any "crowned
head in Europe, and you know it."[28]

For his idea of the one-man power, Douglass drew on Charles
Sumner's "The One Man Power *vs.* Congress: The Present Situation,"
a lecture the Massachusetts senator delivered to a predominantly
white audience at Boston's Music Hall on October 2, 1866. Sumner
sent a copy of the speech to Douglass, who responded in a letter: "I
wish I knew how to express my sense of its excellence without seeming extravagant." Sumner's speech called for impartial Black suffrage
and bemoaned Johnson's practice of "installing ex-Rebels in political power." Unlike some of his colleagues, Sumner expressed genuine
concern about the suffering of Blacks in the South, arguing that Johnson's policies and rhetoric encouraged anti-Black violence. Johnson's
"words," Sumner said, "were dragon's teeth, which have sprung up
armed men. Witness Memphis; witness New Orleans. Who can doubt
that the President is author of these tragedies?" Sumner's blaming of
Johnson for these notorious massacres would have appealed to Douglass. But in this particular speech Douglass found most compelling the
argument contained in its title: "The One Man Power *vs.* Congress."

From Sumner's point of view, Johnson had commandeered power illegally. "Where in the Constitution," Sumner asked, "do you find any sanction of the One Man Power?"[29] In "Sources of Danger," Douglass extended and revised Sumner's constitutional analysis by suggesting that the senator got one thing wrong: Johnson had done nothing illegal in assuming the one-man power.

As Douglass explained to his audience in Philadelphia, Johnson had managed to consolidate his monarchical rule partly because the Constitution provided no checks on the president's granting of pardons and patronage. Douglass was especially troubled by the latter, which he called "the *immense* patronage in the hands of the President. A hundred millions of dollars per annum in times of peace. . . . What a power!" That money corrupted both the president and those who received such patronage. "Who does not see," Douglass prophetically remarked, "that it is corrupting, in that it holds out a temptation to a man to agree with the President, not because of the wisdom and justice of his position, but because in that way he can get something in exchange for his soul."[30]

Douglass similarly warned of the leverage that the Constitution gave to the president's "pardoning power."[31] He had in mind Johnson's efforts, starting in May 1865, to pardon what many in the North regarded as southern traitors, such as Confederate leaders. There was nothing inherently wrong with pardoning the deserving, Douglass said, but by placing an unchecked pardoning prerogative solely in the hands of the president, the Constitution allowed presidents like Johnson to use it for their own political ends. Inevitably that led to corruption.

Concerned about the excessive power that the Constitution lodged in the presidency, Douglass rejected the "two terms principle," which he described as "one of the very worst elements of our Constitution." His main argument, at a time when there were no term limits on the presidency, was that first-term presidents inevitably pursued a second term and made reelection (and not the nation) their top priority. In that respect, a newly elected president was "partly President, and partly chief of the Presidential party"—the very party created and consolidated with the help of patronage and pardons.[32]

Given Johnson's regular vetoes of all civil rights legislation and just about any other legislation intended to help African Americans, Douglass also raised questions about the Constitution's formulation of the veto power, which allowed the president to veto any bill coming out of Congress lacking two-thirds support. As Douglass presented it, the veto gave to the single vote of the president more weight than the votes of the congressional representatives of hundreds of thousands of people. The presidential veto was especially noxious when a "bad man" held the presidency. Such a man, Douglass explained, "full of ambition, full of pride, self-conceit, finds in [the veto power] a means of constantly gratifying his love of notoriety, by flinging himself in opposition to the Congress of the United States."[33] The veto also posed dangers when deployed by a man completely unsupportive of "the unrepresented," by which Douglass meant most Blacks in the North and all Blacks in the South.

In one of the strangest moments of his lecture, Douglass argued that the Constitution also got things wrong in establishing a vice presidency. Initially he made the comical point that "there is no necessity for a ready-made President at all, no more than it would be for a wife to have a ready-made husband." But then he moved to a more darkly conspiratorial vision of the vice president as one heartbeat away from the presidency and wanting that heartbeat to stop. The vice president's "ambition," Douglass explained, "will be instantly subserved by the death of the President, however that death may be brought about." The *Evening Telegraph* described the "sensation" that followed from this insinuation. Douglass even suggested that some vice presidents may want "to procure an assassin."[34]

But he stopped short of suggesting that Johnson had commissioned Lincoln's assassination. Instead, he presented a conspiracy theory that was met by "great and enthusiastic applause," and which he included in all extant versions of the lecture after this one. He proposed that the man who presented himself as a Moses to Black people, the man who seemed exceptionally brave in taking an antislavery position in the South, the man who gained Lincoln's admiration for his commitment to the Union—that man was not the real Andrew Johnson, and Lincoln's assassins understood that. "The man who assassinated Abraham Lincoln," Douglass declared, "knew Andrew Johnson then as we know him now."[35] In this wildly paranoiac fantasy, Johnson may not have directly plotted with the assassins, but they were aware, as Lincoln and others were not, that he was a southern sympathizer and racist. Perhaps the assassins planted Johnson in the White House. Johnson's actions of the past twenty months, Douglass suggested, would support such a claim.

So should Johnson be impeached? Some Republicans and newspaper editors had called for impeachment after Johnson's Swing around the Circle. Even before that lecture tour, the *National Anti-Slavery Standard* had been publishing articles urging Congress to consider impeachment on the grounds that Johnson's policies endangered African Americans. Raising the issue of impeachment at the end of the lecture, Douglass noted that, according to the Constitution, "if the President commits high crimes and misdemeanors, we have the power in our own hands; we can impeach."[36] Johnson promulgated policies that Douglass abhorred, but if the Constitution sanctioned the one-man power, did the president's actions amount to high crimes and misdemeanors? Over the next year, as Douglass and other African American speakers and writers addressed that question, an argument developed in the Black press and elsewhere that Johnson was literally responsible for the deaths of Black people in the South. If murder was not a high crime, what was?

In this lecture, however, Douglass pointed to problems with impeachment. Here, too, he spoke prophetically. Precisely because of the president's control over patronage and pardons, taking him to trial would mean confronting an entire establishment of the powerful, and not simply Johnson. "At the very mention of impeachment," Douglass explained, "Wall Street turns pale." Some Republicans worried that Johnson might attempt a coup d'état to take control of the government, but Douglass suggested that had already happened with the help of the Constitution. For that reason, impeachment would be a dangerous proposition, and for that reason, too, Douglass urged a cautious, more moderate approach. "What we want is not the impeachment of the President," he said, "but a limitation of the one-man power."[37] He advised that constitutional reform would be the more sensible option, and he proclaimed that one of the virtues of "the unmitigated calamity" of the Johnson presidency was that it would inspire Americans "to revise the Constitution of the United States." Meanwhile, the adoption of impartial Black suffrage, with the help of congressional action, would ensure that Johnson would not gain a second term.

Douglass introduced ideas in Philadelphia that he adopted in subsequent versions of "Sources of Danger." But he distinctively shaped the January version for a Black audience. In the militant spirit of such antebellum Black activists as David Walker and Henry Highland Garnet, Douglass underscored the value of Black anger, urging his auditors to "hate as you love." Anger can create community, he said, and it can also prompt political engagement. Douglass expressed his own "great anger" at the end of the lecture by attacking, as he had in his second *Atlantic* essay, not Johnson but the Republicans for their compromises on the Fourteenth Amendment. Those compromises, he charged, left "each of these Rebel States the right to determine whether or not the Black man shall have any political rights at all. Shame on Congress if she admits a single Rebel State upon the adoption of that amendment."[38]

Douglass would later concede in *Life and Times* that the Fourteenth Amendment, by granting birthright citizenship to African Americans, did crucial work in leading the way to the Fifteenth Amendment, which in 1870 made Black male suffrage the law of the land. But early in 1867, no one could foresee the passage of the Fifteenth Amendment, and Douglass believed that Congress had betrayed African Americans by not making federally mandated voting rights part of the Fourteenth Amendment. Speaking in Philadelphia, he nonetheless singled out an exemplary congressman who continued to put Black suffrage at the center of his Reconstruction agenda: "that matchless old hero of Pennsylvania, Thad. Stevens." Douglass's tribute to this local hero was met with "enthusiastic cheering."[39]

"The High Constructive Talent of the Anglo-Saxon Race"

Douglass went on to give versions of "Sources of Danger to the Republic" in Missouri, Ohio, Illinois, Iowa, New York (in several cities), Minnesota, and New Jersey, among other venues.[40] The newspaper coverage was overwhelmingly positive, even in St. Louis, a city where slavery wasn't abolished until January 1865, and where one might have expected more support for Johnson. According to a newspaper account of his February 7, 1867, lecture to a packed house in St. Louis's Turner's Hall, Douglass was "cordially applauded at frequent intervals of his masterly address. . . . The subject, the sources of danger to the republic, in itself of deepest interest, received masterly treatment, and commanded a profound attention." Douglass's presentation in St. Louis so soon after Philadelphia displayed his skill in adapting a lecture to a predominantly white audience of what the *Daily Missouri Democrat* termed "our very best citizens."[41]

In this version of the lecture, which developed a similar analysis of the shortcomings of the Constitution, there was no mocking mention of "Massa Johnson." When Douglass alluded to the massacres in Memphis and New Orleans, he emphasized the need to punish the murderers, since the white audience wouldn't see themselves in the murdered. Again and again he did something that he didn't need to do in Philadelphia: he referred to himself as a Black man—"a member of a despised, outraged, and down-trodden race"—and described his work as a Black abolitionist before the Civil War.[42] As in the Philadelphia lecture, he provided extensive commentary on the problems of patronage and the pardoning power, claiming that Johnson had done extensive damage to the nation. As in the Philadelphia lecture, he set forth the conspiracy theory that Lincoln's assassins knew John-son would advance their southern restorationist agenda.

But Douglass in the St. Louis "Sources of Danger" built to a very different conclusion. Emphasizing that he was a Black man talking to white people, he placed the burden of action on the whites them-selves. "The negro has done his part if he succeeds in pointing out the sources of danger to the republic," he told the crowd. "You will have done your part when you have removed or corrected these sources of danger." In the Philadelphia lecture, Douglass encouraged his predominantly African American auditors to express anger as they pursued their rights; in St. Louis, he flattered his white audience by maintaining that "this matter of reconstruction" can be left to "the high constructive talent of this Anglo-Saxon race." But he made clear what he wanted his white auditors to do: commit themselves to con-stitutional reform, vote for Republican candidates, and support Black suffrage. "We may now do from choice and from sacred choice," he said, "what we did by military necessity."[43]

Harper presented her "National Salvation" lecture several more times after its premiere in the Philadelphia lecture series. She contin-ued to speak out against Johnson through 1867 and beyond. Douglass delivered versions of "Sources of Danger to the Republic" through October 1867. As he traveled around the country, Johnson's advis-ers and friends, who had previously warned him about Douglass,[44] may well have sent reports to the president about this popular lecture. Johnson's specific knowledge of Douglass's activities during the first half of 1867 remains unclear, but we can say unequivocally that the president regarded Douglass as the best-known and most influential African American leader attacking his presidency, which is to say that he probably continued to regard him as "that d—d Douglass."

And yet in July 1867 Johnson reached out to Douglass to see if he would be willing to become the next commissioner of the Freedmen's Bureau. The president clearly hated him, and he also hated the Freed-men's Bureau, which he wanted abolished. Why attempt to make this appointment? Perhaps he was trying to rein Douglass in by offering him a job. In one of the more bizarre twists in the story of Douglass and Johnson, the job offer was intimately connected to the controversies surrounding the new Tenure of Office Act—the very controversies that would lead to Johnson's impeachment.

PART FOUR

---◆---

Impeachment in
Black and White

10

A JOB OFFER

FROM THE MOMENT Andrew Johnson entered the White House, his critics talked of removal or impeachment. His drunken remarks at Lincoln's second inauguration led a number of newspaper editors to call for his resignation or even firing. But the pace picked up in 1866. The *National Anti-Slavery Standard* regularly ran articles either headlined with or including the word "impeachment" in response to what contributing editor Wendell Phillips regarded as Johnson's racist efforts to undermine Reconstruction. As conflict between Congress and the president intensified, the House Judiciary Committee took up several impeachment resolutions. In January 1867, Ohio representative James Mitchell Ashley called for Johnson's impeachment, accusing him of usurping the power of the legislative branch. After much internal discussion, the Judiciary Committee rejected that charge over Thaddeus Stevens's objections. The same committee narrowly approved an impeachment resolution in November 1867, but the full House resoundingly voted it down.

Republicans remained angered by Johnson's efforts to thwart congressional Reconstruction and continued to entertain the possibility of impeachment. Some said that Johnson's fitness for office should be the issue; others contended that his refusal to honor the coequal roles of the legislative and presidential branches was enough to impeach; and still others maintained that his policies had contributed to the loss of Black lives in Memphis, New Orleans, and elsewhere (meaning that he was indirectly guilty of murder). Most Republicans believed, however, that impeachment could be justified only if Johnson were guilty in a legalistic sense of what the Constitution, in Section 4 of Article II, called "high Crimes and Misdemeanors." When the House finally voted to impeach Johnson in February 1868, the main charge against him was dryly legalistic: he had broken the law by violating the Tenure of Office Act.

Passed by Congress over Johnson's veto in March 1867, the Tenure of Office Act made it illegal for the president to dismiss anyone in the federal government whose appointment had been approved by the Senate. The act dictated that the Senate had to concur with the dismissal, not just ratify the replacement. When the House drew up the articles of impeachment against Johnson, ten of the eleven articles addressed the Tenure of Office Act or the main actors connected to Johnson's violation of that act. For that reason, it could appear that Johnson was impeached mainly for firing Secretary of War Edwin M. Stanton in February 1868. Johnson could be impeached for that firing because, eleven months earlier, the Republicans had created a law that made such a firing illegal. Johnson believed the Tenure of Office Act was unconstitutional (a view that would be affirmed by the Supreme Court two decades later) and decided to ignore it. In doing so, he invited his impeachment.

The impeachment scenario could have been different. Frederick Douglass, who in the summer of 1867 was indirectly offered the position of commissioner of the Freedmen's Bureau, could have stood at the center of an impeachment trial, though the issues would have been different. In Douglass's case, the Tenure of Office Act would not have been precisely applicable. That said, if Douglass had accepted the offer, Johnson would have had to dismiss the popular current commissioner, General Oliver Otis Howard, a man who had lost his right arm during a Civil War battle in Virginia and was known as the "Christian General."

Would Congress have chosen to regard such a firing as a violation of the Tenure of Office Act or as impeachable on its own terms? Congress had established the Freedmen's Bureau in March 1865, during Lincoln's presidency, but Howard was appointed in May 1865 by Johnson himself. The position did not need the approval of the Senate. Still, Howard in effect served Congress, which had conceived and funded the bureau in the first place. By 1867, the Freedmen's Bureau was seen as Congress's agency, especially after Congress overrode Johnson's second veto of the funding bill and sustained the life of the bureau. Had Johnson fired Howard in order to appoint Douglass, he might well have triggered an impeachment resolution in the House Judiciary Committee on grounds other than the Tenure of Office Act. In that hypothetical case, the issue would have been that Johnson had dismissed an administrator and undercut an agency that had the support of Congress and was central to Reconstruction. Such a scenario would have further added to Douglass's celebrity, but it did not come to pass.

Even so, Douglass had a central place in the Tenure of Office Act controversy as it began to play out among Secretary of War Edwin M. Stanton, General Ulysses S. Grant, and President Johnson in the summer of 1867.

"By and with the Advice and Consent of the Senate"

Central to the impeachment and to Douglass's interactions with Johnson, the Tenure of Office Act became law in March 1867, at a time when the Republicans had the votes and determination to take control of Reconstruction. Just one month earlier, in February 1867, the same month Douglass delivered "Sources of Danger to the Republic" in St. Louis, the Republican-dominated Congress passed the First Reconstruction Act over Johnson's veto. That legislation, and the several Reconstruction Acts that followed, signaled yet another moment when congressional Reconstruction trumped presidential restoration. The First Reconstruction Act created five military districts out of the ten former Confederate states still not formally readmitted by the U.S. Congress, subjecting them to martial law. The eleventh ex-Confederate state, Tennessee, had been readmitted after approving the Fourteenth Amendment in July 1866, and thus was not placed under the authority of a military commander. In another broad irony of the Johnson presidency, the man who did everything he could to discourage the ex-Confederate states from approving that amendment failed to persuade leaders of his home state to do so.

The First Reconstruction Act mandated that all of the states under military rule must allow both Blacks and whites to vote for delegates to their constitutional conventions. For full representation in Congress, the states were then required to create new constitutions that included Black suffrage, and they were also required to approve the Fourteenth Amendment on birthright citizenship. Historian Eric Foner calls the First Reconstruction Act "a stunning and unprecedented experiment in interracial democracy."[1] The experiment did not last very long, and that was not because of Johnson. As Douglass observed in post-1870 speeches and writings, both sections, North and South, lacked the moral resolve to sustain an interracial democracy. But at the time, the Reconstruction Acts opened up new possibilities for the freedpeople to participate in the political process by buttressing the Republicans' policies with military and legal force.[2]

Not surprisingly, Johnson, driven by his constitutional belief in the limited role of the federal government, his southern sympathies, his preference for the Democratic Party, and his racism, did everything he could to undermine the Reconstruction Acts. Johnson's racist friend and adviser Montgomery Blair warned him that the Reconstruction Acts mainly served the political ends of the Republican Party, authorizing "the military to reconstruct the whole South so as to vote the Radical ticket in '68." In his veto of the First Reconstruction Act, which was quickly overridden by Congress, Johnson asserted that the

military governments were "in palpable conflict with the plainest provisions of the Constitution." In his veto of the Second Reconstruction
Act, also quickly overridden, he continued to invoke the Constitution,
and race relations as well. For Johnson, "complete negro enfranchisement" ultimately meant "white disenfranchisement," as whites in half
of these states, he warned, would become minority voters. Following
Blair's lead, he said in his second veto message that the goal of both
acts was "to make the constitution of a State 'loyal and republican.'"
Once again he affirmed his belief that decisions about Black suffrage
should be left to the states.[3]

With this new legislation, Congress took control of Reconstruction—
but within limits. As commander in chief, Johnson maintained authority over the officers who supervised the five military districts despite
his veto. He could appoint men who were sympathetic to his policies,
such as Major General John Schofield, commander of the First District (which included Virginia), who resisted federally mandated Black
suffrage. General of the U.S. Army Ulysses S. Grant initially thought
that Blacks should have a probation period before they got the right
to vote, but around this time he changed his mind, regarding African
Americans as more loyal than the ex-Confederates treated so leniently
by Johnson. Grant departed from Johnson on a number of issues, but
he was a good soldier and knew his place in the chain of command.
He exerted significant control over the workings of the military, but
even he reported to Johnson.

Congress created the Tenure of Office Act to constrain Johnson,
putting a check on his ability to dismiss and appoint high-level officials. The act could not stop him from firing postmasters and the like,
but it reasserted congressional control over those officials who had
earlier received Senate confirmation, making it difficult for Johnson
to fire cabinet members, such as Secretary of War Edwin M. Stanton,
who favored Republican Reconstruction, or to appoint anyone for a
position subject to Senate approval who had Confederate sympathies.

The Tenure of Office Act consisted of nine sections. Two of these
became especially relevant during the summer of 1867, around the

time Johnson reached out to Douglass to head the Freedmen's Bureau. They also figured in the impeachment of Johnson in February 1868. Section 1 stated that "every person holding any civil office to which he has been appointed by and with the advice and consent of the Senate . . . shall be entitled to hold such office until a successor shall have been in like manner appointed and duly qualified." By "like manner," Congress meant that all such appointments were "subject to removal by and with the advice and consent of the Senate."⁴ This first section addressed the problem of the president's patronage power that Douglass had called attention to in "Sources of Danger," and it also sought to put limits on a president who tended to act impulsively. Congress would eventually use this section of the Tenure of Office Act to challenge Johnson's firing of Stanton (which became, at least nominally, the main reason for Johnson's impeachment), but the section contained an ambiguity, or exclusion, that later muddied the case. Stanton had been appointed by Lincoln and not Johnson, so his firing wasn't clearly covered by the phrasing of section 1. But Johnson's subsequent decision to replace Stanton with Lorenzo Thomas without asking for congressional approval left the president vulnerable to the charge that he had violated this section of the act.

Another section of the Tenure of Office Act added legalistic and coercive language to the same overarching effort to force the president to work with Congress on high-level appointments and dismissals. Section 6 stipulated that all presidential dismissals and appointments violating the terms of the act would be regarded as "high misdemeanors." The section went on to declare that anyone participating in such violations would be fined up to $10,000 and face "imprisonment not exceeding five years, or both said punishments."⁵ Congress made a bold preemptive strike by writing into the act such a massive fine and the possibility of imprisonment. The terms of section 6 would eventually stop Ulysses S. Grant from doing Johnson's bidding in removing Stanton from office. Grant worried that he would end up financially broken and in prison. But the most important part of this section was the reference to "high misdemeanors." For those Republicans who had been calling for Johnson's impeachment, here was the perfect trap: if Johnson violated the Tenure of Office Act, which became law in March 1867, he would have committed a "high misdemeanor," precisely what the Constitution said justified impeachment.

But if a president were to be impeached for violating the Tenure of Office Act, would anyone care? That became an issue in 1868. While there was much support for Johnson's impeachment, few newspaper reporters and commentators focused on the Tenure of Office Act itself. That was especially the case for Johnson's African American critics, whose brief against Johnson centered not on the firing of a white man but on the self-proclaimed Moses's betrayal of African Americans. Central to that betrayal was Johnson's unwillingness to support the Freedmen's Bureau, the agency with the greatest power to improve the lives of the freedpeople.

The Freedmen's Bureau Redux

The various bills passed by Congress in February and March 1867 threw Johnson into a righteous fury about what he perceived as the overstepping of the legislative branch. He vetoed the Tenure of Office Act on the grounds that "the power of removal is constitutionally vested in the President of the United States," and he made similar constitutional arguments when he vetoed the Reconstruction Acts.[6] In his anger at Congress's overriding of his vetoes, Johnson turned his attention to the Freedmen's Bureau, which, as a result of the Reconstruction Acts, had gained an even greater role in monitoring the interactions of the freedpeople with southern whites. The Freedmen's Bureau had also become part of the command structure of the five military districts, with added juridical authority to create military tribunals. Johnson increasingly saw the commissioner of the Freedmen's Bureau, General Oliver Otis Howard, as his enemy, and by

Oliver Otis Howard, c. 1865. Photographer unknown. (*Courtesy of the Library of Congress, Prints and Photographs Division.*)

the summer of 1867 wanted him gone, along with any military commander sympathetic to Radical Reconstruction and the workings of the bureau.

Johnson's disdain for the Freedmen's Bureau was not new. He had vetoed the first measure to extend the bureau in February 1866, and he never relinquished the argument he made in that veto message: that the job of aiding and protecting the freedpeople belonged to the states, not the federal government. Congress failed to overturn the president's first veto, but a few months later passed a second measure to extend the bureau. Johnson vetoed that measure, too, attaching a message expressing his anger at how the bureau worked hand in hand with the occupying federal troops and the military commanders. Again, he appealed to the authority of the states, declaring, falsely, that Blacks had the same protections as whites in the ex-Confederate states, and that there was therefore no need for the "dangerous expedient of 'military tribunals.'"[7] Those tribunals particularly bothered Johnson, and after Congress overrode his veto in June 1866 and resanctioned the bureau, he did what he could to thwart its work, using his presidential power to protect the property of southern white landowners while harassing and even firing bureau officials.

Johnson became still more activist with his use of presidential power to undermine the Freedmen's Bureau after the passage of the Reconstruction Acts of 1867. He was encouraged by the November 1866 Supreme Court decision in *Ex parte Milligan*, which ruled that the military courts established by the bureau lacked authority if state courts were already in operation. In the spirit of Johnson, the Supreme Court prioritized the civil over the federal, the local over the national. The *Milligan* decision cut into the power of the federal government to monitor the South, and in the process, Thaddeus Stevens pronounced in Congress, "unsheathed the dagger of the assassin," placing "the knife of the rebel at the throat of every man who dares proclaim himself to be now, or to have been heretofore, a loyal Union man."[8] Johnson, on the other hand, welcomed the *Milligan* decision as timely support for his belief that the Radical Republicans had overstepped their authority. From Johnson's perspective, the Freedmen's Bureau had become a military and legal arm of the Radical Republicans, and, given *Milligan*, an unconstitutional one at that. It wasn't long afterward that Johnson considered purging the bureau of its commissioner, General Oliver Howard, who was admired by Blacks and whites alike.

But in one of those unpredictable moments that make the story of this presidency so compelling and contradictory, Johnson, before taking up the problem of Howard and the bureau, addressed an individual case with unusual generosity. In March 1867, the president received a letter from Samuel Johnson, one of his former enslaved people, informing him that he had recently been appointed a commissioner of a Tennessee branch of the Freedmen's Bureau and was now raising money to buy "a suitable Lot on which to build a School House for the education of the Coloured children of Greeneville." Samuel

Samuel Johnson, c. 1880s.
Photographer unknown.
(*Courtesy of the Andrew
Johnson National Historic
Site, National Park Service.*)

was the half brother of Dolly, the first person Johnson purchased as a
slave during the late 1830s or early 1840s, and Johnson had purchased
Samuel in order to bring the siblings together. Samuel chose to stay
in Greeneville after Johnson freed his small group of enslaved people, and the evidence suggests that the two men remained on friendly
terms. Samuel's specific reason for writing his former master was to
see about the possibility of buying a one-acre lot from Johnson's property, located "close to the Reble [*sic*] Graveyard," in order to build a
Black school there.[9]

One might assume that Samuel's connection to the Freedmen's
Bureau would infuriate Johnson, and that he would be especially disturbed by the specter of a Black school being built on his own property
by a Confederate graveyard. But Johnson did not just grant Samuel's
request; he went beyond it. In a letter of April 27, Johnson instructed

the Presbyterian minister John P. Holtsinger to survey the land, draw up a deed, and "send the instrument to me. I will convey the land to them without charge." Johnson did this despite having just received a letter from a Georgia supporter charging that the bureau and the military governors were attempting "to *Stir up the Niggers against us*."[10] At his most paranoid, angry, and racist, Johnson moved in the direction of that supporter, but there remained a part of him that kept faith, in a gradualist manner, in the possibilities of Black uplift. He also had affection for Samuel, a Black man who continued to speak well of the president who had owned him as a slave.

Johnson made the paternalistic gesture to help Samuel, but that did not stop him from regarding the Freedmen's Bureau as an occupying force doing unconstitutional work. And in General Howard, he saw an ambitious man who did the bidding of Congress. In August 1867, Johnson received a long letter from one of his supporters, J. McClary Perkins, accusing Howard of corruption. Perkins claimed that Howard, in addition to pushing objectionable policies, engaged in financial speculations with Black schools that "enhance[d] his own personal interests." Perkins advised the president that "the removal of the 'commissioner' of [the] Freedmen's Bureau would cure all the evils growing out of his official misconduct."[11] Perkins called not for the end of the Freedmen's Bureau, just the firing of Howard. Johnson had serious reservations about the bureau, but he also scorned Howard as a sanctimonious surrogate of the Radical Republicans.

Johnson's unofficial and indirect offer to Douglass to replace Howard as head of the Freedmen's Bureau occurred in the summer of 1867, just as the president had begun to fight back against the Republicans' Reconstruction Acts by firing military commanders he didn't trust. The attempt to, in effect, bring Douglass into the Johnson administration also overlapped and intersected with the controversy over Secretary of War Stanton and the Tenure of Office Act. Johnson's offer to Douglass came with ambiguities. Was it a sincere effort to mollify the Radicals or a cynical ploy to destroy the Freedmen's Bureau? One might also ask: Did Douglass seriously consider the offer? And what would have happened if he had agreed to assume the commissioner-ship of the bureau and Howard was subsequently fired?

"It Would Be a Good Thing to Appoint Fred Douglass"

Johnson never directly contacted Douglass about the job, but as Orville Hickman Browning, then secretary of the interior, reported in a diary entry of July 15, 1867, Johnson himself said at a cabinet meeting that "he believed it would be a good thing to appoint Fred Douglas [sic] Commr of the Freedmans Bureau." This meeting took place just two weeks before Johnson fired the popular military commander General Philip Sheridan, so Johnson may have thought the appointment would forestall anger about that decision. He may have also thought some-thing good could come of such a high-profile appointment of a Black man. But General Howard was already immensely popular with Afri-can Americans. There is some mystery here, compounded by the fact that Browning wrote in the same diary entry that he had suggested the appointment to Johnson several months earlier, while failing to explain why he thought the appointment would benefit the president.[12]

Browning was concerned about Johnson's reputation, and he sug-gested that before nominating Douglass for the position, "we had bet-ter ascertain whether he would accept." Urging secrecy and stealth, he hoped to spare the president the embarrassment of being turned down publicly by a Black man. In his diary, Browning wrote that he was charged to find out Douglass's thoughts on the matter.[13] He and his associates decided that the best way to proceed was with the help of Douglass's son Charles Remond.

The youngest son of Anna and Frederick Douglass, Charles had served with his brother Lewis in the 54th Massachusetts Volunteer Infantry Regiment during the Civil War. He struggled financially after the war, but in 1867, just months before he was asked by the pres-ident's men to reach out to his father, he received a clerkship in the

Charles Remond
Douglass, c. 1867.
Photographer unknown.
(*Courtesy of the National
Park Service, Frederick
Douglass National
Historic Site, Washington,
D.C., FRDO 3908.*)

Washington, D.C., Freedmen's Bureau paying $100 a month. Because
he was concerned about his ability to support a family, he left his preg-
nant wife in Rochester to take the job, and in his letters from Washington to his father he regularly mentioned his concerns about money,
at one point asking his father to invest $1,800 in a building association
that would save him the monthly costs of a boardinghouse. (Douglass
declined, and Charles wrote his father in May 1867 that he agreed he
should wait on buying a house "until I am able to do it with my own
earnings.") Initially Charles took a room in a boardinghouse for $25
a month, but he wrote his father on July 14 that he had found new
lodgings for just $12 a month. He also informed his father that "Genl.
Howard is very well pleased with me thus far and I mean to keep on
his right side if possible."[14]

Over the next few months Charles shared his concerns about keeping the job, especially if—as gossip suggested—Johnson planned to

fire Howard. "My position here will depend on the policy of the successor of General Howard," he wrote his father in August.[15] All of which helps to explain why Charles, in a letter written just three days after the cabinet meeting described by Browning, was willing to ask his father to consider the job. Charles believed Douglass would be a great commissioner of the Freedmen's Bureau, but he also believed that his own position at the bureau would remain secure or even improve with his father at the helm.

Charles's letter was roundabout and conditional. He wrote his father on July 18 that Ward Hill Lamon, ex-marshal of the District of Columbia under Lincoln, who had probably been charged by Browning, had asked Charles's friend and fellow Freedmen's Bureau worker Carter Stewart to see if Charles would ask his father, "in a quiet way," whether he would "accept the position as Chief of the Freedmen's Bureau (the place that Genl. Howard now occupies) if tendered you." This series of inquiries had something in common with the children's game of telephone, but Charles got the message, telling his father that "an immediate reply is requested, either by telegraph to me or letter," to an offer that nonetheless remained hypothetical ("if tendered you"). Charles, who for many years was financially dependent on his father, may have enjoyed having the power to offer his father a job. In the same letter, he urged his father to accept the conditional offer: "You possess more than the necessary qualifications for the management of it . . . and the work is easier than lecturing and travelling. My hope is, that you wont [sic] refuse the position if tendered."[16]

But the job was not actually tendered by virtue of Charles's letter, and there is no extant record of Douglass's response. We can assume that Charles never passed along a response to officials in the Johnson administration because Johnson at a cabinet meeting on July 26 once more raised the possibility of offering the job to Douglass. Gideon Welles, Johnson's secretary of the navy, noted in his diary that the president seemed increasingly insistent about replacing the head of the Freedmen's Bureau with Douglass. Welles, who was no friend of the Black man, said that if Johnson "proposed to appoint negroes to any office, that perhaps would be as appropriate as any," and he made no objection to Douglass taking over for Howard. Like Johnson, Welles regarded Howard as "intensely Radical" and wanted him removed. Dismissing Howard, he believed, would contribute to Johnson's efforts to rid himself of those who seemed sympathetic to the Radical Republicans. Welles shared with his diary his personal objection to appointing anyone to a federal position simply because he was "a negro or a mulatto." But appointing a Black person to head the Freedmen's Bureau would appear to have been Johnson's intention, as he would eventually try to get other Black men to take the job.[17] It remains unclear why Welles, who ultimately supported Johnson's desire to recruit Douglass, thought this particular Black person would be any less radical than Howard, who was doing his job well and ultimately wasn't all that radical.

Johnson's consultation with Welles led to a second roundabout and conditional job offer to Douglass. In a letter of July 29, 1867, written on Executive Mansion stationery, William Slade, a Black steward at the White House who had previously served under Lincoln, took on the guise of a cabinet official entrusted with offering the job, while also watching out for Johnson by requesting that Douglass not leak news of the offer. Slade advised Douglass that he wrote "in a *Private* and confidential manner," and such were his concerns about protecting Johnson from potential embarrassment that he added a cautionary postscript to "keep this Private & Confidential." In the letter itself, he attempted to persuade Douglass to take the job by raising concerns about Howard. Slade claimed Howard was "timid" and deficient in "moral courage." By way of contrast, Slade implied in his flattering recruitment letter, Douglass had always acted bravely for what he believed. For that reason, Slade declared to Douglass, "I know of no man—white or colored [who] would be better adapted to the Place than your Humble Self."[18]

Slade's letter conveyed his own sentiments, not those of Browning, Welles, or Johnson. The last thing they wanted at the Freedmen's Bureau was a leader bolder than Howard. Slade may have been recruited by others to contact Douglass, but the case he made for Douglass's suitability was decidedly his own.

In many ways, heading the Freedmen's Bureau would have been an appealing job for Douglass. It paid $3,000 a year and would put him in charge of approximately two thousand employees. But if he had taken the job, he would have had to work with Johnson, and his status as commissioner would have served to legitimate Johnson's administration. In a letter sent from Rochester on August 12, Douglass responded to Slade as if it were Slade himself who had made the offer, thanking him for the job that "in your kindness you would procure for me." He then elaborated on the advantages of the position and on the circumstances under which he might consider taking it, emphasizing that he would be eager to help "our newly emancipated people, especially if I should be assisted—I undoubtedly should be—by President Johnson, if appointed by him." Douglass appeared to be keeping a window open on the possibility of taking the job, but that was deceptive, for he demanded complete support from Johnson, and it's difficult not to read irony into the "I undoubtedly should be." Douglass was smart enough to know that he would never have Johnson's full support, and for that reason, after expressing his satisfaction with Howard's performance on the job, he declined the offer. Continuing to write in an ironic mode, Douglass told Slade that if Johnson managed to appoint a Black man to head the bureau, "it would more than all other acts of his demonstrate his purpose of being the Moses of the colored race in the United States."[19]

Slade refused to take no for an answer, and he followed up with a letter asking Douglass to reconsider. Three days after Slade sent that letter, Charles wrote his father that he had heard from friends and "reporters of the press" that "if you would accept the position as Comm. of this Bureau, it would be at once given you." But no one ever officially offered Douglass the job, and Johnson never got directly involved with the recruitment. Douglass stood by his decision to decline the non-offer, and Charles wrote his father ten days later confirming that people assumed he would reject it.[20]

Douglass wanted that refusal even better known. Choosing to ignore Slade's request that he keep the job offer secret, he wrote Theodore Tilton, the man who had bravely walked the streets of Philadelphia with him at the Southern Loyalists' Convention. Tilton continued to edit the New York newspaper the *Independent*, which was strongly opposed to Johnson. In a letter of September 2, 1867, Douglass told Tilton about the job offer, describing it as "among the strange things which have come to me this summer." Rejecting the thrust of Slade's attack on the current head of the bureau, Douglass insisted that he did not want to participate in the removal of "a man so just and good as General Howard." He also did not want to place himself "under any oblegations [*sic*]" to Johnson. If we accept Douglass's account—and I think we should—he wasn't for a moment tempted to take the job and refused the indirect offer "at once." His contempt for Johnson and his policies had intensified, and he worried about the future. He asked Tilton: "Have we reached the end of Johnson's wrath or may we look for more?"[21]

Not surprisingly, Tilton decided to print Douglass's letter in his newspaper in an article titled "Frederick Douglass," which included Tilton's editorial commentary. "The greatest black man in the nation did not consent to become a tool of the meanest white," Tilton wrote. "For this prudence and firmness, Mr. Douglass is entitled to the thanks of the country." Shortly after the publication of this article and letter, Douglass confided to his friend Gerrit Smith that "Tilton has made a little too much of my declining the Freedmen's Bureau." As for the publication of his letter to Tilton in the *Independent*, Douglass told Smith: "My note to him though not marked private was not intended for publication."[22] This seems disingenuous. Surely Douglass knew what would happen to such a letter when sent to a newspaper editor.

Johnson meanwhile remained intent on appointing a Black man as commissioner of the Freedmen's Bureau. After Douglass spurned him, Johnson offered the job to his friend John Langston, the Black activist who had visited him in Nashville in 1864 shortly after his Moses speech and then interviewed him in the White House in 1865. Langston at the time was working for the Freedmen's Bureau as inspector of Black schools. In his autobiography, Langston described having a "full and free talk with the president" about the possibility of succeeding Howard, frankly telling him that he was troubled by his "extremely severe, sometimes blasphemous" criticism of the commissioner. This was a man, Langston told the president, who was "in every way sagacious, wise and efficient." Taking Howard's character and accomplishments into account, he advised Johnson: "The highest interests of the colored people . . . require the continuance of General Howard at the head of the Bureau."[23] Langston declined the job a day or two after this White House meeting.

In a letter to his father, Charles, who did not know about Johnson's offer to Langston, said that the president next attempted to interest Henry Highland Garnet in the position, but there is no evidence to support that claim. We do know that Johnson tried the Philadelphian Robert Purvis, an organizer of the American Anti-Slavery Society who remained a highly regarded Black leader after the Civil War. Purvis was approached indirectly, as Douglass had been. One of Johnson's secretaries, George B. Halsted, told Purvis that Johnson wanted a "colored man" for the job and inquired about his interest. Unsure about what to do, Purvis wrote Johnson's fierce critic Wendell Phillips, who responded on September 9 with trenchant words about Johnson's underlying motivation to appoint a Black commissioner. Phillips told Purvis that he would have to make his own decision, but he urged him to decline because he believed Johnson was plotting to destroy the Freedmen's Bureau. "The South, Johnson's ally, will never allow a colored man in that place," Phillips explained. "Half the officers would refuse to serve under him." If that were the case, the bureau would fall apart, which would have dire consequences for the freedpeople. Phillips also advised Purvis that Johnson at this moment in his presidency wanted to preserve his reputation as someone who cared about Black people. "You see," Phillips said, "by formally appointing you, & then having two or three southern statesmen remonstrate & a dozen officers refuse to serve under you Johnson *gets* all the *credit* of a radical."[24]

Phillips's letter illuminated the situation for Purvis, who responded that he could "now see, that the whole purpose of this execrable Excellency, to put a 'colored man' in Gen. Howard's place is a mere 'trick.'" Like Douglass and Langston, Purvis turned down the job. Howard, who was admired by African Americans in all sections of the country, managed to hold on to the commissioner's position until 1872, when a more conservative Congress, much to Howard's frustration, voted against extending funding for the bureau. Before then, he had a role in establishing a number of schools for Blacks, including Howard University, which was named in his honor.[25]

Howard kept his job at the bureau for another five years at least partly because of African American support. Langston did more than just decline. He betrayed the president, thinking it his duty to inform Howard that Johnson was secretly trying to replace him.[26] Perhaps Langston's subterfuge helped Howard remain in his job and out of the fray, or perhaps Johnson simply lost interest in replacing Howard as tensions increased among himself, Stanton, and Grant. Langston's

Edwin M. Stanton, c. 1865. (*Brady's National Photographic Portrait Galleries. Courtesy of the Library of Congress, Prints and Photographs Division.*)

account of his betrayal of Johnson, whom he sometimes called a friend, reveals the extent to which Johnson's effort to appoint a prominent African American as Freedmen's Bureau commissioner became entangled with the developing controversy involving Secretary of War Stanton and the Tenure of Office Act.

In July 1867, when Johnson arranged to offer Douglass the job of commissioner of the Freedmen's Bureau, the president had already decided to remove Stanton from his position as secretary of war and Philip Sheridan from the military command of the Fifth District. Johnson objected to Stanton because his views on Reconstruction increasingly coincided with those of the Radical Republicans. He objected to Sheridan because he had blamed whites for the New Orleans massacre and then dismissed state and local officials, actions that Johnson believed crossed the line that had been established by the Supreme Court's *Ex parte Milligan* decision.

Johnson shared his plans to fire Stanton and Sheridan with Ulysses S. Grant, and on August 1, Grant advised Johnson that, because of the Tenure of Office Act, Stanton's removal could not "be effected against his will without the consent of the Senate." In the same letter Grant told Johnson that it would also be a mistake to remove Sheridan because he was "universally, and deservedly, beloved." Even the normally supportive Gideon Welles warned Johnson that removing Sheridan would be politically dangerous. Johnson proceeded anyway. He ordered Grant to use his position as general of the U.S. Army to remove Sheridan from his military command. Grant had no choice in the matter. Still, on August 17, he urged Johnson to change his mind. "Gen. Sheridan has performed his civil duties faithfully and intelligently," Grant advised Johnson. "His removal will only be regarded as an effort to defeat the laws of Congress."[27] Johnson did not change his mind, and after Grant relieved Sheridan of his duties, Johnson appointed Major Winfield Scott Hancock, a Democrat who immediately reinstated the officials that Sheridan had removed from office.

Before the Sheridan drama unfolded, Johnson had proceeded on another front. He wrote Stanton on August 5 to inform him that "your resignation as Secretary of War will be accepted." In response, Stanton invoked the Tenure of Office Act, informing Johnson that he refused to leave his post and would await Congress's reconvening in December. This occurred at the time when Douglass, on August 12, sent his letter to Slade declining the Freedmen's Bureau position. That same day (which would have been before Slade received Douglass's letter), Johnson wrote Grant that he had suspended the recalcitrant Stanton from his job and appointed Grant "Secretary of War ad interim." Stanton responded to his suspension with outrage, and again invoked the Tenure of Office Act. "I am compelled to deny your right under the Constitution and Laws of the United States, without the advice and Consent of the Senate," he wrote Johnson.[28]

If a Black man had accepted the commissioner position, would that have diverted attention from these dismissals? Might Johnson suddenly have appeared to care about African Americans in a way that would have quieted Radical Republican opposition? Probably not, and Douglass, Langston, and Purvis knew that. They also knew that Howard was well liked and doing a good job, which would help to explain why they chose to keep their distance from Johnson as he tried to dismantle Reconstruction by making it difficult to enforce the Republicans' policies. Stanton did what he could to keep his job, refusing to resign. As articulated in the eleven articles of impeachment that Congress drew up the next year, the Johnson-Stanton standoff, which began in August 1867, would become the principal reason for Johnson's impeachment. Stanton's status as secretary of war would not be resolved until *after* the impeachment trial.

These machinations over a cabinet appointment can seem small and petty in the larger scheme of things. But for the Republicans the Stanton controversy addressed issues of fundamental importance. Johnson, who had been constrained by the Reconstruction Acts and the Tenure of Office Act, had managed to find ways to continue to undermine congressional Reconstruction: by firing the military commanders who were sympathetic to the Radical Republicans and replacing them with military people supportive of his policies, and by suspending the cabinet official most aligned with the Republicans' approach to Reconstruction. In late 1867 and in the opening months of 1868, the Republicans faced a challenge. They needed to convince the public that something urgent was at stake with how Johnson handled dismissals—indeed, that something urgent was at stake with the Tenure of Office Act itself.

11

THE TRIALS OF
IMPEACHMENT

OUGLASS DID NOT comment specifically on the drama surrounding the secretary of war, Edwin M. Stanton, but he
continued to speak out against the excesses of executive power in his
"Sources of Danger to the Republic" lectures. He gave the last known
iteration of that lecture in Newark, New Jersey, in October 1867. In
this version, Douglass covered familiar ground: "the defects in the
Constitution"; "the one-man power"; the need to eliminate the vice
presidency; and his conspiracy theory that Lincoln's assassins knew
of Johnson's sympathies for the ex-Confederates. As Frances Harper
did in her "National Salvation" lecture, Douglass also addressed the
problem of racism in a northern state where Black people still could
not vote. Surveying electoral developments in the fall 1867 midterm
elections, he reported: "Ohio has gone unmistakably against [Black]
suffrage. It is likely, it is probable, I do not say possible, that New York
will do the same." Douglass lamented the "prejudice here in New Jersey and prejudice all over." It is easy "to hate the nigger," he said, "and
it can be brought into an election with telling effect."[1]

That hatred had an effect on the fall 1867 elections. Republicans lost seats in Congress and in state legislatures. As Douglass predicted, New York voted against impartial Black suffrage, as would Michigan early in 1868. The policies of the Radical Republicans had begun to disillusion northern white men, who had little interest in initiatives to help the freedpeople. In Ohio, voters turned the state legislature over to the Democrats. Because state legislatures (and not the voting public) elected U.S. senators, that change meant Radical Republican senator Benjamin Wade would be out of a job in 1869.

Wade had become the president pro tempore of the Senate in March 1867, and thus the man who would assume the presidency if Johnson, who did not have a vice president, were impeached and convicted. During a newspaper interview in the fall, Wade offered a brutally frank assessment of what had happened in Ohio's recent elections. "The nigger whipped us," he said. "We went in on principle, and got whipped." Wade confessed his surprise "that there were so many Republicans in Ohio who were willing to see negro suffrage in the South, but wouldn't let the few niggers of Ohio vote."[2] Wade had his own problems with racial prejudice, but notwithstanding his language (which was vulgar even then), he owned up to what Harper, Douglass, and other African Americans had been saying all along: that the race problem was not limited to the ex-Confederate states.

Douglass knew firsthand of the difficulties Black people faced even in states with Radical Republicans in office. That is why he wanted the federal government to mandate Black suffrage through a constitutional amendment, and that is why Black suffrage remained central to his writings and lectures of the period. He regularly denounced Johnson for resisting the Radical Republicans' efforts to promote Black citizenship, but he had nothing much to say about the controversy surrounding Stanton and the Tenure of Office Act.[3] As in the New Jersey version of "Sources of Danger," he portrayed the nation as facing even greater challenges than its president. Nevertheless, Douglass came to believe that Johnson deserved to be impeached, though not necessarily for violating the Tenure of Office Act.

"The Eyes of the Whole World Are Fixed upon Congress"

The standoff between President Johnson and Secretary of War Edwin M. Stanton, which threatened to bring the Tenure of Office Act into play, showed no signs of letting up in late 1867. Stanton refused to resign and general of the U.S. Army Ulysses S. Grant refused to fire him. By November 1867, Johnson began to crack under the pressure of the ongoing dispute. His memo "To the Cabinet," written when the elections suggested he would gain supporters, offers insight into his increasingly paranoid and defensive thinking as he dealt with the stress of the Stanton situation. Johnson warned his closest associates "that the Constitution has been set aside and repudiated by Congress." In the Radical Republicans, he discerned an aristocratic conspiracy, a "combination of men" who sought to be the "absolute masters of all the wealth of a country, the richest in the world." For Johnson, the parallel between the Radical Republicans and the secessionists was clear: "So, in 1861, were the People of the South . . . mis-led by a few designing men and forced into a disastrous revolution."[4]

Johnson's racism emerged in its baldest form when he was under stress. Recall his outburst against Douglass shortly after his White House meeting with the Black delegation. Johnson's Third Annual Message to Congress of December 3, 1867, is another grotesque example. Eric Foner calls this message "probably the most blatantly racist pronouncement ever to appear in an official state paper of an American president." Central to the message was Johnson's extraordinarily racist warnings about the dangers that Black suffrage posed to the nation. In 1865, Johnson had urged southern provisional governors to consider limited Black suffrage; now he stated that fully enfranchising southern Blacks would in effect disenfranchise southern whites by making them into a voting minority subject to "negro domination." The Republicans' policies, he stated in alarmist fashion, would "Africanize the half of our country." Such a development would bring disaster to the South, he explained, because "negroes have shown less capacity for government than any other race of people" and tended "to relapse into barbarism." Johnson followed this logic to a set of dire warnings about the future of the nation, and the South in particular. He insisted that Blacks would govern only to serve their own interests, and he again raised the specter of a race war. Black people, he reported, "are taught to regard as an enemy every white man who has any respect for the rights of his own race."[5]

Johnson's crude appeal to racial fears to attract white supporters abraded against his more generous remarks about African Americans in the same message to Congress. Even in a report that ominously imagined an Africanized United States, Johnson expressed his "willingness to join in any plan within the scope of our constitutional authority which promises to better the condition of the negroes in the South." Such plans included "encouraging them in industry, enlightening their minds, improving their morals, and giving protection to all their just rights as freedmen."[6] Johnson sounded paternalistic here, but not very different from his Republican opposition. Ever the savvy politician, he remained hard to pin down.

Perhaps aware that his more incendiary comments about Black people hurt his public image, Johnson granted an interview to the *Cincinnati Commercial* shortly after submitting his annual message. In a section of the interview titled "THE 'MOSES' BUSINESS," Johnson once again presented himself as a leader of Black people. He explained that he "wanted the negroes to be free and enjoy their rights." But, as in his recent message to Congress, he expressed his concerns about Black voting majorities in the southern states. He was all for equality, but not for what he called "negro supremacy."[7]

This more subdued interview notwithstanding, Johnson's remarks about Black "barbarism" caught the eye of Republicans and African Americans. Congressional Republicans discussed the possibility of impeachment, though they must have realized there would be difficulties placing racism under the rubric of "high Crimes and Misdemeanors." When they did impeach him, the Republicans would stop short of making that case.

African American commentators addressed Johnson's racism more directly than the Republicans. A censorious response to his 1867 message to Congress appeared in the December 13 issue of *The Elevator*, an African American newspaper published in San Francisco by the New York–born Black activist Philip A. Bell, whom Douglass had met at Black conventions before Bell's move west. After receiving Johnson's annual message "in full by telegraph," Bell called it "the most disgraceful State paper ever issued from the Executive Department," comparing it to "a third-rate Democratic speech at a Ward meeting." An editorial in the December *Christian Recorder* mocked Johnson's persistence in proffering himself as a biblical leader. "The 'Moses' of the colored people has again spoken," the newspaper said of Johnson's message. "The Lord deliver us!" Johnson's remarks about Black barbarism particularly nettled the editors of the paper. " 'Barbarism!' " the editorial scoffed. "Let him apply that term to his own government." In the view of the *Christian Recorder*, it was precisely the barbarism of Johnson's government that made it necessary to impeach this president, who regularly undermined the lives and aspirations of African Americans in the way of a lawbreaker. "He is guilty," the paper thundered from its editorial column, "and the eyes of the whole world are fixed upon Congress, to see whether that body has the nerve to . . . bring him to trial and punishment."[8]

Congress remained uneasy about calling Johnson to account for anything having to do with his racist words and actions. Senator Benjamin Wade's comments on the recent elections, which acknowledged that Johnson was hardly the only white racist in America, made clear why congressional hesitation persisted, and also why the Tenure of Office Act had such a seductive appeal for the Republican opposition. It had the potential to focus attention on Johnson as a lawbreaker without having to address the vexed matter of race. In the context of the racism that crossed all regions of the country, the Tenure of Office

Act concealed a deliberate political calculus: it allowed Congress to impeach Johnson not for doing harm to hundreds of thousands of Black people in the South but for firing a white man. That is precisely what happened as the jockeying between Johnson and Ulysses S. Grant intensified in January and February of 1868.

Johnson by this point wanted to rid himself of Stanton, who had been reinstated as secretary of war by Congress. Grant committed himself to the rule of law as elaborated in the Tenure of Office Act. Because the act decreed that anyone involved with dismissing government officials subject to approval by the Senate would be punished with up to five years in jail and a $10,000 fine, Grant refused to use his

Ulysses S. Grant. Color lithograph by Samuel S. Frizzell, published by Charles H. Crosby, 1868. (*Courtesy of the Library of Congress, Prints and Photographs Division.*)

position as general of the U.S. Army to fire Stanton, even though Johnson offered to pay his fine (he said nothing about serving his prison time). But the fine and prison term were not the main issues for Grant. In a searing letter to Johnson of February 3, he explained that he defied the president's orders mainly because he saw them "as an attempt to involve me in the resistance of law." The law-abiding soldier accused Johnson of trying "to destroy my character before the country."[9] Grant's refusal to do Johnson's bidding not only preserved his reputation but also positioned him as the most likely Republican presidential candidate in the upcoming election.

The back-and-forth between Johnson and Grant over Stanton became great political theater once their dispute went public. Congress, which had rejected Johnson's efforts to make Grant acting secretary of war, requested their letters and leaked them to newspapers. The *Christian Recorder* sided with Grant, applauding "the bold stance taken by Congress in reinstating Mr. Stanton, and the prompt and hearty loyalty of General Grant in seconding their action." The editors of this Black newspaper saw in Grant's resistance to Johnson an important new development—a more independent general and Congress—that would benefit the freedpeople. "Now help yourself, Andy," the newspaper taunted. "The Reconstruction can and will go on. . . . The colored people must have their rights."[10]

Meanwhile, Douglass from his home base in Rochester followed the unfolding events in Washington through various newspapers. But perhaps just as importantly, he kept up through the firsthand accounts he received in letters from his son Charles, who continued to work in the Washington office of the Freedmen's Bureau. Charles's letters constitute a hitherto untapped resource for considering Blacks' perspectives on the Johnson impeachment just a year after Black men in the District of Columbia had gained the franchise. As newly enfranchised voters, Charles and his Black male colleagues took an intense interest in politics, knowing that they had a voice in who would be representing them, at least on the local level. They were a politically engaged group in a workforce increasingly populated by African Americans.

Charles's letters to his father conveyed his personal opinions, but he regularly noted that conversations with his fellow civil service workers had an impact on his thinking. Accordingly, the letters open a window onto the larger world of Black Washington, D.C.[11]

Charles, like everyone else in his bureau office, was absorbed by the Johnson-Grant-Stanton imbroglio. "There is quite a stir here in political circles occasioned by the correspondence between the President and Genl. Grant," Charles told his father in February 1868. He confessed that there were days when he and his colleagues couldn't keep their focus on work while wondering what would happen next between Johnson and Grant. Conflicting reports made it difficult to choose sides. Charles initially viewed Grant as a showboater, but he also heard rumors that there was "a deep laid plot to crush Grant" before he could emerge as the Republicans' choice for the presidency over Johnson. With the presidential election slated for later that year, Charles disdained Johnson, favoring Chief Justice Salmon P. Chase as the Republican nominee over Grant. Based on his conversations with his fellow office workers, he thought Chase would win if nominated.[12] What Charles couldn't anticipate at the time was Chase's compromised role in the Johnson impeachment trial once it got underway.

Shortly after Charles wrote this letter, Johnson precipitated the events that led to his impeachment. Convinced that he had the constitutional authority to act on his own, he fired Secretary of War Stanton without Grant's assistance. He then asked General William T. Sherman to take the job, but Sherman, who was Grant's former comrade-in-arms, wanted no part of the controversy. So Johnson named as *ad interim* secretary of war the adjutant general Lorenzo Thomas, a man described by historian Brenda Wineapple as "a bumbling desk officer, . . . vain, weak, and completely incapable of performing any public service credible to the country."[13] Thomas subsequently demanded that Stanton vacate the War Office, but Stanton told him he was staying put. The flustered Thomas repaired to a local tavern, and the next day Stanton ordered him arrested for violating the Tenure of Office Act. The charge was quickly dropped, but the feisty Stanton refused to leave the premises, locking himself in his office at the War Department, which was located in the Old Executive Office Building just west of the White House. In a striking display of civil disobedience, he remained in his office for the entirety of the impeachment trial, eating and sleeping there while Congress deliberated on what to do about Johnson and, by extension, his own cabinet position.

Johnson took the risk of firing Stanton and appointing Thomas because he believed the Tenure of Office Act was unconstitutional. However, that act was the law of the land. For that reason, most Republicans viewed Johnson's actions as a godsend. Charles Douglass captured the spirit of the moment in a letter to his father, in which he analogized Johnson's sacking of Stanton and appointment of Thomas to an act of intemperance: "The city is in the wildest excitement in consequence of Johnsons [*sic*] last drunk. Before you receive this, Johnson will be impeached."[14] Simultaneously shocked and delighted by Johnson's brazen disregard of the law, the Republicans leaped at the opportunity to rid themselves of a president they loathed. All of this happened quickly, with Johnson cocky at the start, convinced that Americans, and even the Republicans in Congress, wouldn't care about the dismissal of a cabinet official. Then he resigned himself to the inevitable. Three days after Johnson's violation of the Tenure of Office Act, before a packed gallery of spectators who regarded the proceedings as great theater, the House voted in favor of a resolution to impeach Johnson by a vote of 126 to 47 (seventeen members didn't vote).

Republicans across the Northeast were initially thrilled by the vote, and abolitionist and Black newspapers were ecstatic. The *Loyal Georgian*, a Black newspaper published in Augusta, celebrated the impeachment as vindication for a Congress whose failure to impeach Johnson up to this point had been "not a blunder but a crime." But excitement about the impeachment quickly died down, and most mainstream newspapers raised questions about an impeachment centered on a cabinet appointment. The *New York Herald*, for instance, asserted that the impeachment was "only the insane dream of men who, in indulging an intense party passion, have driven away from them the guides of reason and judgment." The nation may have been divided on the impeachment, but the House Judiciary Committee quickly drew up eleven articles of impeachment, ten of which specifically mentioned the Tenure of Office Act, Stanton, or Lorenzo Thomas, with the outlier article focusing on Johnson's unpresidential behavior. Thaddeus Stevens complained privately that the articles lacked "any real vigor," but Charles Sumner was pleased with the impeachment, telling a friend that he regretted only that "A. J. was not impeached a year ago." He told another friend: "One of the great blunders of our history was that the Presdt. was not impeached two years ago."[15] Sumner saw Johnson as guilty of impeachable offenses well before the Senate created the Tenure of Office Act, but that act would set the course of the impeachment trial. In his letters to his father, Charles never mentioned the Tenure of Office Act. As was the case with Sumner, other issues were at stake for the worker at the Freedmen's Bureau, such as the president's opposition to Reconstruction policies that advanced Blacks' civil rights.

As Congress worked on the articles of impeachment, Douglass journeyed to Meriden, Connecticut, to lecture on Blacks' civil rights—and he found himself in an appalling confrontation there that directly threatened his own civil rights. According to a report in the *Baltimore Sun*, Stephen Ives, the proprietor of Meriden House, where Douglass had taken a room, "called Frederick Douglass a 'nigger' and ejected him from his public table." When the editor of the local newspaper came to Douglass's defense, Ives assaulted the editor and was arrested. The incident was widely reported. The *New York Times*, generally not sympathetic to Black causes, referred to the attack as a "disgraceful affair" and praised Douglass for giving "the landlord a lesson in politeness by remaining in the house." Ives, described by the *Times* as "a Democrat of the ancient pro-slavery school," showed that the proslavery school was neither ancient nor limited to the South.[16] This ugly incident occurred in a New England state where Black people could not vote, and it took place just a few days before Johnson's formal impeachment on February 24. It would have shown Douglass yet again that, with respect to Blacks' rights, northerners could be as much of a problem as Johnson for African Americans in the years immediately after the Civil War.

"Tedious Even to the Galleries"

The impeachment trial of Andrew Johnson took place in Senate chambers from late March to late May, following the constitutional mandate that a House managing committee present the case before the full Senate. Given the nature of the articles of impeachment, the House managers (that is, Johnson's prosecutors from the House of Representatives) would have to spend most of their time demonstrating that Johnson had violated the terms of the Tenure of Office Act in order to convict. The Republican legislators were angry at Johnson for obstructing and undermining Reconstruction, and there was support for their position in the Northeast and elsewhere. But the legalistic focus on the Tenure of Office Act in the articles of impeachment seemed strangely calculated to have as little impact on public opinion as possible. That became apparent when the articles were first formally presented in Congress on March 5. According to the *New York Tribune*, "the Senate's galleries were choking full" with visitors palpably excited to hear the accusations against the president. But as House manager John Bingham of Ohio recited the articles, the senators in chamber read newspapers and wrote letters, seemingly bored by what they were hearing. They were not alone. The *Tribune* reported that the articles "became tedious even to the galleries before the conclusion, there being such an endless repetition of phrases about Year of the Lord and said Andrew Johnson, etc."[17]

The opening sentence of Article 1, for instance, the article from which the other ten articles emerged, has 359 words and forty clauses. One expects circuitous legalese in such documents, but the writers of the articles took that legalese to extremes, to the point where it could seem that nothing much was at stake in the articles, at least as they were presented to the public. Article 1 starts out strongly, with the assertion that Johnson had been "unmindful of the high duties of his oath of office and of the requirements of the Constitution." That sounds impeachable. But as the article proceeds with its numerous running clauses about the firing of Stanton against the strictures of the Tenure of Office Act, it quickly loses exigency:

> . . . said Andrew Johnson, President of the United States, on the 12th day of August, in the year of our Lord 1867, and during the recess of said Senate, having suspended by his order Edwin M. Stanton from said office, and within twenty days after the first day of the next meeting of said Senate, on the 12th day of December, in the year last aforesaid, having reported to said Senate such suspension, with the evidence and reasons for his action in the case, and the name of the person designated to perform the duties of such office temporarily, until the next meeting of the Senate, and said Senate therafterwards, on the 13th day of January, in the year of our Lord 1868, having duly considered the evidence and reasons reported by said Andrew Johnson for said suspension, did refuse to concur in said suspension; . . . whereby said Andrew Johnson, President of the United States, did then and there commit, and was guilty of a high misdemeanor in office . . .

When you cut through all of the words and syntactical circling (and this is just a portion of Article 1), it sounds as if Johnson had done what most of his predecessors had done: taken steps to dismiss his own cabinet officer. The conservative *Baltimore Sun* sarcastically asserted that "if Frederick Douglass were elected president, or fell heir in any way to this office, we could claim for him the right to select his own cabinet, and to change the members thereof at his discretion." It is difficult to imagine the general public even bothering to read Article 1, or the subsequent ten, all the way through.[18]

Article 10 moved in a different direction from those that emphasized the Tenure of Office Act. It accused Johnson of attempting "to bring into disgrace, ridicule, hatred, contempt and reproach, the Congress of the United States," especially through the inflammatory speeches he made in Cleveland and elsewhere during his 1866 Swing around the Circle lecture tour. In the tradition of his political hero Andrew Jackson, Johnson used salty language to express his displeasure with Congress. One could imagine that such rhetoric would upset the targeted congressmen, but would ordinary citizens care that a president who admired Jackson had blustered about his enemies? The committee drawing up the articles attempted to raise the stakes of Article 10 with the suggestion that Johnson's contempt contributed to "resentment of all good people of the United States against Congress and the laws by it duly and constitutionally enacted." But the committee could have clarified that such resentment came mainly from the South, and was hurtful less to members of Congress than to the freedpeople. The committee tried to do that by quoting extensively from Johnson's St. Louis speech of September 8, 1866, when he blamed the anti-Black violence in New Orleans on Congress. But the charge against Johnson stated simply that the speech was "peculiarly indecent and unbecoming," which was hardly a misdemeanor, let alone a high crime.[19] During the trial, Johnson's defense team had the relatively easy task of using the First Amendment to brush away that charge.

Article 11 was more complicated because, at its core, it accused Johnson of not fulfilling the duties of his office when he attempted to undermine congressional legislation, such as the Reconstruction Acts. But that article was diluted by yet another mention of the Tenure of Office Act.

Because the articles of impeachment focused almost entirely on the Tenure of Office Act, the Republicans found it difficult over the course of the ensuing trial to condemn Johnson for the consequences of his policies. They also found it difficult to raise questions about his racism or fitness for office, or even to explore the philosophical conflict between presidential restoration and congressional Reconstruction.

This is not to say that such issues didn't come up, but over the more than two months of the trial, recorded in the approximately 1,200-page trial transcript, the House managers only occasionally spoke bluntly about what the Tenure of Office Act represented: an effort to restrain a president who had been doing everything in his power to support white supremacist southerners, many of them former Confederate leaders, by thwarting congressional initiatives that sought to improve the condition of the freedpeople.

The actual trial began on March 13, and then was postponed to March 23. Eight hundred tickets were made available each day to government workers and others interested in attending. Charles and his fellow employees at the Freedmen's Bureau had ready access to those tickets. His letters over the next few months conveyed his confidence, bolstered by what he had been hearing from his fellow workers at the

"The Senate as a Court of Impeachment," *Harper's Weekly*,
April 11, 1868. Sketch by Theodore R. Davis. (*Courtesy of the
Library of Congress, Prints and Photographs Division.*)

bureau, that the trial would have a happy outcome. "We are all well here," Charles wrote his father later in March. "We have no doubt here, that Johnson will be convicted."[20]

But right from the start the Republican House managers encountered difficulties in making their case. Charles reported to his father that those difficulties had much to do with the man he had earlier touted for the White House but now deeply suspected as a Johnson apologist: Chief Justice Salmon Chase, the presiding judge at the trial. "Republicans in this quarter seem to be a little shy of Chf. Justice Chase," Charles wrote. "He has favored the attempt to delay the trial of Johnson, and his course looks as though he is not well pleased with the turn of affairs in regard to the nomination for the next Presidency."[21] In other words, Chase had begun to pick up on the likelihood of Grant becoming the Republicans' presidential nominee.

Chase had aspired to the presidency since the late 1850s. In 1864, suspecting that Chase wanted his job, Abraham Lincoln removed him from his cabinet post of secretary of the Treasury and nomi-

Salmon Portland Chase, c. 1868. (*Brady-Handy Collection. Courtesy of the Library of Congress, Prints and Photographs Division.*)

nated him to replace the recently deceased Roger Taney as chief justice of the Supreme Court, hoping that would satisfy his political ambitions. It didn't. Still looking toward the presidency in 1868, and sensing that Grant was going to be the Republicans' presidential nominee, Chase sought to ingratiate himself with the moderates of the Republican Party, as well as with the Democratic Party. If he couldn't get the Republican nomination for the presidency, maybe the Democrats would want him. But that would mean this longtime abolitionist would have to change his politics, though perhaps not so dramatically, for he had come to oppose the federal occupation of the South. "I do not believe in military domination any more than I do in slaveholding oligarchy," he wrote a friend in March 1868. To fellow abolitionist Gerrit Smith he confided that in his view the Tenure of Office Act lacked constitutional authority and that "the President has a perfect right, and, indeed . . . the highest obligation, to remove Mr. Stanton."[22] The former abolitionist appeared to think that Johnson had no obligation to keep a cabinet member who was at odds with his policies, but as indicated by his opposition to federal oversight of the South, Chase had become considerably more conservative than the man who had visited Johnson in 1865 to promote Black suffrage. Chase probably should have recused himself from presiding over a trial that centered on an action that he approved of: Johnson's removal of Stanton. Without knowing Chase's private views, Charles worried that Chase's apparent deference to Johnson's legal team betrayed his sympathy for Johnson, and even his efforts to shape the trial to bring about an acquittal. Douglass would echo and further develop his son's concerns about Chase, but not until after the trial.

The trial proceedings proved a grueling affair. Johnson's defense was led by a skilled team of lawyers, the most distinguished being Benjamin Robbins Curtis, who had served on the Supreme Court and resigned in disgust after dissenting from then–Chief Justice Taney's *Dred Scott* decision of 1857, which had deprived African Americans of the rights of U.S. citizenship. Though he had disagreed with that lamentable ruling, Curtis was no passionate abolitionist; he had earlier supported the 1850 Fugitive Slave Act. Another of Johnson's distinguished lawyers was William M. Evarts, a moderate Republican with a prestigious private practice in New York. The House of Representatives had put together its own distinguished impeachment management team. Ohio's John Bingham was the nominal leader of the group, but Massachusetts representative Benjamin Butler, known for his aggressive rhetoric and demeanor, took on the major role of prosecuting the case against Johnson.[23]

As might be expected from the articles of impeachment, much of the trial focused on evidence linked to the firing of Stanton and the appointment of Thomas. Did presidents have the right to appoint and dismiss their own cabinet officials? In terms of precedent, the answer was yes, with the obligatory approval of the Senate. But in terms of the Tenure of Office Act, the answer was no. The question boiled down to whether Johnson had made the right decision to test the constitutionality of the law by breaking it.

Article 10, which charged Johnson with verbally attacking Congress and disregarding its authority, had the potential to lead to larger issues concerning Reconstruction, but the trial rarely moved in that direction. Given the legal skill of Curtis and Evarts, and the relative lack of trial experience among the House managers, the trial quickly came to focus on small details in which little seemed to be of consequence. Overseeing the trial, as a possible Johnson supporter or aspirant for the Republican or Democratic presidential nomination, Chief Justice Chase didn't help matters. He allowed the defense team numerous delays and insisted that the House managers keep their focus on legalistic points of contention directly relevant to the Tenure of Office Act, even though at least two of the articles of impeachment addressed broader failings of the Johnson presidency.

Typical of the trial was a direct examination by House manager Benjamin Butler of James K. Moorhead, a member of the House of Representatives. Moorhead was supposedly in Edwin Stanton's office

when Lorenzo Thomas "came in there to make some demand." The
Senate transcript gives a good sense of what those in the gallery, and
those who read about the trial, had to deal with:

> **Q.** Did you get into the room as soon as Mr. Stanton?
> **A.** Immediately after him.
> **Q.** Did you get there before any conversation began?
> **A.** I think about the time. I followed immediately, and there
> was no conversation of any marked significance until that
> which I have mentioned.
> **Q.** What was the conversation, significant or not, that took
> place between Mr. Stanton and General Thomas after you
> got into that room?
> **A.** I cannot recite it, because, as I told you, I did not take a
> memorandum of it, and it was not important enough to be
> impressed on my mind. I do not recollect.
> **Q.** But you have an impression that there was some?
> **A.** I think there was some—perhaps joking, or something of
> that kind. They appeared to be in a pretty good humor with
> each other.
> **Q.** That is, the parties did not seem to be in any passion, at all?
> **A.** Not hostile.
> **Q.** But in good humor?
> **A.** Yes, sir.
> **Q.** Joking?
> **A.** Yes, sir.
> **Q.** Do you recollect any of the jokes that passed?
> **A.** No, sir.[24]

Butler persisted awhile longer, with much of the questioning focusing on the question of what Johnson had in mind when he dismissed Stanton.

And if Johnson's dismissal of Stanton wasn't at issue, then there
was the matter of how Johnson treated Congress. In a fairly typical

exchange relevant to Article 10, which accused Johnson of speaking disparagingly of some Republican members of Congress, Butler this time questioned William N. Hudson, who had written a newspaper account about Johnson's notorious speech in Cleveland during his late summer 1866 Swing around the Circle. After asking Hudson to confirm his status as a journalist writing for the *Cleveland Leader*, Butler attempted to move to the heart of the matter:

> **Q.** Did you hear the speech that President Johnson made there [in Cleveland] from the balcony of a hotel?
> **A.** I did.
> **Q.** Did you report it?
> **A.** I did, with the assistance of another reporter.
> **Q.** Who is he?
> **A.** His name is Johnson.
> **Q.** Was your report published in the paper the next day?
> **A.** It was.
> **Q.** Have you a copy?
> **A.** I have.

But Hudson did not have his original notes, and when asked about the accuracy of the report, he confessed that it was "not a *verbatim* report." As Butler pressed his questions about Johnson, the president's defense lawyers claimed to be confused about Butler's reference to Johnson:

> **Mr. STANBERY.** Whom do you mean by Johnson?
> **Mr. EVARTS.** There was another Johnson mentioned.
> **Mr. Manager BUTLER.** Not on this occasion.
> **Mr. EVARTS.** Yes, reporter Johnson.
> **Mr. Manager BUTLER.** I mean Andrew Johnson "last aforesaid."[25]

Here the trial got caught up with an unintended comedy of names. Eventually, Evarts got Hudson to concede that the newspaper had a bias against Johnson. Even if Hudson had managed to get the president's words verbatim, Johnson's lawyers defended the president's First Amendment right to speak out against Congress.

This sort of testimony went on for weeks. The *Christian Recorder* reported that the trial centered on "legal quibbles" concerning the Tenure of Office Act.[26] Even the impassioned Thaddeus Stevens, a House manager who was so ill that two men carried him in on a chair for each day of the trial, succumbed to the torpor of the event. His major speech at the trial was an exceptionally long, detailed, and dry affair that he began by saying, "I shall discuss but a single article," Article 2. That article made it illegal for the president to fire a Senate appointee when the Senate was not in session. Where were the big issues that had led Stevens in January 1867 to declare before Congress that "it was impossible to reconstruct the South with ANDREW JOHNSON as president"?[27] Now Stevens was reduced to providing a painstaking, chronological account of the firing of Stanton and the appointment of Thomas, a succession that was rehashed on numerous occasions during a trial that seemed intent on wearing everyone down.[28] Johnson couldn't have hoped for a better scenario.

12

"DEMENTED MOSES
OF TENNESSEE"

How did African Americans understand the issues central to
Johnson's impeachment? The Republicans enmeshed in the
trial thought of it mainly in relation to the Tenure of Office Act.
That aspect had little interest for African Americans. After all, the
articles of impeachment, en masse, seemed to imply that Andrew
Johnson would have been doing just fine if he hadn't dismissed Secretary of War Edwin M. Stanton. Of course the Radical Republicans
didn't believe that, but they had found a way of impeaching Johnson
through their recently passed act, and they remained committed to
the path mapped out by the articles of impeachment. The articles also
addressed the separation of powers and evidence of Johnson's misconduct, but those larger issues got relatively little attention during
the trial.

Like many African Americans, Frederick Douglass seemed uncon-
cerned about the specifics of the Tenure of Office Act. For him and
other Black activists, there was something much more compelling at
stake than Johnson's firing of Stanton. In African American and Radical Republican newspapers and publications, Johnson was seen as

deserving of conviction for being a failed Reconstruction president who brought death and suffering to the freedpeople. As one Black clergyman was quoted as saying, Johnson merited conviction for being the "demented Moses of Tennessee"—the white president who promised to be the leader of Black people and turned out to be their oppressor.[1]

The Radical Republicans who impeached Johnson were brave and idealistic, and indeed dreamed of helping to create a better America.[2] But they were often hamstrung at the trial because of the articles of impeachment they had developed and now had to focus on for their prosecution of the president. Their emphasis on the Tenure of Office Act could seem timid at times, or just bloodlessly pragmatic. That was the risk the Republicans took in going for what they thought would be the sure thing of convicting the president for violating the new law. But there were times when the Radical Republicans made their case against Johnson in a way that complemented and enhanced the position of the African Americans hoping for conviction. One such instance came during a speech by House manager Benjamin Butler on the day that Charles Douglass and his father had tickets for the trial. On April 16, 1868, Butler cut through the rigmarole of the Tenure of Office Act to say something sharp and passionate about what Douglass, his son, and most Radical Republicans and Black activists believed the trial really was about: the impeachment of a president for whom Black lives did not matter.

Benjamin Butler Will Not Be Interrupted

Douglass made plans to attend the trial on April 16 as a guest of his son, booking a room with one Mrs. Parker, who kept "the 'Davis Hotel.'"[3] Charles, who wanted to take advantage of his good fortune in obtaining the tickets, no doubt arranged for part of the day off from the Washington, D.C., office of the Freedmen's Bureau.

The impeachment trial had so far lacked the excitement that the eight hundred daily spectators had been hoping for, and April 16 seemed as if it would be more of the same. The proceedings began with Charles Sumner asking the court secretary to read into the transcript his request "that all evidence offered on either side not trivial or obviously irrelevant in nature shall be received without objection." Sumner's request was approved by a vote of the Senate. Most of the rest of the day focused on minutiae linked to the Tenure of Office Act. From the point of view of Johnson's legal team, led by Evarts and Curtis, presidents had a long history of appointing and dismissing cabinet and other White House officials on their own. The lawyers introduced into evidence all such appointments and dismissals between 1853 and 1868, having earlier provided a similar list for 1789 through 1852. They also introduced into evidence a document that included the beginning and end of each legislative session of Congress from 1789 to 1865.

Following these preliminaries, Johnson's defense lawyer Benjamin Curtis requested in writing "to raise judicially the question of Mr. Stanton's legal right to continue to hold the office of Secretary for the Department of War against the authority of the President." That led to an additional dull hour of interrogation and conversation about what House manager Butler termed "the doctrine of estoppel." The discussion got increasingly legalistic, confusing, and eye-glazing. The main issue for Butler and the other House managers continued to be that on February 21, 1868, Johnson, in violation of the Tenure of Office Act, removed Stanton from his position as secretary of war and appointed Thomas to the job. The House managers argued that Johnson knew that he had violated the law, and they charged that he deliberately sought "to raise in the courts the question of the constitutionality of the tenure-of-office act."[4] Johnson, they asserted, should have explored the constitutionality of the act *before* breaking the law. The discussion went on for a considerable while longer.

But then House manager Benjamin Butler decided he had had enough parsing of detail, and the day finally got interesting. At the end of the long session, Butler let loose with his frustrations about all of the legalisms—indeed, about the Tenure of Office Act itself—and also about the president's lawyers' call for yet another delay in the trial because of the illness of former attorney general Henry Stanbery (who had resigned from his office in order to serve on Johnson's defense team). For a few minutes, Butler offered a glimpse of what many Radical Republicans and African Americans thought the impeachment of Johnson should have been addressing from the beginning: Johnson's efforts to thwart Reconstruction and undo the work of the Civil War. Butler cut to the core of what was wrong with Johnson's presidency in a remarkable rhetorical display.

Butler was a big man with droopy eyes, but his placid looks belied his capacity for bullheadedness. He first addressed the defense's request for a delay by linking the trial to the Civil War itself. "Gentlemen of the Senate," he announced, "this is the closing up of a war wherein three hundred thousand men laid down their lives to save the country." Johnson's counsel Evarts interrupted Butler in mid-speech to object to the "relevancy" of the war to the trial, and Butler quickly responded: "The relevancy of it is this, that while we are waiting for the Attorney General to get well, and you are asking to delay this trial for that reason, numbers of our fellow-citizens are being murdered day

Benjamin Franklin Butler, c. 1870. (*Brady-Handy Collection. Courtesy of the Library of Congress, Prints and Photographs Division.*)

by day. There is not a man here who does not know that the moment justice is done on this great criminal these murders will cease."⁵ In this formulation, as had been suggested by African American orators and journalists, Johnson could be thought of as something like a murderer. The outraged Curtis attempted once again to bring a halt to Butler's speech, but Butler pushed on with a rousing peroration:

> I cannot be interrupted. . . . While we are being courteous the true Union men of the south are being murdered, and on our heads and on our skirts is this blood if we remain any longer idle. . . .
>
> Now, I say, for the safety of the finances of the people, for the progress of the legislation of the people, for the safety of the true and loyal men, black and white, in the south who have per- illed their lives for four years; yea, five years; yea, six years; yea, seven years, in your behalf; for the good of the country, for all that is dear to any man and patriot, I pray let this trial proceed; let us come to a determination of this issue. If the President of the United States goes free and [is] acquit, then the country must deal with that state of facts as it arises; but if he, as the House of Rep- resentatives instructs me, and as I believe, is guilty; if on his head rests the responsibility; if from his policy, from his obstruction of the peace of the country, all this corruption and all these murders come, in the name of Heaven let us have an end of them and see to it that we can sit at least four hours a day to attend to this, the great business of the people.⁶

The previous four hours had focused on details connected to the Ten- ure of Office Act. In this stirring moment at day's end, Butler under- scored the stakes of Articles 10 and 11—the only articles that raised questions about the implications of Johnson's policies. But those arti- cles hardly did so in such stark terms; the situation of the freedpeople wasn't explicitly mentioned anywhere in the House's indictment of Johnson and now Butler was talking about whites and Blacks together.

In his radically visionary declamation, Butler suggested that the Civil War had not come to an end, and that the South at this point was winning. The two months of the trial had featured not a single statement from a Black person. In this respect the impeachment trial implicitly followed the racist practices of the nation's many states that disallowed Black testimony in court cases. Butler's mention of "true and loyal men, black and white," in effect crossed a line established by the articles of impeachment and Judge Chase's legalistic handling of the trial. It was an effort, by this white congressman, to bring a Black perspective into the trial.

Recognizing that Butler had strayed into arguments that seemed irrelevant to the eleven articles of impeachment, Evarts responded: "I have never heard such a harangue before in a court of justice." Evarts's objection led to a testy exchange on "whether the word 'harangue' be in order here," and counsel on both sides, perhaps recognizing that Butler had violated some sort of protocol, requested an adjournment until 10 a.m. the next day, which Justice Chase granted.[7] But how inspiring Butler's declamations would have been for Frederick Douglass had he been in attendance that day.

Charles almost certainly was there, but Douglass never showed up. Charles wrote his father on April 24: "I was much disappointed in not seeing you here on the 16th, thinking that your desire to witness a portion of the trial would induce you to come on for a day at least." Douglass may have taken on a new speaking engagement, or he may have had second thoughts about how his attendance would affect the trial. Had he attended, all eyes would have been on him, and that's precisely what he didn't want. Back in fall 1864, after he had decided to support Lincoln's reelection, he chose not to campaign for the president because, as he confided to Theodore Tilton, he didn't want to expose Republicans "to the charge of being the 'N___r' party."[8] At the last minute he may have had similar concerns about the impact of his presence on an impeachment trial that the Republicans were prosecuting as if it wasn't about race. He wouldn't have wanted to jeopardize the possibility of obtaining a conviction by "exposing" the Republicans as caring about Black people, and he wouldn't have wanted his celebrity status to serve as a distraction.

Charles probably told his father about Butler's speech the next time they got together.

"The Negroes Praying for Conviction"

Douglass disappointed his son and missed out on Butler's inspiring speech. Had he made the trip to Washington, he could have also offered counsel to his friend George T. Downing, for Downing had recently received threats from the Ku Klux Klan. Founded in Johnson's home state of Tennessee in 1866, along with other white supremacist groups, the Klan deployed violence against the freedpeople as a way of resisting congressional Reconstruction and now sought to intimidate Blacks in Washington, D.C., as well. An article in the April 13, 1868, issue of the *New York Herald* had the ominous headline, "The Ku Klux Klan in Washington: Downing, the Oysterman, and Bob, the Bootblack, Doomed." Using the demeaning imagery of minstrelsy, the reporter wrote of how the Klan's threats induced in these Black men "a shaking and a shivering worse than swamp chills and fever." The article included a letter Downing had received from the Klan, which stated, "If you're in Washington ten days after this reaches you it will be as a corpse." Signed "Assassin," the letter urged Downing to "remember Lincoln." The reporter deferred throughout to the authority and fearsomeness of the Klan, stating that "in his pensive moments Downing upbraids himself for ever having anything to do with the War Department, even in the way of furnishing poor Stanton with a lunch of oyster soup."[9]

The mention of Stanton is significant, for it puts the Klan's threat to Downing into the larger context of the impeachment trial. Amid its tone of jocular racism, the article, in spite of itself, provides another African American perspective on the impeachment. Downing, the manager of the House cafeteria, was among those who brought food to Stanton while he remained barricaded in the War Office. Because the Klan had no foothold in Washington, with its large African American population, Downing probably didn't have second thoughts about helping Stanton while the trial remained in progress. Downing's February 1866 visit to Johnson with the Black delegation had already established that he had major concerns about Johnson's policies even before the president violated the Tenure of Office Act. But Downing's solidarity with Stanton, which had a human dimension, suggests that he took that aspect of the trial seriously, too.

The article on Downing and the Ku Klux Klan was not the only racist piece in the *New York Herald* that both revealed and distorted African American perspectives on the impeachment trial. As the trial approached the moment when the senators would be voting on Article 11, the newspaper printed a piece about an African Methodist Episcopal (AME) Church convention in Washington, D.C. Like Charles Douglass, those at the conference were confident that the senators would convict. After all, for the past two years their newspaper, the *Christian Recorder*, had been exposing how Johnson's policies harmed the freedpeople. Surely those policies would lead senators to remove the president from office. In a section of the *Herald* article titled "The Negroes Praying for Conviction," a contemptuous reporter described the Black conventioneers on May 15, 1868, as they awaited the verdict. Desirous of a conviction, they voted to spend the day in "fasting and prayer to the Almighty to throw around the Senate of the United States 'the girdling of the Holy Spirit,' that a verdict may be passed in the interest of the Freedmen's Bureau, the impecunious carpet baggers and the starving set of office seekers." According to the reporter, "All Methodistical darkydom is supposed to be groaning in the flesh to-day." One of the AME leaders, the Reverend Sampson Jones, hoped "de Lord would stiffen wid de grace of fortitude de doubtful backbone of de waverly Senators, and dat Andrew Johnson, de demented Moses of Tennessee, would be disremoved by de sanctimonious voice ob de Senate to whar de wicked cease from troublin and de weary am at rest." The reporter's use of dialect was meant to demean Jones, but the terms of the clergyman's anger at the duplicitous president came through nonetheless. The conference participants concurred in their desire that the Senate remove Johnson from office; they also asked for a "special place of excruciating torture in the realm of Hades for such republican Senators as voted for acquittal." The day's praying and fasting concluded with "a public demonstration in favor of impeachment."[10]

To be sure, the *Herald*'s account of Black hostility to Johnson was condescending, dismissive, and racist. But one can read against the grain of the racism to see that Blacks at this convention had strong views about Johnson that weren't represented at the trial. Even with the author's decision to use dialect, the Reverend Sampson Jones's reference to "de demented Moses of Tennessee" said a good deal about Johnson's betrayal of Black people. The participants at the AME Church conference believed that the betrayal was serious enough to merit an eternity in hell for any senator who voted for acquittal. From the point of view of the African Americans mentioned in this article, the removal of Johnson would make a strong statement about the insidious policies that had led to the violence against the freedpeople in Memphis, New Orleans, and elsewhere. Conviction and removal might even help to bring forth better days for Blacks in the United States.

But this article, again because of its racism, also reveals the challenge of bringing forth those better days. The article didn't appear in a backwater newspaper in the Deep South but in one of the most widely read newspapers in New York City, where African Americans without significant property were not allowed to vote. A Black perspective came through in the article, but the reporter did not take it seriously. The mocking tone pointed to one of Douglass's large concerns during the Reconstruction period: that white Americans had trouble viewing Blacks as fully human.

Given that concern, both the article on the Black conventioneers and the article on Downing and the KKK shed additional light on the Republicans' impeachment strategy. One might criticize the Republicans for not being more forthright about their problems with Johnson, and for not offering charges more highly specific about the impact of his intransigence and racism on the freedpeople. Johnson's dismissal of Stanton was a relatively small thing, but what about his firing of the various military commanders presiding over the five military districts and his replacement of those officers with Confederate sympathizers? (Those dismissals and appointments were addressed in Article 11, but only obliquely.) A case could be made that Johnson worked to undermine the Freedmen's Bureau, to dismantle other Reconstruction initiatives, and to prevent African Americans from attaining equal rights through federal legislation. Were these actions not worthy of being mentioned in the articles of impeachment? The *New York Herald*'s reportage suggests why the Republicans chose to say nothing about such specifics in the eleven articles. In 1868, many white people in the United States shared Johnson's racism. Thaddeus Stevens knew that, and that's why, when he wanted to advance his progressive agenda, he objected to Douglass's participation at the Southern Loyalists' Convention in 1866. African American leaders knew that as well. A bolder Republican strategy to address the issues that Benjamin Butler brought up on April 16 might have made a better case for the impeachment of Johnson. But that is one big hypothetical—and made in hindsight.

"The Work before Us"

While his son followed and sometimes attended the impeachment trial in Washington, Douglass remained on the road, continuing his advocacy of Black suffrage. Even so, Johnson was very much on Douglass's mind at a vexed moment in his own career. On May 14, 1868, two days before the vote on whether to convict the president on Article 11, Douglass was in New York City participating in the American Equal Rights Association convention, which was devoted to the cause of women's suffrage. He had attended the first women's rights conven-

tion in Seneca Falls, New York, in 1848, and had long supported voting rights for women. But his relationship with leading women's rights
advocates had begun to fray. He wanted the "male" in male suffrage
to be extended to Black men; women's rights advocates such as Olym-
pia Brown and Susan B. Anthony insisted that educated white women
deserved the vote before uneducated Black men. The issue for Douglass and Anthony, who shared a commitment to Black and women's
suffrage, was who should get the franchise first.

At the convention, Douglass was put on the defensive by Olym-
pia Brown, the first woman ordained as a minister by the Unitarian
Church (in 1863) and a prominent lecturer on women's rights. Brown
had recently given a number of speeches in Kansas on women's suffrage, accompanied by George Francis Train, a Democrat, business
entrepreneur, and avowed advocate of women's rights. When Brown
criticized Douglass for not joining her in Kansas, Douglass, in a
speech at the Equal Rights convention, assailed Train. He "hates the
negro," Douglass said, "and that is what stimulates him to substitute
the cry of emancipation for women." He added that Train's "Democratic Party opposes the impeachment of Johnson and desires a 'white
man's government.'"[11]

With these comments, Douglass made clear that he saw the
impeachment of Johnson as a challenge to white supremacy. At the
American Equal Rights convention, to the dismay of the women's
rights advocates, he argued that impartial Black suffrage was the best
way to fight white supremacists like Train and Johnson. Black male
suffrage, he said, which involved simply extending the male vote to
Black men, should be the initial goal of everyone at the convention.
Douglass supported women's suffrage, but not at the expense of delay-
ing the reform he had been advocating since the Civil War.

Douglass's remarks at the convention showed that he had been
paying attention to the impeachment trial. They also suggested that
he shared the view of his journalistic friend Philip A. Bell, the editor of
the Black newspaper *The Elevator*. Bell thought that the Republicans'
focus on the Tenure of Office Act was misconceived. A day before the

verdict, he lamented that the Republicans failed to follow through on a vigorous impeachment of the president, and were instead "quibbling about technicalities, and standing in the way of the reform which his removal would produce." Douglass had no apparent interest in the Tenure of Office Act but, like his son (who had recently written, with his usual optimism, "We here are confident of a conviction"), anticipated conviction for reasons that weren't limited to the act. Convicting this president, he said at the women's rights convention, "will be a hopeful indication of the triumph of our right to vote . . . and mean that the fair South shall no longer by governed by Regulators and the Ku-Klux Klan, but by fair and impartial law."[12]

Douglass's reference to the Ku Klux Klan and other racist groups (which he termed "Regulators") was almost certainly motivated by the Klan's public threat to his friend George T. Downing. That threat was a present reminder of what Douglass believed the impeachment trial was about. The Tenure of Office Act might dominate the articles of impeachment, but he thought the Republicans would convict in order to take a stand against Johnson's racist actions and continue the work of Reconstruction.

On May 16, 1868, the House managers requested a vote on a single article of impeachment. The Senate at that time consisted of fifty-four members—forty-five Republicans and nine Democrats—from twenty-seven states, with Tennessee still the only ex-Confederate state readmitted to the Union. The House managers believed they had their best chance of conviction with Article 11 because it was the widest-ranging article, addressing the Tenure of Office Act but also accusing Johnson of working against the Reconstruction legislation passed by Congress. Ten Republicans voted not to convict, including seven moderate Republicans who the House managers hoped would support the cause. That left the vote 35 in favor and 19 against, one short of the two-thirds majority required for conviction. Moderate Republican James Grimes of Iowa, who voted against conviction, explained himself as follows: "I cannot agree to destroy the harmonious working of the Constitution for the sake of getting rid of an Unacceptable

President." Grimes and other of his moderate colleagues believed that the House managers had overreached and presented an exaggerated picture of Johnson's malfeasance. But their dissent was not just about constitutional principles; the evidence suggests that there was much dealmaking (and possible bribery) in the final few days before the Senate vote. Moreover, some of the senators who voted in favor of conviction may have done so only after they counted heads and saw that Johnson would be acquitted. Had their votes been needed, they may well have voted to acquit, too. As circumstances turned out, these waffling senators got credit for voting to convict while fulfilling their desire to keep Johnson in office out of concern about his successor.[13]

Though they didn't come right out and say it, by the time of the vote a number of Republican senators wanted Johnson acquitted because they hated the idea of the pro tempore leader of the Senate, Ohio's Benjamin Wade, ascending to the presidency. Over the years, Wade's brash style had irritated many of his colleagues. That he had just lost his senatorial seat and would be out of office in January 1869 was fine with most of them. The Republican Party was known for championing Reconstruction, but it was also a party of economic conservatism supported by northern and western businessmen. Such men viewed Wade as an extremist whose economic proposals verged on socialism. After all, Wade, who supported trade unions, had declared in a July 1867 interview with the *New York Times*: *"We must elevate the laborer and give him a share of the proceeds of his labor."* Wade's support for Blacks' rights in the North and South, along with his advocacy of women's suffrage, didn't help his cause among moderate Republicans, either. A Texas newspaper from the Democratic side predicted that if Wade were to become president, he would appoint African Americans John Langston as postmaster general and "Frederick Douglass, of New York—Secretary of the Interior."[14] Moderate Republicans had similar concerns about what they regarded as the potential extremism of a Wade presidency.

In addition, many Republicans worried about the role that Wade might play in the upcoming Republican presidential convention, scheduled to begin just four days after the vote on Article 11. Johnson had no chance of gaining the nomination for a second term; most Republicans favored Ulysses S. Grant. If Johnson was convicted and Wade became president, he could control the convention, conceivably taking the nomination from Grant, or even emerging as the vice presidential nominee. That was a nightmare that a significant cohort of Republicans didn't want to experience.

All of which is to say that though the trial did not officially end with Johnson's acquittal on Article 11, in a sense it did. Enough Republicans had made the decision not to convict, and they were not to be moved. Ten days after this first vote, the House managers called for votes on two additional articles, 2 and 3, which concerned aspects of the Tenure of Office Act. Both got the same vote of 35 in favor and 19 opposed, and that led the House managers to end the trial on May 26, 1868, with votes on just three of the eleven articles. Disappointment in newspapers like the *National Anti-Slavery Standard* and the Black press was palpable. Furious at the Republican senators who acquitted the president, an anonymous editorialist for the *Standard* remarked: "We defy the cunningest lawyer among the Republican traitors to sit down and, after full deliberation, paint a President who *would* be worthy of impeachment and not have the picture a striking likeness of Andrew Johnson." Frances Harper, in a novel serialized in the *Christian Recorder*, best captured what the acquittal meant to African Americans in the larger context of developments that did not bode well for Reconstruction:

> The impeachment had failed. State after State in the North had voted against enfranchising the colored man in their midst. The spirit of the lost cause revived, murders multiplied. The Ku Klux spread terror and death around. Every item of Northern meanness to the colored people in their midst was a message of hope to the rebel element of the South. . . . Men advocating equal rights did so at the peril of their lives, for violence and murder were rampant in the land. . . . If Johnson was clasping hands with reb-

els and traitors was there no power in Congress to give, at least, security to life?

Harper describes the persistent racism and violence that African Americans faced in the North and South, even as she (correctly) imagines conditions further deteriorating with the end of Reconstruction. Nevertheless, one of the main characters of her novel, a Black man, declares: "We must trust and hope for better things."[15]

The Republican senators themselves hoped for better things, even with Johnson still in office. To the relief of many, including Douglass, Grant emerged as the Republicans' presidential nominee, receiving a unanimous vote on the first ballot. The convention gave Grant his personal choice for vice president, Indiana's longtime antislavery advocate Schuyler Colfax, then Speaker of the House of Representatives. Grant and Colfax both supported Black suffrage, but even so, the Republicans' caution—or cowardice—prevailed, and Black suffrage was not included in the party platform.

Still, the trial had done its office. It restrained Johnson for much of 1868, which is another reason some Republicans willingly settled for impeachment without conviction. One month after the trial ended, Congress readmitted seven of the ex-Confederate states to the Union in an omnibus bill of June 25, 1868, despite Johnson's veto and objections to the conditions that Congress set on readmission: support for the Reconstruction Acts and the Thirteenth and Fourteenth Amendments. Stanton finally left the War Office in late May and was replaced by General John Schofield, a more acceptable choice to congressional Republicans than Lorenzo Thomas. In July, Johnson vetoed yet another extension of the Freedmen's Bureau. Congress overturned that veto on the same day. The Fourteenth Amendment was ratified in July 1868.

In his letters from Washington to his father, Charles didn't comment on the acquittal, or if he did, that letter hasn't survived. But he did send a letter on May 29, three days after the impeachment trial had formally ended, that affected his father's understanding of what had happened. Charles, who had initially expressed his support for Chief Justice Chase, and then grown wary of how he handled the trial, now spoke out against him. Charles went as far as blaming the chief justice, who was angling for the presidential nomination from the Democratic Party, for the failure to convict. "I am not for Chase or any other man who would help to secure the acquittal of Andrew Johnson," said Charles. "I did think at one time that Mr. Chase was all right and that we could rely upon him, but now, as the investigation continues in the House I can see him and understand him more clearly. If I had a vote to cast next fall I would cast it for Grant & Colfax." Like many Republicans, Charles believed that Chase helped "to secure the acquittal" by slowing down the pace of the trial and keeping the questioning focused on the Tenure of Office Act. There had also been talk in Republican circles that Chase had become close with Johnson, even attending a party for his family at the White House just as the trial commenced.[16] Earlier in the year Charles had regarded Chase as a possible presidential candidate; now he saw him as a traitor.

Two months after the anticlimactic conclusion to the trial, Douglass took up his son's critique of Chase in an essay published in the *National Anti-Slavery Standard* and at least four other newspapers, including Bell's *The Elevator*. In Douglass's most important statement on the impeachment trial, he went one step further than his son and accused his former friend of "apostasy."[17]

For Douglass, Chase's career exemplified everything that was wrong with politics in the age of Andrew Johnson, and he vented his anger and frustration at what he had seen since 1865. Chase, an "Abolitionist of thirty years standing," had sold his soul to the white man's party in order to further his political ambitions. Chase's courtship of the Democratic Party, Douglass remarked, was "certainly one of the saddest spectacles which can afflict the eyes of men." After doing what he could to thwart the Republican House managers at the impeachment trial, Chase was now "piteously imploring the Democratic party to nominate him as their candidate for the Presidency." His brilliant past had given way to an effort "to put the government into the hands of the Democratic Party the next four years." Douglass presented Chase as attempting to turn back the clock on the Civil War by joining forces with Johnson, the man whose presidency he preserved. As it turned out, the Democrats at their convention in early July 1868 chose Horatio Seymour of New York, a candidate more racist and opportunistic than Chase. Chase's failed machinations, Douglass said, led him to the "gutter."[18]

Douglass's venomous essay showed what he believed was at stake in the impeachment of Johnson. Compared to Chase's treachery, Douglass said ironically, Johnson's own "whitens into innocence." Douglass was so angry at Chase that he worked with conventional stereotypes to "blacken" him, sparing Johnson by comparison. Chase, he declared, "brought the whole influence of his position and learning to shield Andrew Johnson from deserved impeachment." (By "deserved impeachment," Douglass meant deserved conviction, as the House had impeached the president before Chase was summoned to preside over the trial.) Johnson deserved to be convicted for the same reason that Douglass now associated with Chase: for "hostility to the negro" and for attempting to place Black people "in a condition only less wretched than the slavery from which the war for the Union had rescued" them.[19] According to Douglass, Johnson had done much worse than violate the Tenure of Office Act, but conviction, even if only through that new law, would have pleased him.

Douglass's essay highlighted his rationale for impeachment and conviction, but it also cast light on the moment in the summer of 1867 when the president's men offered him the job of commissioner of the Freedmen's Bureau. Douglass may well have understood Chase's ambitions because he had been tempted to take that job. Surely there was a moment when he thought about the power, influence, and salary that would have come with it. But he realized then, as he argued about Chase now, that to succumb to such ambition would mean surrendering high ground to the enemy. That, Douglass told his readers, was what Chase had done at a time when the Senate's acquittal of Johnson showed that Blacks' freedom struggles were hardly over.

The best advice he could now offer his readers was simply to ignore the chief justice, "a deserter from our ranks" whose "degradation is complete."[20]

Douglass was done with Chase, but he continued to brood over the impeachment. He returned to it on several occasions in lectures and essays over the years, usually at moments when he despaired about the failure of Reconstruction. But he offered one more reflection in 1868 in "The Work before Us," an essay that endorsed the Republican ticket of Ulysses S. Grant and Schuyler Colfax over the Democratic ticket of Horatio Seymour and Frank P. Blair. Seymour had supported President James K. Polk's aim to extend slavery, while Blair had advised Johnson on various matters and was known for his unabashed racism. Douglass's concern, as in his essay on Chase, was that present circumstances increasingly indicated that the Civil War was not over. "In the ranks of Seymour and Blair," Douglass pronounced, "is the rebel army, without its arms."[21]

That the Democrats could put forth such a ticket in 1868 demonstrated that the Thirteenth Amendment—which ended slavery—did not mark the end of slavery's regime. Garrison and his abolitionist allies had hailed the passage of the Thirteenth Amendment as a symbol of the Union's triumph, but their celebration had been premature, to say the least. Douglass remained concerned that the unsettled, never-ending war would have dire consequences for African Americans. He observed that "the slaveholding rebels, struck down by Gen. Grant," persisted with "one purpose, and one purpose alone," and that was to secure "permanent control over the black laborers of the South." Chattel slavery may have been outlawed, but white supremacy, through peonage and Black Codes, still reigned in the South. The Senate's failure to convict on any grounds, Douglass said, had consequences, for the acquittal further encouraged racist outrages. Douglass grimly assessed the post-acquittal moment in late summer 1868:

The South to-day is a field of blood. Murder runs riot in Texas, Tennessee, Mississippi, and Louisiana. Assassination has taken place of insurrection. Armed bands of rebels stalk abroad at midnight with blackened faces, and thus disguised go forth to shoot, stab, and murder their loyal neighbors.

Douglass didn't have to mention the earlier anti-Black violence in Memphis and New Orleans. His point was that the Senate had implicitly exculpated Johnson for policies that had led to such violence. Douglass's evocation of the context of that violence served less as a critique of Johnson than of the Republicans for their reluctance to name the harm that Johnson had done to African Americans. Johnson, Douglass claimed, pressed on with the "scene of war" from "the presidential chair" by "feeding the rebel imagination with a prospect of regaining through politics what they lost by the sword."[22]

Douglass detested Johnson and thought he should have been convicted. But in his writings of 1868 and beyond, he saw white Americans as complicit in the racist practices that thwarted Blacks' freedom struggles. As the title "The Work before Us" suggests, Douglass believed much work still needed to be done by "us," whom he broadly conceived as "every loyal man and woman in the country." For that work to be accomplished, he advised, "the connection of the present with the past" could neither "be ignored nor forgotten."[23] America had been a slave culture and would remain a slave culture until Americans honestly confronted the history and legacy of slavery. Douglass came back to this theme repeatedly after Johnson completed his term of office, typically by invoking the Johnson presidency as an episode threatening to repeat itself. The history of race relations over the remainder of the nineteenth century, and indeed into the twentieth and twenty-first centuries, sadly confirms Douglass's status as one of the nation's prophets.

Epilogue

"WE HAVE A FIGHT
ON OUR HANDS"

ANDREW JOHNSON SURVIVED the impeachment trial, but his
presidency was never the same. The deals and compromises
that garnered the votes needed to avoid conviction left him something
of an onlooker in the remaining months of his presidency. He would
not receive the Republican nomination for president; that went to
Ulysses S. Grant. The Democrats, too, lost interest in Johnson and
chose Horatio Seymour, a former governor of New York, as their presidential candidate. Johnson continued to veto bills that came his way
from the Republicans who had taken charge of Reconstruction, and
most of those vetoes were quickly overridden. The Republicans who
impeached Johnson essentially got what they wanted even without the
conviction: a declawed president. In the larger scheme of things, however, Johnson got what he wanted, for the Democrats, the party that
he now identified with, made significant gains in the fall elections.
White Americans in all regions of the country showed their disapproval of the policies of the Radical Republicans. Moreover, Johnson
continued to enjoy a platform to express his ideas about Congress's
"departure from the letter and spirit of the Constitution," as he put

it in his Farewell Address of March 4, 1869. That document included Johnson's testimonial to himself: "Calmly reviewing my administration of the Government, I feel that, with a sense of accountability to God, having conscientiously endeavored to discharge my whole duty, I have nothing to regret."[1]

Shortly after submitting his Farewell Address, Johnson returned home to Greeneville, Tennessee. But he had no intention of settling into a quiet presidential retirement. Almost immediately after he arrived, he sought to revitalize his political career.

Four years earlier, in March 1865, Johnson had moved from Nashville to Washington, D.C., to assume the vice presidency. A few weeks before he left, a group of Nashville's Black leaders visited him at the statehouse to award him a gold watch for his "Untiring Energy in the Cause of Freedom." As described a year later in an article in the *Christian Recorder* with the teasing title "That Watch! Mr. President!," the group gave him the timepiece in recognition of his October 1864 speech in which he "thrilled the heart of every colored man in Nashville by promising to be a 'Moses' for the colored race." By 1866, Johnson had lost the support of that Black constituency. Following his Swing around the Circle lecture tour, Nashville's Black leaders, believing that Johnson was "not exactly modelled after the ancient Moses, but rather a very excellent type of Pharaoh," sent "a committee to . . . request the return of that watch." Did this really happen? According to an article in the *Christian Recorder*, Johnson, who was always keen to meet with Black people, greeted the committee and made an effort to locate the timepiece. The article reported: "But, alas! The watch had proved such a good goer, that it had left the donor's sight forever! The committee's errand proved a futile one; for 'Moses' said unto the children of African descent, 'Stand still and see the salvation that cometh by the means of "My Policy."'" In this comical and probably fictional account of the president and his former admirers, published in the nation's most widely read African American newspaper, the author passed a final judgment:

Unlike the Moses of Egypt, the "Moses" of Tennessee has entered the Promised Land himself, and kicked his children out. What an example of parental affection does he set! Yet may he behold, like at the midnight hour, the dire handwriting of an angry God upon the wall,—"Thou art weighed in the balance and found wanting!"[2]

As this writer understood the situation, Johnson would go to hell.

Johnson never stopped conceiving of himself as a Moses to Black people. In March 1869, at age sixty-one, he hoped to become a senator or congressman. He gave speeches in Knoxville, Memphis, and elsewhere, looking for vindication and often focusing on what he regarded as the unfair charge that he was hostile to African Americans. He calculated that he had enough credibility with Tennessee's Blacks that he could appeal to them for their support, hoping that the approximately fifty thousand Black men who had been added to the state's voting rolls would lead him to victory. Speaking in Knoxville in April 1869, Johnson directed himself to the Blacks in the audience, telling them that "the time is coming when you will know who your friends are." For the skeptics in the crowd, he trotted out his favorite piece of evidence of his long-standing concern for African Americans: "the subject of Moses."[3]

Johnson's forensics were all too familiar. "I want the colored men to listen to me," he proclaimed, and then he made the case he had elaborated many times before:

Who set the colored men free? Was it done by President Lincoln in his proclamation? No, for you will find that Tennessee was excepted from that proclamation. Who was it, who, standing there upon the Capitol steps at Nashville, in the midst of war and tumult and strife, declared freedom to the colored men of Tennessee. Look to the record and you will see that I declared their freedom then, and that after declaring the colored men free, I

said if there was none other more capable than I, I would be their
Moses and lead them from captivity. Have not they been led from
captivity?

As obtuse as ever, Johnson regarded himself as a leader of Black people and as enlightened on civil rights. Having now returned home,
he told his Black auditors that he had taken more risks over the past
six years than any other white southern leader in supporting African
Americans. He had even been "accused of favoring negro suffrage."
The irony, he said, was that the Republicans now claimed he was
against it. "Where is the proof of that?" he asked.[4]

Douglass could have offered plenty of proof, but Johnson continued to maintain that the states and not the federal government should
set policy on voting rights for African Americans. That position, he
argued, did not mean that he opposed Black suffrage. But it surely
meant that he failed to acknowledge the depth of whites' resistance to
Black suffrage in the southern states, and indeed elsewhere across the
nation. It was precisely that resistance that led Douglass and the Radical Republicans to champion the Fifteenth Amendment, ratified in
1870, that protected Black voting rights at the federal and state levels.

But this was 1869, and as part of his effort to revive his political
career, Johnson continued his attempt to appeal to the Black people
of Tennessee. He spoke to another mixed-race audience in Memphis
in April 1869. As in Knoxville, Johnson turned to the matter of slavery and race. "I want the colored people to understand," he said. "I
want them to understand who is their best friend." To make his case,
he brought from his pocket newspaper accounts of his October 1864
Moses speech, and informed the crowd that "when men were being
shot down in hearing of the shrieks of the wounded and dying, I made
this speech and proclamation." Whereupon he selectively quoted from
one of the accounts, and again reminded his public that less than five
years earlier the Blacks of Nashville had hailed him as their savior. He
took special pride in reading a flattering snippet from a newspaper
article. "'You are our Moses,'" he quoted the Blacks at that gathering

as saying, "and the exclamation was caught up and cheered until the Capitol rang again." Johnson lifted his eyes from the newspaper clipping, gazed outward at the sea of faces, and declared, "I want the colored people to hear me." As if delusional, he announced to the Blacks in the audience: "Your Moses has come to free you again."[5]

There is more than a little pathos here. Johnson appeared briefly to have moved beyond metaphor: he actually conceived of himself as a liberator of Black people who had already been freed. But that's where the speech got interesting, for Johnson made a sudden and surprising turn. He announced that he now sought to liberate the Blacks of Tennessee not from slavery but from peonage.

Johnson was racist, paranoid, and narcissistic, but he understood class conflict and continued to disdain moneyed plantation owners. Ironically, those owners remained wealthy because of Johnson's May 1865 presidential Amnesty Proclamation that allowed them to keep their land. Johnson chose to support the plantation owners over the Radical Republicans, whom he disdained even more. Most of those owners now wanted Blacks to remain on the plantations as low-wage workers under the system of peonage, a practice that eventually evolved into sharecropping. Peonage threatened to keep Black families in perpetuity on plantations by fixing wages at or below their living expenses.

Consistent with his long-standing resentment of wealthy plantation owners, Johnson challenged peonage in this speech, with apparent sympathy for the Blacks who were trapped by it. "Now you have nothing," he said to the Blacks in the audience. "They have taken your money and your trinkets, and you are the slaves of those worse than taskmasters. They have a mortgage upon you and a bill of sale."[6] Johnson couldn't put a stop to the evolving social and economic system that served the master class, but the Black people in the crowd may have respected his willingness to critique peonage as a form of slavery. Still, as any political operative could have predicted, his trafficking of himself as a Moses to Blacks didn't help him with Tennessee's white voters. Johnson lost every election that he ran for until 1875, when the Democrat-controlled state legislature, not the people of Tennessee, elected him a U.S. senator by a single vote on the fifty-fourth ballot.

When Johnson returned to Washington, D.C., in March 1875, much had changed. Democrats were now the majority party in the House of Representatives. After several years in which Black people had achieved some representation in Congress and statehouses, Reconstruction was fading away and southern states had returned to repressive rule. Their state legislatures had begun creating a series of barriers that made it difficult, if not impossible, for Blacks to vote and run for office. President Ulysses S. Grant had supported Force Bills in the early 1870s that put federal muscle behind enforcing the Fifteenth Amendment and quashing the Ku Klux Klan and other white supremacist organizations. But those bills increasingly failed to stop southern whites' racist and often violent reactions against Republicans' efforts to enhance Blacks' civil rights in the ex-Confederate states. The only way of guaranteeing those rights would have been to send thousands of occupying federal troops, and there simply was no will to do that. By the mid-1870s, Reconstruction had been thwarted through the combined efforts of southern and northern Democrats, the daily violence of southern whites against Blacks, and the complacency of whites across the nation. White "Redemption" governments took hold in the South; Black ghettoization remained the norm in the North.

Johnson was greeted warmly on his return to Congress. He took the oath of office from Vice President Henry Wilson of Massachusetts, who in 1868 had been one of the Republican senators calling for Johnson's conviction. There seemed to be no hard feelings. In his first Senate speech after his return, Johnson said what he had been saying since 1861, when he rejected southern secession: "I warn the people of the United States against encroachments upon, against violations of, and against the total disregard of the Constitution of the United States." In terms of policy, Johnson had earlier taken a stand against Grant's Force Bills. But surprisingly he offered tentative support for Congress's recently passed Civil Rights Act, which was intended to shore up enforcement of the Fourteenth Amendment. That legislation was championed by Johnson's former nemesis Benjamin Butler. In a newspaper interview, Johnson called for some modifications of the act, while recommending "a policy of moderation and calmness."[7] Four months later, while visiting his daughter Mary at her farm near Elizabethton, Tennessee, he died from a stroke. He was sixty-six years old. The New York printmaking firm of Currier and Ives honored the death of a senator and former president who continued to have many admirers.

Johnson undermined Radical Reconstruction, but he alone can't be blamed for its failure. When he left office, the presidency was in the hands of Ulysses S. Grant, a man who supported the Radical Republicans. The Radicals still prevailed in Congress, and the Fourteenth Amendment to the Constitution granting birthright citizenship had just been ratified. The Fifteenth Amendment on Black suffrage was on the verge of ratification. What went wrong over the next three decades

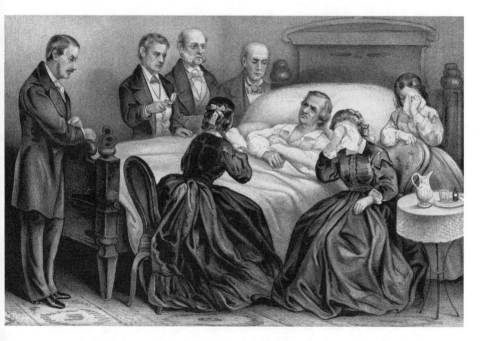

"Death of the Hon. Andrew Johnson," Currier & Ives, 1875. (*Courtesy of the Library of Congress, Prints and Photographs Division.*)

and more? It certainly wasn't Andrew Johnson, though his legacy had an impact. At a moment in American history when there was opportunity for change, his actions as president damaged the prospects of the freedpeople and encouraged resistance to the far-reaching programs of the Radical Republicans. Ironically, however, it was Johnson's intransigence that led the Republicans to formulate and ratify the Fourteenth and Fifteenth Amendments. That might not have happened under the Lincoln administration, or at least not as quickly, and those amendments offered the essential framework for a reconstructed nation.[8]

In spite of Johnson, and in paradoxical ways with the help of Johnson's opposition, the Radical Republicans achieved much in the years immediately following the Confederate surrender at Appomattox. But Reconstruction still failed, in large part because Johnson was not the only white racist in post–Civil War America. Most historians regard his fantasy of being a Moses to Black people as laughable and contemptible, but that fantasy also revealed a tantalizing aspect of Johnson. At key moments in his career, including in 1869 when he challenged the peonage system, we see a man who could have done much less harm to the country than he did. We can even see, as most Radical Republicans did in April 1865, someone who had the potential to do good. That Johnson showed such promise and then failed in just about every respect made him not the incarnation of evil but, as W. E. B. Du Bois put it, "the most pitiable figure of American history."[9]

There is something shortsighted in conceiving of the failure of Reconstruction as the fault of one white man. The stigmatization of Johnson allows for speculation that a different leader would have guided the nation to interracial reconciliation. But such a speculation asks that we close our eyes to the endemic, debilitating, cruel, and destructive racism that was everywhere in the United States in the post–Civil War period. That racism has not gone away. Some historians celebrate the idealistic representatives and senators who impeached the president and brought him to trial, imagining that, had it not been for Johnson, the United States would have discovered its better self. I mean not to defend Johnson but rather to call attention to the differing perspectives of African Americans. Frances Harper, George T. Downing, Martin Delany, Douglass, the writers for the *Christian Recorder* and other African American newspapers, and the participants at Black conventions all considered Johnson in the larger context of the history of slavery and racism in the United States. In their view, Johnson was a symptom of endemic national problems that would not quickly go away.

Douglass addressed the persistence of racism in many of his lectures and essays in the years and decades following the Johnson presidency. He ranged from remarks on the difficulties his son Lewis Henry faced during the late 1860s, because of racial discrimination, in obtaining a printing job in Washington, D.C., to his outrage at the rise of lynching during the 1880s and 1890s. In between, during the 1870s and 1880s, Douglass lamented the nation's retreat from the accomplishments of Reconstruction. He saw progress, but of the kind that Nathaniel Hawthorne, in a very different context, termed "an ascending spiral curve."[10] There was progress and regression, with Andrew Johnson symbolizing the latter soon after the Civil War. But regression, Douglass liked to think, was always followed by an advance. For that reason, he was capable of bursts of optimism even during bleak times. He increasingly spoke of the failed promise of Reconstruction, but he never gave up on that promise.

In a May 1868 speech delivered just days before Johnson's acquittal, Douglass identified the problem that was larger than the president. "There is no such thing as instantaneous emancipation," he said three years after the Thirteenth Amendment ended slavery in the United States. "The links of the chain may be broken in an instant, but it will take not less than a century to obliterate all traces of the institution." Douglass offered similarly cautionary thoughts in an 1870 essay celebrating the ratification of the Fifteenth Amendment. He stated that the passage of the amendment on Black suffrage was not a "miracle." The true miracle, he observed, would be to "obliterate all traces of two hundred and fifty years of slavery." That's what he hoped for, but in an 1872 essay titled "Give Us the Freedom Intended for Us," he protested that African Americans continued to be denied equal access to schools, transportation, and voting booths. He made a plea to Congress similar to the requests he had made during the Johnson years: "We ask this Congress to carry out the intention of this Nation as expressed in the thirteenth, fourteenth and fifteenth amendments. We are not free. We cannot be free without the appropriate legislation provided for in the above amendments." In the coming years, Douglass would sometimes speak optimistically about the possibilities for African Americans in the United States, but his recurring theme, as he put it in 1893, was that although slavery had been abolished in 1865, "its asserted spirit remains."[11]

From the 1870s until his death in 1895, Douglass did what he could to confront that spirit. In a Cincinnati speech in 1876, the year of the nation's centennial, he identified the problem particularly poignantly. "You have emancipated us," he said to his white audience. "I thank you for it. You have enfranchised us, and I thank you for it. But what is your emancipation—what is your enfranchisement? What does it all amount to, if the black man, after having been made free by the letter of your law, is unable to exercise that freedom?"[12] Even after the passage of the Fifteenth Amendment, Douglass pointed out, Blacks in the South voted at the risk of their lives.

As he had during the Johnson presidency, Douglass regularly attacked national lawmakers for failing to take action to protect Blacks' civil rights. The "footprints" of slavery, he told his audience at the Douglass Institute in 1877, can be seen "in the general exercise of force and cruelty" of the legislation, or lack of legislation, coming out of Congress. For those who needed to be reminded of how white supremacists sustained their power in Washington after the Civil War, Douglass offered the example of Andrew Johnson. The slave power, he asserted, "stood between President Johnson and deserved impeachment, and cheered him on in his ministry of disorganization."[13]

Douglass was hardly obsessed with the impeachment of Johnson, but he regularly presented Johnson as the embodiment of what had gone wrong with Reconstruction. Even after the Compromise of 1877, which made Republican Rutherford B. Hayes president at the cost of further federal troop withdrawals from the South, Douglass continued to work for Reconstruction and warn against politicians cut from the same cloth as Johnson. In 1880, he cautioned that the Democratic nominee for the presidency, Winfield S. Hancock, resembled Johnson in his desire to place the federal government "subordinate to the civil power." Hancock's advocacy of the local over the federal, Douglass said, had its sources in the mid-1860s, when a similar view

> was uttered in the South, when the embers of rebellion were still smoking; when Andrew Johnson, the Moses of the colored race, had betrayed that race into the blood-stained hands of the old master class; when he had betrayed the Republican party, by which he had been elected; when he was plotting the organization of a new party upon its ruins; when he was seeking the destruction of the Freedmen's Bureau; when outrage, riot and murder held sway in the South; when the only protection to the colored people of the South was the arm of the Federal soldier. And it was uttered with a view to deprive our people even of this imperfect protection, and to make their subjection to the old master class full and complete.[14]

In these stemwinding, slow-burning sentences summarizing the dark history of the Johnson presidency, Douglass signaled that efforts at such "subjection" had not come to an end. Vigilance was needed. Perhaps thanks in part to Douglass's efforts, Hancock was defeated by James A. Garfield.

Three years later, however, Douglass thought that Reconstruction itself had been defeated. On October 15, 1883, the Supreme Court ruled that the Civil Rights Act of 1875 was unconstitutional. Douglass linked the decision to the spirit of Andrew Johnson. The Fourteenth Amendment, which Johnson had opposed, brought birthright citizenship and equal rights to African Americans, at least on paper. But the amendment was difficult to enforce because of its vagueness.

Frederick Douglass, 1877. (*Annotated negative: Brady-Handy Collection. Courtesy of the Library of Congress, Prints and Photographs Division.*)

Congress's Civil Rights Act of 1875 attempted to buttress the Fourteenth Amendment by specifying that equal rights meant equal access to schools, transportation, and public accommodations such as hotels, along with the right to serve on juries. In response, the Supreme Court ruled that private individuals and groups could discriminate against Blacks, and that the amendment applied only to official state practices. Douglass regarded this decision as a nullification of the Fourteenth Amendment itself. Speaking before a packed house of over two thousand whites and Blacks at Washington, D.C.'s Lincoln Hall, he lamented that the court's ruling left African Americans "naked and defenceless against the action of a malignant, vulgar, and pitiless prejudice." Overturning the Civil Rights Act of 1875 in effect took the nation back to "the administration of President Johnson." Douglass recalled "the conflict which then took place between the National Executive and the National Congress, when the will of the people was again and again met by the Executive veto, and when the country seemed upon the verge of another revolution." Warning of the parallels between the Johnson presidential years and the current moment, Douglass concluded: "No patriot, however bold, can wish for his country a repetition of those gloomy days."[15]

But repetition was what Douglass saw during the 1880s and 1890s. Johnson and his epoch were neither dead nor past. Worse, Johnson was apparently winning his fight against the Republicans posthumously. "At no period since the abolition of slavery in the District of Columbia, have the moral, social and political surroundings of the colored people of this country been more solemn and foreboding than they are this day," Douglass declared in an 1889 speech, which took up such topics as "OUR CITIZENSHIP A DELUSION" and "THE SOUTH IS STILL THE SOUTH." Although he did not mention Johnson in this speech, he referred to "the sources of danger" to the republic, the same tag phrase he had used when he spoke out against Johnson in 1867. In Douglass's view in this 1889 speech, "the rights and liberties of the colored people in this country have PASSED BEYOND THE DANGER LINE."[16]

Douglass's concerns about the dangers to the republic led him to update his 1881 *Life and Times of Frederick Douglass.* In that autobiography, he had told a mostly affirmative story about his and the nation's journey from slavery to freedom. As a result of disturbing developments during the 1880s and early 1890s, he decided to add a new, darker section about the lost gains of Reconstruction. He wanted to extend the story of himself and the country because "my emancipated brothers and sisters . . . are yet oppressed and are in as much need of an advocate as before they were set free." Part of the new section focused on the Supreme Court's 1883 ruling against the Civil Rights Act, which he termed "the most flagrant example of this national deterioration." He once again invoked Andrew Johnson in his assertion that the Supreme Court had moved the nation backward, "defeating the manifest purpose of the Constitution, nullifying the Fourteenth Amendment, and placing itself on the side of prejudice, proscription, and persecution." He stated that the current moment was about the living "history of the administration of President Johnson."[17]

Johnson, many African Americans had said, was responsible for southern violence against Black people, especially the 1866 attacks in Memphis and New Orleans. There was a marked increase of violence in the late 1860s and early 1870s, which Grant's Force Bills addressed. But lynching surged during the 1880s and 1890s, especially in the South, and most of the victims were Black. In his most famous lecture of the 1890s, "Lessons of the Hour" (1894), Douglass addressed lynching directly, but he also continued to think about the crises facing African Americans because of Johnson's unwillingness to complete the victory of the Civil War. "The pit of hell is said to be bottomless," Douglass remarked in the way of a preacher. "Principles which we all thought to have been firmly and permanently settled by the late war, have been boldly assaulted and overthrown by the defeated party. Rebel rule is now nearly complete in many States and it is gradually capturing the nation's Congress." In "Lessons of the Hour," he offered a battle cry for the struggle he was leading still and again: "We have a fight on our hands right here, a fight for the whole race."[18]

Douglass died in 1895 at the age of seventy-seven, a year before the Supreme Court's ruling on *Plessy v. Ferguson* (1896), which established the segregationist principle of "separate but equal" for the next sixty years. Segregationism had structured free Blacks' lived experience in the South and elsewhere since the end of the Civil War, and Homer Plessy began his legal case against racial segregation on Louisiana passenger trains in 1892, the year of the publication of Douglass's revised and updated edition of *Life and Times*. Shortly after the book's publication, De Witt Miller, a minister and avid book collector, asked Douglass to sign his copy of the autobiography. Douglass obliged with these words:

> Not a Negro problem, not a race problem, but a national problem; whether the American people will ultimately administer equal justice to all the varieties of the human race in this Republic.
> From Frederick Douglass.[19]

Had an admirer asked Douglass to sign a copy of any of his publications during Johnson's presidency, he could have written the same thing.

———

AT ONE OF the many rhetorically skillful moments in his 1867 "Sources of Danger to the Republic," Douglass, to laughter and cheers, referred to the current president as he "who shall be nameless." To invoke Douglass's theme of historical repetition: I have written this book during 2017–2020 under the shadow of he who shall be nameless. Pundits have linked our nameless one to Johnson in terms of their shared commitment to policies that advance white nationalism and their similarly polarizing, paranoiac, and nonnegotiable styles of political leadership.[20] I recognize some of these similarities, but I also see differences, which I have tried to tease out by paying close attention to Johnson's words. There was promise in Johnson, even in his career-shaping delusion of himself as a Moses to Black people. There was promise in his bold decision to adopt an antislavery position in the Confederate South, in his interactions with John Langston, in his Lincoln-like proposals for limited Black suffrage at a time when any Black suffrage would have been revolutionary, and, late in his career, in his attack on peonage and his willingness to negotiate on the Civil Rights Act. With his rigid version of constitutionalism and blinkered racism, Johnson destroyed that promise during his presidential term. But through it all, he was never driven by greed. When his presidential term came to an end, the man who some said wanted to be king quietly stepped down. I have tried to present a more complex Johnson who was both partly responsible for, and the incarnation of, the failed promise of Reconstruction.

Douglass has a more prophetic and inspirational role in this story. Nearly thirty years after the inauguration of Andrew Johnson, Reconstruction remained for Douglass less a failed promise than an unfulfilled promise. It remains unfulfilled to this day. There has been progress along the "ascending spiral curve" that is racial relations in the United States, but the struggle remains a fundamental challenge facing a nation that was built on slavery.[21]

Andrew Johnson was not unique. There would be more Johnsons to come, and Douglass knew that. But Douglass, with his determination to persist in the effort to achieve the promise of Reconstruction, continues to appeal to what Lincoln in his first inaugural address called "the better angels of our nature." There are moments when Douglass is so eloquent, prescient, and wise that the best we can do is listen without comment. In this story of the failed promise of Reconstruction, Douglass gets the last word. Here's a short excerpt from the end of his 1894 anti-lynching lecture, which he seems to have written with twenty-first-century Americans in mind. We need to listen, and then we need to resume Douglass's struggle, because it remains our own:

> Put away your race prejudice. Banish the idea that one class must rule over another. Recognize the fact that the rights of the humblest citizen are as worthy of protection as those of the highest, and your problem will be solved; and, whatever may be in store for it in the future, whether prosperity, or adversity; whether it shall have foes without, or foes within, whether there shall be peace, or war; based upon the external principles of truth, justice, and humanity, and with no class having any cause of complaint or grievance, your Republic will stand and flourish forever.[22]

APPENDIX

Frederick Douglass on Reconstruction, Andrew Johnson, and the Constitution

This section reprints for the first time the version of "Sources of Danger to the Republic" that Douglass delivered on January 3, 1867, as part of a Black-sponsored lecture series in Philadelphia. Discussed in chapter 9 of this book, "Sources of Danger" is one of Douglass's most powerful speeches from the period of Johnson's presidency. Douglass presented various versions of the speech from December 1866 through October 1867. A transcription of the January 3 version appeared a day later in the *Philadelphia Daily Evening Telegraph*. The lecture sheds considerable light on Douglass's ideas about Reconstruction, Johnson, and the Constitution, as well as on how he framed arguments for Black audiences. Speaking in a Black lecture series, he used oratorical flourishes, humor, and appeals to pathos to link himself with Philadelphia's African Americans, who were continuing to face racism in the North while aspiring for change across the country. As in many of his lectures and essays of the time, he underscored the need for Black suffrage, while using his thoughts about the "one-man power" of Andrew Johnson to address the future of the country as well. What can Americans do when a "bad man" becomes president? Are there flaws in the Constitution that allow such a man to assume king-like powers at great cost to the Republic? How can we ensure that democracy will continue to flourish? The prophetic Douglass addressed such questions in 1867 while impelling us to consider similar questions in our own time as well.

SOURCES OF DANGER TO THE REPUBLIC*

RISING OF THE AFRIC.
"Sources of Danger to the Republic."
Frederick Douglass' Great Lecture Last Night.
"Down with the One-Man Power."
The Democracy that Saves Us.
"No More Vice-Presidential Succession."
The Hopes and Fears of Our Country.
"Constitutional Amendment a Swindle."
Etc., Etc., Etc., Etc., Etc., Etc.

[SPECIALLY REPORTED FOR EVENING TELEGRAPH]

National Hall was literally packed last night with people to hear Mr. Douglass' address. The speaker was frequently interrupted with applause, and he evidently made the best effort of his life. The eloquence and searching political analysis of Fred. Douglass last evening took some of his warmest admirers by surprise.

Miss Greenwood,† the "Black Swan," sang several arias and ballads during the evening with great acceptability.

---

* *Philadelphia Daily Evening Telegraph,* January 4, 1867. Obvious printer's or transcription errors have been corrected.

† Known as the "Black Swan," Elizabeth Taylor Greenfield (c. 1820–1876), mistakenly called "Greenwood" here, was a renowned African American singer.

Mr. Douglass was introduced by Mr. William Still,* President of the Social, Civil, and Statistical Association of the Colored People of Pennsylvania, and the great freedman† spoke as follows:—

THE GREAT AND all-commanding thought of patriotic citizens of the United States is, as to how this republic can be rendered enduring, beneficent, and permanent. I am here this evening to discuss some of its dangers and sorrows, or weaknesses. In all political institutions the subject is to some extent an unwelcome one to many, for it is common on great occasions to hear men speak of the republican institutions of our republican Government as the best Government on earth, an admirable piece of mechanism, destined at some future period, not far distant or remote, to supersede all other forms of government.

Many men, when our eulogistic orators would appear somewhat recondite as well as patriotic, tell us of the change and the distribution of the various powers under our form of government. I am certainly not here this evening rudely to call in question the very pleasing assumptions of governmental superiority on our part which it is natural to indulge, however unwise it may be this time.

They are consonant with national pride, consonant with national self-love; and when they are not employed, as they too often are, in the service of a blind, unreasoning, stubborn, and obstinate fanaticism and conservatism, they are comparatively harmless, although they may not always be consonant with good taste.

It is, however, well to remind this class of American hearers and speakers that they are not alone in this species of eulogy, that there are other men reputed wise and good in other parts of the planet who appear just as confident of the excellent qualities of their peculiar government, or monarchical aristocracy or autocracy, as we are of the

* The Philadelphia-based Black abolitionist William Still (1821–1902) had been a leader of the Underground Railroad (the informal network that helped enslaved persons escape to the North).
† Frederick Douglass.

good qualities of our own, and not a few of these have already voted our republican experiment a failure; they already have detected signs of decay, and have predicted that at some day, not very distant, our beautiful republican institutions will have to give place to another Government, a stronger and more absolute Government than the one we have. Those who entertain these opinions are not entirely without reason for them. And every Republican, every lover of his country, must wish these reasons fewer and less visible than they are. The fact is that the ballot-box, upon which we have relied as a protection from the passions of the multitude, has failed us, broken down under us.

That a large sectional minority of the people, united and animated by sectional interest, have combined, and for four long years have resisted the constitutional authority of this Government, is regarded as a telling argument against the travelling assumptions of Americans in favor of the permanence and stability of our republican institutions. But this is not the only reason which they have arrayed against us. They point us to the fact that we did not meet this trouble, this resistance to the constitutional authority of the Government, in anything like a manly, heroic, comprehensive, and wise spirit; that, in fact, we met it with apathy, tardiness, hesitation, doubt, a feeling of uncertainty which no Government in Europe ever exhibited in the presence of a combination to overthrow it; and they regard that as an evidence of our decay as a nation, and of the final substitution of some other form of government for the present one.

They point us, also, to the hesitation, the doubt, the apparent want of courage on the part of this Government in the matter of reconstruction, now that the Rebellion has been put down. They point us, moreover, to the fact (apparently at least) that the American Government has yet to demonstrate to the world its ability and its disposition to punish traitors on the one hand, and reward loyalty on the other hand; a Government that cannot hate cannot love; and a Government that cannot hate traitors, cannot love and respect loyal men. (Cheers.) They point us to the fact that the bristling bayonets of this Government of ours are no longer a protection for loyal men in the Rebel

States; that loyal men by the score—by the hundred—have been deliberately slaughtered in the presence of the Star-Spangled Banner in New Orleans; and that at this hour the murderers are still at large, unquestioned by the law, unpunished by justice, unrebuked by the public opinion of the neighborhood where they lived.

No such thing as this could exist in any other Government on earth. They point us, moreover, to the fact that there is an absence of national honor and national gratitude in the Government, which, in its extremity, invoked the iron arm of the negro in its defense; and has deliberately, since the war, placed that same loyal class under the political heel of the former traitors (cheers)—they point us to the low standard of political morality everywhere prevalent in this country; how riotous swindlers can climb to the high places in the nation. The best pattern of a member of Congress in some districts is a fist—(laughter and applause)—the worst elements of American society come uppermost.

They point us also to the antagonisms that exist between the Executive and Legislative branches of our Government, the indecent haste with which we sacrifice permanent interest for mere temporary trials, and they regard all these as signs of a decline and fall of our great republican experiment; they tell us that the lives of republics have been unsatisfactory, short, stormy, and that our Government will prove no exception to the general rule.

Now, why do I refer to this unfavorable judgment of our political institutions? Not certainly to indorse them, nor to combat them, but simply as a reason, and to weigh them very fully, and with a more impartial judgment, than we have hitherto done. I find in these things a motive for searching out the defects of our Government; to ascertain, if possible, how far the machine is responsible for the developments of character to which I have alluded; or how these developments can be traced to another cause—whether, in fact, the fault is in the machine, or in the men who run the machine. For we must all admit that republican governments undermine and destroy manly character if they foster baseness, or cherish and feed ingratitude and meanness. If they destroy manly character instead of elevating manly character, let us have done with republican and install some other form of government more favorable to the development of manhood.

Let me state the whole of the case in this inquiry. Now that our Government is broken up, as it were, and the work of reconstruction is taking place, I am here to-night to defend the theory of radical, complete, and comprehensive reconstruction, which shall set our Government right. We American citizens have to decide the form of our Government; and we can at least examine our Government. We are at liberty to discuss every feature of it, to examine and try and test it by every rule of law and reason and logic. There is nothing more thoroughly established in this country than the right of free inquiry.

The material with which some men would appear to weigh or discuss the importance of our institutions is decidedly splendid. We can have no superstitious reverence for our Constitution. This is [not]* the time to generate such a reverence. Place it on such a foundation that neither darkness, nor smoke, nor thunder, nor lightning, nor whirlwind, nor tempest, nor any other disturbance can shake it. And it will be reverenced.

While we respect it for what it is, we affirm of it that it was the creation of man—men like unto ourselves. In one respect, however, we can afford to say something of the fundamental structure of our Government. It was a man's contrivance, as I have alleged, designed with more or less wisdom to make society happy, promote liberty and order, and, in the language of the Constitution itself, to form a more perfect union, and establish justice, promote the general welfare, provide for the common defense, and secure the blessings of liberty to ourselves and to our posterity. It is, at least, an honest Constitution. It does not ask respect on any ground of a superstitious character, but it is a human instrument, made to promote human objects.

While I discard all the Fourth-of-July extravagances, I cannot but offer my humble gratitude to the fathers who framed the Constitution,

---

* The context suggests that Douglass said "not," but that was missed by the reporter who transcribed the speech.

that they were able to put into it as much of wisdom, truth, and goodness as they did. My early experience in life was not favorable to the
development of patriotism, or reverence for our institutions, and the
like, and yet I can say that this Constitution, in many of its features, is
based upon the eternal rock of ages.

I think the men who framed it are entitled to the profoundest gratitude of mankind, if for nothing more than this, that, against the temptation to do otherwise, they have given to us a Constitution free from
bigotry, free from sectarianism, free from complexional distinctions.
In the eye of that great instrument there are neither Jews nor Greeks,
barbarians or Scythians, but fellow citizens of a common country.
There is neither black nor white—we are all one, and our Constitution was so framed purposely. Whenever the galling chains of bondage burst from about the bodies of the enslaved, each and all of them
immediately rise to any position in the common country for which
their talents and character might fit them. (Cheers.)

But wise as this great paper is on this and many other points, it
is but a human instrument, and, like all human performances, has
its defects. It is the work of men struggling for their independence,
with their full proportion of the prejudices and limitations of men,
time, and experience; and the ever-increasing light of knowledge has
revealed defects and errors in our Constitution which, in my judgment, must be removed, or prove fatal to every institution alike.

The national complacency with which we contemplated the Constitution under the aspect of the war of the Rebellion, so that that
check, apparently, seems likely to be about as transient in duration
as it was violent in its inception—the complacency arising from the
fact that we met the Rebellion, that we conquered the Rebels, ground
them to powder, scattered them to the four winds, showed the vigor
and strength of the structure of our Government, I think is all wrong.
The right view of that struggle is, that instead of disclosing to us the
inherent strength of our institutions, it only reveals to us their serious
weakness in a more glaring light than we have ever before seen them.
It should lead us to search out the sources of national weakness, and in

this hour to go to work like sensible and patriotic men to make weak places strong, and the strong places stronger.

The suppression of the Rebellion was a grand achievement, but applauded as that was, I utterly deny that it reflected the least credit upon the structure of our Government and Constitution. And how are we to explain our success? There is only one way. It is this—that during the last two years of the Rebellion our gallant armies fought on the side of human nature, liberty and fraternity, and human brotherhood, and in proportion as our Government was faithful to these grand soul-inspiring ideas, so were its victories and so its reverses. (Cheers.) The Rebels fought well. They fought desperately. Invisible chains were about them, entangled by the chains of their own bondmen, and deep down in their own souls there was an agonizing voice that cried tremblingly to them. They struggled, not merely with gigantic armies and the skill of our veteran generals, but they struggled with the moral sense of the nineteenth century, and hence their failure, in my judgment.

Another secret of our success was this:—We happened, for it was only a happening, to have in the Presidential chair an honest man. (Cheers.) It was our exceedingly good fortune that Abraham Lincoln, and not William H. Seward received the nomination in 1860. Had William H. Seward, had Millard Fillmore, had John Tyler,* or had that vilest embodiment of ingratitude and baseness, who shall be nameless now (laughter and cheers), occupied the Presidential chair, the Government of which we are so proud to-day, might have been only a matter of history.

I regard the last three months of Mr. Buchanan's administration† as most instructive, especially in regard to the sources of danger and

---

* William H. Seward (1801–1872) served as secretary of state under Lincoln and Johnson from 1861 to 1869; Millard Filmore (1800–1874), was the thirteenth president of the United States (1850–1853); and John Tyler (1790–1862) was the tenth president of the United States (1841–1845).

† James Buchanan (1791–1868) was the fifteenth president of the United States (1857–1861).

weakness in our republican form of government. It showed how completely the liberties of the American people are at the mercy of a bad and wicked President and his Cabinet. (A voice, "That's so.") We saw during those three months our army, navy, and munitions of war either scattered to the four winds, or placed at the disposal of wicked men who were plotting the destruction of the Government, and we were compelled to sit helpless. We could neither move hand not foot; we sat biting our thumbs in silence, unable to help ourselves during the time. We were in a mighty stream, with all our liberties at stake, a faithless pilot on board; in a mighty stream, whose current we neither could resist nor control. We were in a helpless manner swept on and on towards an awful cataract of ruin, then thundering in the distance; we saw no help for the Republic until the honest man, Abraham Lincoln, came to the rescue. (Cheers.)

But it is sad to think that half the glory, honor, and moral advantage to this nation of the great beneficent measures already adopted were lost—lost in the meanness of their performance. Even for the abolition of slavery we have no one to thank; we have not the nation to thank for that by any means. What was done in that direction was done reluctantly. We are about as justly required to thank the American people for emancipating the slaves as Pharaoh of old was entitled to the thanks of the Israelites for releasing them from bondage. (Cheers.) For it was not until judgment, wide spreading, far reaching, and overwhelming, overtook us—it was not until we saw the Southern horizon studded all around with military disasters, that we consented to part with our reverence for slavery, and to arm the black man in defense of the flag. (Cheers.)

Oh that we could have done this from a holy, sacred choice of right for the right's sake, for the truth's sake, for man's sake! Oh that it could have been done from a high and holy motive of disinterested benevolence! As it was, it has gone into history as simply a piece of military strategy or necessity. Justice had but little to do with it.

Well, I am taking a long time without coming to the subject of the evening, the Sources of Danger to our Republic.

I take these to be of two classes. The first may be described as interior, and the second as exterior. I shall discuss them in the order now stated.

Mr. President,* let me observe, at the outset, that in this comprehensive statement I concede nothing to those who hold to the doctrine of the inherent weakness of the republic. Our sources of danger and weakness are not necessarily connected with republicanism; they are not essential to it; they are alien to our republican institutions; they are deadly poisons taken into our system by accident.

Our Government was framed under conditions favorable to a purely republican government. The result was, the Constitution was projected and completed under the shadow of monarchical institutions and slavery institutions, and it has received its coloring largely from both these sources. Nor is this to be wondered at. A man's surroundings may exert but a limited influence upon him; he may easily throw them off, but only a hero can throw off entirely the influence of early surroundings and training; and mankind can never immediately be emancipated either from slavery or monarchy; and a century is not too much to obliterate all traces of a former bondage.

The fathers of this republic, born in the presence of slavery, or under monarchical institutions, also naturally enough, while they conceived the great principles of the Declaration of Independence as the law of this Government, when they came to the practical work for making a Government, we all know that they did plant something of the aristocratic element of the Government under which they had formerly lived. This was their mistake, and it must now be corrected, or you must make up your mind to bid farewell to your republican Government. You must have either a purely republican Government or you must have a monarchical Government, one or the other.

The eclectic principle may work well in medicine, but it does not work well in matters of government. Here we must have unity of idea

---

* Douglass refers to the president of the lecture series, William Still.

and object—a concord of method, as well as of principle—in order to [produce] a permanent and prosperous result. Now, so far am I from conceding anything to those who hold that republican governments are weak in themselves. I believe that a republican form of government is the strongest government on earth. (Cheers.)

I am here to-night, a genuine Democrat, to advocate democracy in its purity. So far from regarding a republican Government as necessarily weak, it is the strongest and best Government known to the children of men. I am here, in fact, to advocate a genuine republic as against a false and spurious and sham republic. (Cheers.) Only make this republic a genuine republic, eliminating all foreign elements; strike out from all your form of government everything looking to autocracy; make it in fact, as it is in theory, a Government of the people, by the people, for the people and the whole people. (Cheers.)

Pull out from it everything that looks away from the people to the individual, or to the oligarchy; strike out everything that makes it rest upon a class; let it be a Government each for all, and all for each—the black man for the white, and the white man for the black. Drive no man from the ballot-box because of his color, and keep no woman from it on account of her sex. (Applause.)

Let the Government rest squarely down upon the shoulders of the people; let there be no shoulder in the land that does not bear its full proportion of the Government; let there be no intellect, no heart, no soul in the land but is directly and practically responsible, to the full share of its capacity, for the honor, wisdom, and virtue of the Government. (Cheers.)

Let it be completely democratic, resting upon the whole people. Take from it everything that limits its power or its benevolence, or mars its beauty. Let it rest squarely down upon the whole people, and I see no reason why this Government may not stand and flourish while the world endures.

The first source of danger to which I will call your attention, and which has been spoken of a great deal of late, is the one-man power. I rejoice to know that the nation is at last startled into the consciousness of the existence of the one-man power. If Jeff. Davis* taught us the folly of fostering the slave power, Andy Johnson has taught us, beyond wisdom, the absurdity of fostering in our form of Government the one-man power; and if his reign shall inspire us with a determination to revise the Constitution of the United States at this point, and to limit and circumscribe this one-man power, his accidental occupancy of the Presidential chair will not prove the unmitigated calamity we have sometimes been accustomed to regard it. (Cheers.)

Mr. Seward has been a great deal laughed at for calling Andrew Johnson king, introducing him to a Michigan audience as King or President, evidently regarding the one title as appropriate as the other. I think he was not far from the truth, and the title was, to some extent at least, appropriate, for the fact is, Andrew Johnson to-day is invested with kingly powers, and exercises them to an extent which would bring to the block almost any potentate in Europe. (Sensation.)

If he has recently overstepped these powers, as some of us think he has, and at times [is] mistaken in the singular condition of his mind (which is quite too frequent), mistaking himself for the United States instead of the President of the United States—(laughter)—the explanation is not to be found entirely in his unbounded egotism, but in our Constitution. But, happily, by this Constitution our king cannot reign during life.

But he can reign long enough to commit any number of mischievous acts, and so defeat the most beneficent measures of our Government. It is true we have the right to choose our President, which is a very important right, and therein is our distinctive advantage over the subjects of a foreign yoke. I admit that it is something to be able to put a man out of authority when he does not behave well, but I have taken a more sober view of the freedom of the American people to elect their officers recently than formerly.

When I was a slave I used to think it quite a large degree of liberty

---

* Jefferson Davis (1808–1889) served as the president of the Confederate States (1861–1865).

that, at the end of each year, if I did not like my master I could get another.* I had the right to choose him again, or another in his place. I was quite delighted, indeed intoxicated, with this precious privilege of selecting another master, and during the year, if I got an extra kick or cuff, the thought would come to me, "Never mind, old fellow, I will shake you off at Christmas." (Laughter.) But after a while, as I grew older, and a trifle wiser, I came to the conclusion that it was not another master that I wanted. Not a new master, or an old one, but no master at all. (Great applause.) That in fact what I wanted was to be my own master.

From this little item of my experience in slavery, I have managed to read quite an elaborate chapter of philosophy, applicable, I think, to the American people at this time. What the American people want is not another master at any time; not a new one, or an old one. But they want the people themselves, ever, at all times, in times of peace and in time of war, to be their own masters, and control their own affairs. (Cheers.)

It is not so now. It is Massa Johnson now. (Laughter.) It is true we are free, and while we are putting a piece of paper in the ballot-box—I will not say how the names get on the paper—that would betray too great an acquaintance with politics—(laughter)—we are free while we are voting, but once he is elected, once he strides the national animal, his feet in the stirrups, his hand upon the reins, and puts the spurs in the sides of the animal, he can rule this country as despotically as any crowned head in Europe, and you know it.

A one-man power is here. You are free before he is elected; but once he is, he is then the master of the situation. Yes, I affirm that the President of the United States can rule this Government with a contempt for the opinions and wishes of the people, at every stage of his administration, which no crowned head in Europe dare manifest towards the wishes and wants of the people who are represented in the Government.

---

* Douglass's Black audience knew that he was joking about enslaved people having the option to choose their masters.

This is the state of the case, and I contend that it ought not to be so. Why, when the Prime Minister of England is outvoted in the House of Commons on any important question, he construes that vote into a vote of want of confidence in him by the country. He says:—"I no longer represent the views and wishes of the country, and for this reason I will lay the seal of my office at the foot of the throne, and require the throne to call some other men to power who can administer the Government more in harmony with the wishes of the people," but you might vote down Andrew Johnson every month, and vote down Seward every morning. (Laughter.) I think he would never resign, or either of them. (Great cheering.)

They are at the head of the people. They say the people are mistaken; they don't know what they want. Over there they respect the opinions of the people; over here they treat them with the utmost contempt. I have seen men invited to resign, but I have never seen a man who has accepted the invitation. Your man Cowan* was invited to resign; he thought you were mistaken. Doolittle† was also invited to resign; he thought his constituents were mistaken. Once in the stirrups, they are there, as the man said to the horse at the foot of the hill. (Cheers.)

Let us examine the questions that enter into the one-man power. The first to which I call your attention is the *immense* patronage in the hands of the President. A hundred millions of dollars per annum in times of peace, and uncounted thousands of millions in times of war, are put in his hands for distribution among his political friends. What a power! What a corrupting power! Now, is there not ingenuity, is there not skill enough in the American people to alter this arrangement, this corrupting arrangement; for while the President can place

---

* Edgar Cowan (1815–1885) served as a Republican senator from Pennsylvania from 1861 to 1867. He was defeated for reelection because of his support for Andrew Johnson.

† James Rood Doolittle (1815–1897), senator from Wisconsin (1857–1869), switched his allegiance from the Republican to Democratic Party because of his support for Johnson.

a man in office because of his political opinions, not for any fitness for the position, and put another out of office because of the difference of opinion, it is for us to see, and to see at once, that this is an assault upon integrity and freedom of opinion.

Who does not see that it is corrupting, in that it holds out a temptation to a man to agree with the President, not because of the wisdom and justice of his position, but because in that way he can get something in exchange for his soul. We don't want this power in the hands of one man to buy up men. At any rate, we can go to this extent, and I am glad Congress is looking in that direction, and that is, that the Constitution of the United States now provides that the President can appoint by and with the consent of the Senate of the United States—we can go to the whole extent of demanding that the whole power required to appoint, as also to remove a man from office, shall be in Congress. (Cheers.)

At present it is not so, for while it requires the President and the Senate to appoint, the President alone removes, and by that means makes of non-effect the constitutional guarantee that the Senate shall be consulted also.

But I must hasten. This vast amount of money lodged anywhere outside of the Government would prove a dangerous lever of destruction to our Government in the hands of an enemy. It has already given rise to the most disgraceful and disgusting immorality in regard to the Government.

Nothing so illustrates the degrading tendency of this patronage than the many proverbs already in circulation concerning it, for to Mr. Marcy is attributed the saying that "To the victor belongs the spoils;" and from ex-Governor Randall, Postmaster-General,* we have the blackguard assertion that no man should eat the President's

---

* Alexander Williams Randall (1819–1872), Wisconsin politician, was appointed by Johnson to the postmaster-general position in 1866 and remained a firm supporter of his policies; New York senator William L. Marcy (1786–1857) made his famous comment about "To the victor belongs the spoils of the enemy" during an 1831 debate in the Senate.

bread and butter that does not indorse the President's policy. It is an attack upon the national integrity, by breaking down individual integrity, by placing the honors and emoluments of office as against independence and judgment. I am for limiting this power in the hands of the President.

Then I am for abolition. I am an old-fashioned Abolitionist. I am for the abolition of the "two terms" principle. Wherever else I may meet with response, here I expect co-operation. The "two terms" principle is, in my humble judgment, one of the very worst elements of our Constitution, in that, so soon as a man is elected to the Presidential chair, he is furnished with a motive to enter upon schemes for his re-election to that office, and he comes up to the duties of that office with a heart and a mind divided, instead of being united in behalf of or in discharge of his duties. He is partly President, and partly chief of the Presidential party. At once it furnishes a motive for such a distribution of the patronage of this Government as shall favor his re-election.

It may be said, as it was said in the Convention by that wise and excellent patriot, Alexander Hamilton,* that the prospect that the President may serve two terms instead of one furnishes to a President a motive for good behavior, for the faithful performance of his duty. I admit the force of the argument. The answer to it is this—that a man who does not find an all-sufficient motive for devoting all his mind and heart and soul to the discharge of the duties of the Presidential office in the first election, may be relied upon not to have such confidence in a second election.

A third element of the weakness of the one-man power to which I wish to call attention, and in favor of abolishing which I am, is the veto power. I want that old, despotic, and aristocratic power of our Government utterly banished from our Constitution. It has no business in a republican form of government. It is anti-democratic, anti-republican,

---

* American politician and one of the Founders of the nation, Alexander Hamilton (c. 1756–1804) served as the first U.S. secretary of the Treasury (1789–1795). He was killed in a duel with Aaron Burr (1756–1836), the vice president at the time.

and anti-common sense. (Sensation.) It is based on a miserable absurdity, that one man is more to be trusted than many men.

While we talk of believing in the people, when we come to promote a Government, we vest one man with a power which only two-thirds of the people can counterbalance. It is an absurdity in itself. It is based upon the idea that one man, with his limited judgment, with his limited abilities and infirmities (and there are some of them that have many of these who get into the Presidential chair); that one man, in his Cabinet in the White House, surrounded by his cliques and clans, his satellites, his comrades, who have no voice to contradict him, that he will bring to bear upon public measures a cooler judgment and power of patriotism than will the Congress of the United States, assembled under the broad light of day, with the flaming sword of the press waving over them, and sworn before high Heaven faithfully to attend to the claims of public measures. It is to think that this one man will act more wisely and more patriotically than will these hundreds of representatives.

A more glaring contradiction to the very idea of republicanism is nowhere found, except in this idea of veto power. (Cheers.) We don't need it; let it go. While I believe that two heads are better than one, I don't believe that one head is better than two or three hundred. Let it go; we can get along without it. It is a remarkable fact that while the veto power is entirely consistent with monarchical institutions, it is entirely inconsistent with democratic institutions.

It has not been exercised in England under a monarchical and aristocratic Government. It has not been exercised there more than once in a century and a half, while here in this republic of the people, where the right of the people to rule is admitted, we can have a little veto every morning—veto on all occasions. It is a powerful lever in the hands of one man to make himself of consequence; and a bad man, full of ambition, full of pride, self-conceit, finds in it a means of constantly gratifying his love of notoriety, by flinging himself in opposition to the Congress of the United States, and in antagonism with the Senate of the United States.

I know not why it is that one man in this country could arrogate to himself this power, while thrones and dominions of the Old World shrink from its exercise. When in a Government where the veto is consistent, it is not used; why in a Government believed to be a Government of the people, professed to be such a Government, where it is inconsistent, should it be used so incessantly?

That the veto power has sometimes been used very beneficially I admit. That it has been the means of arresting hasty legislation I admit. That its peculiar power is sometimes frequently and wisely used, is no proof that we should approve despotic power to the power of the people. I know what is said, that there must be some check upon a fanatical majority. Mr. Johnson himself has been on a pilgrimage of late, sandwiched between two heroes, one of the land and the other of the sea, wending his way from the Atlantic to the Mississippi, preaching to the people of the danger of trusting to majorities.*

Well, if this thing be true, then our republican institutions are at fault. This is an argument against republicanism, if it be true that majorities are likely to be more despotic than individuals. Then let us have an individual Government; let us have Andrew Johnson as Dictator or Emperor; or, let us have something that is arbitrary, that is despotic in its control over us. But don't believe it; I don't believe it; no man believes it. I know that republics and republican majorities can be arbitrary, have been so, but so to whom? If arbitrary at all, they are so to an unrepresented class of men. They have been so towards the black man, towards the slave. They have enforced penalties, enacted laws, that had an element of the direct cruelty and injustice in them. And towards whom? Never towards represented classes, always towards the unrepresented. What, then, is the remedy?

Why it is to have our Government consistent, and have no unrep-

---

* When Johnson made his August–September 1867 speaking tour, dubbed the Swing around the Circle, he was accompanied by the general of the U.S. Army Ulysses S. Grant (1822–1885) and the admiral James Glasgow Farragut (1801–1870), a naval hero during the Civil War.

resented classes in it (great cheers); then the rights of all classes will be sure to be represented. If the Government of Great Britain can be trusted without the interposition of the veto, why may not the United States be entrusted with the Senate of the United States?

I have looked down upon both bodies while in session, and I must say, while I have no desire to bestow any unmerited eulogy on the Americans, that the House and Senate is fully equal to the House of Lords and Commons of Great Britain. In all the elements that go to make up the wise and eloquent and brilliant deliberative assembly, we stand their peers, equal in every respect. (Cheers.) If those may be trusted, why not these here?

A man told me, when in England, that beloved and honored as was Queen Victoria, if she should venture to veto a measure after it had been regularly passed by the House of Commons and House of Lords, it would come near costing her her crown; and yet in this country your President can thwart your House of Representatives, your Congress, at every turn with his veto; and we acquiesce. What a mighty handy set of people generally! (Sensation.)

Another thing I would have done—that is, to abolish his pardoning power. Let us have the pardon, certainly, but let the President have less to do with it. I am in favor of limiting his power at this point. The same argument resorted to against the veto is pertinent as against this pardoning power. During the past year it has been a coin with which to traffic in treason, to win personal friends and co-operation and alliance, instead of loyal obedience to the laws of the land; let us have done with this pardoning power.

I am also for abolishing secret diplomacy, as another Government weakness. You cannot—perhaps it is not necessary you should—know how that is managed. It is a power in the hands of a bad President and a bad Cabinet—for he will be sure to have a bad Cabinet, because he could not get a good one—and this nation might be conducted into the jaws of a terrible war, and be perfectly helpless. We cannot say when the nation is to be at war, and the alternative may be presented at any time. Unwilling that our country should be beaten, we resort to arms under the inspiring motto of "Our country, right or wrong."

In England when the Prime Minister is negotiating with foreign powers, any member of the Cabinet who stands in the House of Commons, and any other member, can rise in his place, and demand to know of that Cabinet Minister what is the policy of Government towards France, towards America, Russia, or towards any other power, and that minister must answer affirmatively, negatively, or evasively, and often the evasive answer is the most expressive; but here in this country, our Executive, with his Cabinet sitting away off in another house, carrying on its private correspondence, may conduct us to the verge of a terrific war, and we are perfectly helpless.

Another thing in our system of government I am for abolishing is the Vice-Presidency of the United States. We have had bad luck with Vice-Presidents. (Laughter and cheers.) There is no sort of necessity for electing Vice-Presidents. When we elect a President, there is no necessity for a ready-made President at all, no more than it would be for a wife to have a ready-made husband. "Sufficient unto the day is the evil thereof."* We don't need another. (Cheers and laughter.)

How I wonder we ever came to do such things, and ever hit upon the plan of appointing one man President at the same time we appointed another who shall take his place upon the instant of his death, resignation, or removal. It was done in utter ignorance, apparently, of human nature. The argument against the Vice-Presidents is this. Men are men, ambition is ambition. The Presidency is a tempting bauble, like the crown of a monarch; is a constant source of temptation to the ambition of a man; and what do you do when you appoint a Vice-President? Why, you appoint a man to stand directly behind the President, and immediately within striking distance of him, whose interests, whose ambition, will be instantly subserved by the death of the President, however that death may be brought about. (Sensation.)

---

* Mathew 6:34; from the Sermon on the Mount.

I believe the President of the United States will sit more securely and safely in his chair when the shadow of the Vice-President ceases to fall upon him. Let us have done with the Vice-President. Let us put men's interest and their duties in the same boat. How easy it is in a country like ours to procure an assassin at any time! There is most sure to be out of every fifty thousand people you can hire one assassin to commit an assassination anywhere.

How easy it would be for a clique and a clan to surround the Vice-President of the United States, immediately upon the election of the President, and ascertain from him how far he sympathizes with the President, and learn from him, without making him a party to their intentions, how he will bestow the patronage of the Government in case he comes in possession of the office of President, and then how easy it would be to procure the men who should send the President staggering to his grave!

I don't want a President to be exposed to this danger; it is a most striking and instructing fact, that of all the Vice-Presidents we have had, not one of them who has succeeded a dead President ever followed in the footsteps of their predecessor. (Cheers.) No! John Tyler did not; you know about that as well as I do.

Harrison* was the first man elected suspected of entertaining anti-slavery proclivities. He did not hold his office for a month and was followed by a man with a policy diametrically opposed to that of the man with whom he was elected. Gen. Taylor† was elected with Millard Fillmore. As soon as it was rumored that he would not favor paying Texas for her claim upon New Mexico, and that he was in favor of California coming into the Union as a free State, if she desired it, the man whom the bullets of Mexico could not kill died, to give his place

---

* William Henry Harrison (1773–1841), ninth president of the United States (March 4, 1841–April 4, 1841). He was succeeded by the proslavery Tyler.

† Zachary Taylor (1784–1850), twelfth president of the United States (March 4, 1849–July 9, 1850).

to a Northern sycophant, whose name is found at the bottom of the Fugitive Slave bill.*

Andrew Johnson and Abraham Lincoln were elected upon the same ticket, and the latter holds his seat to-day by virtue of the assassination of the former. In my belief, the man who assassinated Abraham Lincoln knew Andrew Johnson then as we know him now. (Great and enthusiastic applause.)

It is well enough, perhaps, that you should have somebody to fill the Presidential chair. What is this chair? Can you make an executive? It will be easy in this country of swift travelling to get together the Congress of the United States, and appoint some man to act as President until such time as he can be elected by the people. We could have a vacant chair for six weeks, while the President was swinging around the circle, I think we could afford to have it vacant for six days.

But if the President commits high crimes and misdemeanors, we have the power in our own hands; we can impeach. I wish we could! (Laughter and cheers.) At the very mention of impeachment, Wall Street turns pale. It brings the President before us in a more powerful attitude. The Commander-in-Chief of the Army and Navy, he then comes before us, master of fleet and army, with the purse and sword in his hand, and the necessity of getting a two-thirds vote.

The President here outweighs a majority—almost makes a two-third vote kick the beam. You must have two-thirds in the House and two-thirds in the Senate besides. You have got to get ahead of him some way or another. He is, as Andrew Jackson once said, a co-ordinate branch of the Government. He is sworn to support the Constitution, not as you understand its requirements, but as he understands them.

I hardly deem it possible to make an amendment to the Constitution, to remove from the office as soon as you have no power to command; then secure the soldiers, and hold the Commander-in-Chief of the Army and Navy. You had better think twice before you act in

---

* The Fugitive Slave Act, which made it illegal to harbor escaped enslaved people, was part of the Compromise of 1850.

this matter. It is a mighty easy thing to say to the Senate, Impeach the President. What we want is not the impeachment of the President, but a limitation of the one-man power. We want him simply to be an executive officer, and not a legislative officer. (Cheers.)

I intended to call your attention for a moment to the great danger which now threatens this Government and this country: it is in the Constitutional Amendment.* I think it is but a shade different from that submitted by Andrew Johnson himself. It is a mean, contemptible, base, and most ungrateful betrayal by the people's loyal representatives of your only friends at the South during the war. It leaves to each of these Rebel States the right to determine whether or not the black man shall have any political rights at all. Shame on Congress if she admits a single Rebel State upon the adoption of that amendment!

You are silent now. I wish to God that you American people could hate as you love. I wish you could hate a little now, and there was some honest indignation here. (Applause.) You would sacrifice your friends to make peace with your enemies, but I wish we could only go back to the time of trial and hardship in this war; there was a time when the black man was somebody; when Rebel armies were in the field bold and defiant, then there was room under the American flag for all its defenders. (Great cheering.)

Stand by that matchless old hero of Pennsylvania, Thad. Stevens; uphold the hands in the House of your gallant Judge Kelley (cheers);† rebuke the falterers; strike down the one-man power everywhere (cheers); make your Government lean to the people, and away from the individual or the one-man power; and in proportion as you do this, you make sure the permanence, prosperity, and glory of this great republic. (Enthusiastic cheering.)

---

* The Fourteenth Amendment, which granted birthright citizenship to African Americans. Douglass initially objected to the amendment for not being clearer on African American voting rights.

† Thaddeus Stevens (1792–1868) and William D. Kelley (1814–1890), Pennsylvanian Radical Republicans who served in the U.S. House of Representatives.

ACKNOWLEDGMENTS

I BEGAN THIS BOOK during the first year of the Trump administration and completed it in the midst of a pandemic. These have been unusual, challenging times. I'm grateful for the continued support and collegiality of the English Department at the University of Maryland. A special thanks to my chair, Amanda Bailey, for approving a strategically timed semester's leave. My thanks as well to University of Maryland research librarian Patricia Herron for always being there with the help I need, this time especially with nineteenth-century newspapers.

I have received assistance from a number of Douglass scholars. I am especially grateful to John R. McKivigan, the editor of the *Frederick Douglass Papers* and director of the Douglass Papers archive at Indiana University–Purdue University, Indianapolis. On several occasions Jack allowed me complete access to the archive; he also quickly (and regularly) responded to after-midnight email queries. This book wouldn't exist in its current form without his generosity. I am indebted to the librarians overseeing the Frederick Douglass Papers at the Library of Congress. I am also indebted to the published work of more scholars than I can name, but especially that of David W. Blight, Eric Foner, Hans L. Trefousse, and Brenda Wineapple. Writing this book would have been a lot more difficult without the invaluable volumes of the *Frederick Douglass Papers*, edited by John W. Blassingame, John R. McKivigan, and their editorial teams; and the *Andrew Johnson Papers*, edited by Leroy P. Graf and his editorial team.

I first tried out material in this book at the University of Edinburgh and the University of Paris. My thanks to Celeste-Marie Bernier at Edinburgh and Michaël Roy and Cécile Roudeau at Paris for their kind invitations. A special shout-out to Douglass scholar Celeste-Marie Bernier for her inspiring example and friendship over the years. While in Edinburgh I met Walter O. and Linda Evans, who subsequently allowed me to work with materials from their astonishing Douglass collection, which they recently donated to the Beinecke Library at Yale. Thank you, Walter and Linda, for giving me access to those materials in exchange for a copy of this book, which I look forward to putting in the mail.

My thanks to Eric Gardner for supplying me with key Frances Harper and Douglass documents, and much appreciation also to Andrew Cohen, Jeffery Duvall, Ira Dworkin, John Ernest, Carol Faulkner, Carrie Hyde, Kate Masur, Brook Thomas, and Hannah Yi for their help along the way. Over the years I've been lucky to have the friendship, support, and good counsel of Jonathan Auerbach, Marijean Berry, Anna Brickhouse, Nick Bromell, Chris Castiglia, Russ Castronovo, Jeannine DeLombard, Elizabeth Duquette, Joan Goldberg, Sandra Gustafson, Susan Gillman, Ezra Greenspan, Gordon Hutner, Rodrigo Lazo, Ted Leinwand, Caroline Levander, Marilee Lindemann, Beth Loizeaux, Bill Loizeaux, Peter Mallios, Tom Moser, Samuel Otter, Jean Pfaelzer, Joel Pfister, Sangeeta Ray, Elizabeth Renker (who, even before marketing, came up with the title of the book), Xiomara Santamarina, Jane Schultz, Martha Nell Smith, John Stauffer, Julia Stern, Ernie Suarez, Mary Helen Washington, Rob Watson, Cindy Weinstein, Pam Wesling, and Edlie Wong. Thank you all.

My good friend Lenny Cassuto read what I thought was the finished draft of the book. He returned a manuscript in which virtually no sentence went untouched. I am grateful for his patience, editorial acumen, and wisdom.

At Norton, I've been fortunate to work with senior editor Amy Cherry, who taught me how to bring to the surface the story that I wanted to tell about Douglass and Johnson. My warm thanks for her guidance, support, and good humor. My thanks as well to Julia Reidhead, president of Norton, who long ago invited me to become an editor of *The Norton Anthology of American Literature* and more recently invited me to submit a proposal for this book. I'm glad I did. For their assistance with production matters, thank you to editors Bee Holekamp and Huneeya Siddiqui and expert copyeditor Sarah Johnson.

My wife, Ivy Goodman, read numerous drafts and helped me to the very end of the project with matters both large and small. Our son, Aaron, a data scientist, revealed during one of our conversations a deep vein of knowledge about Andrew Johnson. As always, I am grateful to them for their sustaining love.

NOTES

Abbreviations

FDP: Correspondence   *The Frederick Douglass Papers: Series Three: Correspondence*, ed. John R. McKivigan et al. (New Haven, CT: Yale University Press, 2009–).

FDP: Speeches, Debates, *The Frederick Douglass Papers: Series One: Speeches, Debates,*
and Interviews   *and Interviews*, 5 vols., ed. John W. Blassingame et al. (New Haven, CT: Yale University Press, 1979–1992).

PAJ   *The Papers of Andrew Johnson*, 16 vols., ed. Leroy P. Graf et al. (Knoxville: University of Tennessee Press, 1967–2000).

Introduction

1. Traditionally, historians have viewed the Reconstruction period as running from the end of the Civil War to the Compromise of 1877, but increasingly historians talk about a long Reconstruction that continued into the final decade of the nineteenth century. Allen C. Guelzo terms the years 1877 to 1896 the "Aftermath" of Reconstruction (*Reconstruction: A Concise History* [New York: Oxford University Press, 2018], 14); and Henry Louis Gates Jr. refers to the years spanning late 1865 into the early twentieth century as "the longer Reconstruction era" (*Stony the Road: Reconstruction, White Supremacy, and the Rise of Jim Crow* [New York: Penguin, 2019], 8).

2. For recent studies that emphasize the idealism of the Radical Republicans, see Brenda Wineapple, *The Impeachers: The Trial of Andrew Johnson and the Dream of a Just Nation* (New York: Random House, 2019); and Fergus M. Bor-

dewich, *Congress at War: How Republican Reformers Fought the Civil War, Defied Lincoln, Ended Slavery, and Remade America* (New York: Alfred A. Knopf, 2020).

3. Black voices have a surprisingly small place in studies of the Johnson impeachment. Despite its title, even Hans L. Trefousse's *Impeachment of a President: Andrew Johnson, the Blacks, and Reconstruction* (1975; New York: Fordham University Press, 1999) has little to say about Black perspectives. Two notable books that offer some account of African Americans on Johnson are James M. McPherson, *The Struggle for Equality: Abolitionists and the Negro in the Civil War and Reconstruction* (Princeton, NJ: Princeton University Press, 1964); and especially Hugh Davis, *"We Will Be Satisfied with Nothing Less": The African American Struggle for Equal Rights in the North during Reconstruction* (Ithaca, NY: Cornell University Press, 2011).

4. "Thirty-Second Anniversary of the American Anti-Slavery Society," *Liberator*, May 26, 1865.

5. David W. Blight, *Frederick Douglass: Prophet of Freedom* (New York: Simon & Schuster, 2018), xvii.

6. H. L. Trefousse, *Benjamin Franklin Wade: Radical Republican from Ohio* (New York: Twayne Publishers, 1963), qt. 311; Eric Foner, *The Fiery Trial: Abraham Lincoln and American Slavery* (New York: W. W. Norton, 2010), 257. See also Henry Louis Gates Jr. and Donald Yacovone, eds., *Lincoln on Race and Slavery* (Princeton, NJ: Princeton University Press, 2009).

7. Martin R. Delany to G. T. Downing, William Whipper, Frederick Douglass, John Jones, L. H. Douglass, letter of February 22, 1866, Frank [Frances] A. Rollin, *Life and Public Services of Martin R. Delany* (Boston: Lee and Shepard, 1868), 282.

8. Douglass, "Seeming and Real," *New National Era*, October 6, 1870, in *The Life and Writings of Frederick Douglass*, ed. Philip S. Foner (New York: International Publishers, 1955), IV, 227.

9. The key work that changed our understanding of Reconstruction, and informs my sense of the period, is Eric Foner, *Reconstruction: America's Unfinished Revolution, 1863–1877* (New York: Harper and Row, 1988). See also Foner's *The Second Founding: How the Civil War and Reconstruction Remade the Constitution* (New York: W. W. Norton, 2019); and Gates's *Stony the Road*.

10. Douglass, "Black Freedom Is the Prerequisite of Victory: An Address Delivered in New York, New York, on 13 January 1865," *FDP: Speeches, Debates, and Interviews*, IV, 54.

Prologue: Lincoln's Second Inauguration

1. See Ronald C. White Jr., *Lincoln's Greatest Speech: The Second Inaugural* (New York: Simon & Schuster, 2002), esp. 8–35; and Edward Achorn, *Every Drop of*

Blood: The Momentous Second Inauguration of Abraham Lincoln (New York: Atlantic Monthly Press, 2020).

2. Frederick Douglass, *Life and Times of Frederick Douglass*, ed. Rayford W. Logan (1881, 1891–1892; New York: Collier Books, 1962), 363–64, 366. Douglass's rendering of the concluding lines of Lincoln's second inaugural address varies slightly from other published versions.

3. Douglass, *Life and Times*, 364.

4. Douglass, 330, 325. On Douglass as an autobiographer, see Robert S. Levine, *The Lives of Frederick Douglass* (Cambridge, MA: Harvard University Press, 2016).

5. Douglass, "The Late Election," *Douglass' Monthly*, December 1860; Douglass, "The Inaugural Address," *Douglass' Monthly*, April 1861; Douglass, "The Progress of the War," *Douglass' Monthly*, September 1861; Douglass, "The President and His Speeches," *Douglass' Monthly*, September 1862.

1. Southern Unionist

1. Throughout this study, I am indebted for biographical details to Hans L. Trefousse, *Andrew Johnson: A Biography* (New York: W. W. Norton, 1989).

2. "Gallery of Portraits of Past and Present Members of Congress," *New York Sunday Times*, May 21, 1849, *PAJ*, I, 677, 678.

3. Johnson, "Speech on the Gag Resolution" (January 31, 1844), *PAJ*, I, 135; Johnson, "Exchange with Palfrey of Massachusetts on the Negro" (April 15, 1848), *PAJ*, I, 420; Johnson, "Remarks on the Organization of the House and the Issue of Slavery" (December 14, 1849), *PAJ*, I, 518.

4. Johnson, "Address to State Democratic Convention, Nashville" (January 8, 1856), *PAJ*, II, 354. On Johnson as a slave owner, see Douglas R. Egerton, *The Wars of Reconstruction: The Brief, Violent History of America's Most Progressive Era* (New York: Bloomsbury Press, 2014), 57–59. The idea that "wage slavery" was worse than slavery was promulgated by, among others of the time, Virginia proslavery writer George Fitzhugh in *Sociology for the South* (1854) and *Cannibals All!, or Slaves without Masters* (1857).

5. Johnson, "Speech on Harper's Ferry Incident" (December 12, 1859), *PAJ*, III, 319.

6. Johnson, "Speech on Secession" (December 18–19, 1860), *PAJ*, IV, 45.

7. On the publication of "Speech on Secession," see *PAJ*, IV, 109; the congressional printing office priced it at two dollars per one hundred copies.

8. Lane, qt. in *PAJ*, IV, xxxi; Johnson, "Speech in Reply to Senator Lane" (March 2, 1861), *PAJ*, IV, 354; *PAJ*, IV, xxxii.

9. Johnson, "Speech at Newport, Kentucky" (September 2, 1861), *PAJ*, V, 4.

10. Johnson, "Speech to Davidson County Citizens" (March 22, 1865), *PAJ*, V, 230.

11. Johnson, "Speech to Davidson County Citizens," 231; Johnson, "Speech at Baltimore" (March 20, 1863), *PAJ*, VI, 180; Johnson, "Speech at Indianapolis" (February 26, 1863), *PAJ*, VI, 153.
12. *Indianapolis Journal*, February 27, 1863; *New York Times*, March 2 1863. Both references are quoted in *PAJ*, VI, 157.
13. Johnson, "Speech at Indianapolis," 152; Lincoln to Johnson, letter of March 26, 1863, *PAJ*, VI, 194.
14. Johnson, "Speech at Nashville" (August 29, 1863), *PAJ*, VI, 344; Lincoln to Johnson, letter of September 11, 1863, *PAJ*, VI, 363; Johnson to Edwin M. Stanton, letter of September 17, 1863, *PAJ*, VI, 376.
15. Johnson, "Testimony re Condition of Negroes" (November 23, 1863), *PAJ*, VI, 491; Johnson, "Speech on Slavery and State Suicide" (January 8, 1864), *PAJ*, VI, 550; Johnson, "Speech at Knoxville" (April 12, 1864), *PAJ*, VI, 672.
16. Johnson to Lincoln, letter of April 5, 1864, *PAJ*, VI, 659; Michael Burlingame and John R. Turner Ettlinger, eds., *Inside Lincoln's White House: The Complete Civil War Diary of John Hay* (Carbondale: Southern Illinois University Press, 1997), 199 (entry of June 5, 1864).
17. Johnson, "Speech on Vice-Presidential Nomination" (June 9, 1864), *PAJ*, VI, 724, 723, 725; Johnson, "Acceptance of Vice-Presidential Nomination" (July 2, 1864), *PAJ*, VII, 9.
18. Johnson, "Speech near Gallatin" (July 19, 1864), *PAJ*, VII, 42.
19. Johnson, "Speech at Logansport, Indiana" (October 4, 1864), *PAJ*, VII, 226.
20. Johnson, "'The Moses of the Colored Men' Speech" (October 24, 1864), *PAJ*, VII, 251. Egerton notes that slavery remained legal in Tennessee until February 22, 1865, despite Johnson's Moses speech (*Wars of Reconstruction*, 59).
21. Johnson, "Moses of the Colored Men," 252. This version of the speech appeared in the *Nashville Times and True Union*, October 25, 1864, and November 9, 1864.
22. Johnson, "Moses of the Colored Men," 252, 254, 252–53.
23. Historians have tended to ridicule the speech, especially Johnson's offer to be a Moses to Black people. The editors of the Johnson Papers, who typically write about Johnson with great sympathy, describe the speech as "a bathetic display" and "demagogic" (*PAJ*, VII, li, l). Annette Gordon-Reed is harsher, asserting that the speech was "outrageously mendacious." She goes on to remark that "of course Johnson did not mean a word he said" (*Andrew Johnson* [New York: Henry Holt, 2011], 79, 81). Granted, Johnson's claim to be a Moses for Black people was outrageous, but his speeches of the period suggest that he meant what he said about his hopes for the freedpeople. We need to resist reading him through the lens of his later actions. There are good reasons why Charles Sumner, Thaddeus Stevens, and other Radical Republicans regarded Johnson as such an appealing figure in late 1864 and early 1865.
24. *Nashville Dispatch*, October 25, 1864, and *Nashville Daily Press*, October 27, 1864; see Trefousse, *Andrew Johnson*, 183, 184.

25. "Andrew Johnson's Great Speech to the Colored People: He Proclaims Freedom to All in Tennessee," *Liberator*, November 11, 1864; "Andy Johnson's Speech to the Slaves of Tennessee," *National Anti-Slavery Standard*, November 12, 1864; "Freedom! Freedom! Declared in Tennessee!," *Christian Recorder*, November 12, 1864; "The Conquest," *Christian Recorder*, November 12, 1864.
26. Johnson, "Speech to Nashville Freedmen" (November 12, 1864), *PAJ*, VII, 281, 282. On the importance of temperance to Black reform, see Donald Yacovone, "The Transformation of the Black Temperance Movement, 1827–1854: An Interpretation," *Journal of the Early Republic* 8, no. 3 (1988): 281–97.
27. Johnson, "Speech to Union State Convention" (January 12, 1865), *PAJ*, VII, 395, 396; Johnson to Lincoln, letter of January 13, 1865, *PAJ*, VII, 404; Johnson, "Remarks to the Union State Convention" (January 14, 1865), *PAJ*, VII, 409; *PAJ, VII*, li.

2. The Mission of the War

1. William Lloyd Garrison, "Preface," in *Narrative of the Life of Frederick Douglass, An American Slave* (1845; New York: Penguin Books, 1982), 34.
2. William G. Allen, "Orators and Orations," *Liberator*, October 29, 1852.
3. For a fuller discussion of Douglass's dynamic thinking about the U.S. Constitution, see Nick Bromell, *The Powers of Dignity: The Black Political Philosophy of Frederick Douglass* (Durham, NC: Duke University Press, 2021), chap. 4.
4. Allen, "Orators and Orations."
5. Douglass, "A Letter to the American Slaves from Those Who Have Fled from American Slavery," *North Star*, September 5, 1850, in *Frederick Douglass: Selected Speeches and Writings*, ed. Philip S. Foner and Yuval Taylor (Chicago: Lawrence Hill Books, 1999), 158; Douglass, "Is It Right and Wise to Kill a Kidnapper?," *Frederick Douglass' Paper*, June 2, 1854, in *The Life and Writings of Frederick Douglass*, ed. Philip S. Foner (New York: International Publishers, 1950), II, 287.
6. Qtd. in Eric Foner, *The Story of American Freedom* (New York: W. W. Norton, 1998), 75.
7. Douglass, "Cast Off the Mill Stone," *Douglass' Monthly*, November 1861; Douglass to Gerrit Smith, letter of December 22, 1861, *FDP: Correspondence*, II, 325.
8. In 1817, the American Colonization Society was formed with the express purpose of shipping U.S. Blacks to Africa, specifically Liberia. Black leaders vociferously rejected the goals of the society. Lincoln during the Civil War displayed some interest in removing U.S. Blacks through colonization. See P. J. Staudenraus, *The African Colonization Movement, 1816–1865* (New York: Columbia University Press, 1961); and Phillip W. Magness, *Coloniza-*

tion after Emancipation: Lincoln and the Movement for Black Resettlement (Columbia: University of Missouri Press, 2011).

9. Douglass, "The Proclamation and a Negro Army: An Address Delivered in New York, New York, on 6 February 1863," *FDP: Speeches, Debates, and Interviews*, III, 551.

10. Douglass, "Emancipation, Racism, and the Work before Us: An Address Delivered in Philadelphia, Pennsylvania, on 4 December 1863," *FDP: Speeches, Debates, and Interviews*, III, 607. On Douglass and Lincoln, see James Oakes, *The Radical and the Republican: Frederick Douglass, Abraham Lincoln, and the Triumph of Antislavery Politics* (New York: W. W. Norton, 2007); John Stauffer, *Giants: The Parallel Lives of Frederick Douglass and Abraham Lincoln* (New York: Twelve, 2008); and Robert S. Levine, *The Lives of Frederick Douglass* (Cambridge, MA: Harvard University Press, 2016), chap. 4.

11. Douglass, "The Work of the Future," *Douglass' Monthly*, November 1862.

12. Douglass, "The Mission of the War: An Address Delivered in New York, New York, on 13 January 1864," *FDP: Speeches, Debates, and Interviews*, IV, 4; Abraham Lincoln to Horace Greeley, letter of August 22, 1852, in *The Collected Works of Abraham Lincoln*, ed. Roy P. Basler (Springfield, IL: Abraham Lincoln Association, 1953), V, 388–89; Lincoln, "Annual Message to Congress" (December 8, 1863), in Basler, *Collected Works of Abraham Lincoln*, VII, 49; Douglass, "Mission of the War," 13, 12, 20. David W. Blight describes "The Mission of the War" as perhaps Douglass's "fullest expression of what the Civil War meant to him" (*Frederick Douglass' Civil War: Keeping Faith in Jubilee* [Baton Rouge: Louisiana State University Press, 1989], 175). On Douglass's Civil War, see also Cody Marrs, *Not Even Past: The Stories We Keep Telling about the Civil War* (Baltimore: Johns Hopkins University Press, 2020), 143–48.

13. *Minutes of the National Convention of Colored Citizens: Held at Buffalo, on the 15th, 16th, 17th, 18th and 19th of August, 1843: For the Purpose of Considering Their Moral and Political Condition as American Citizens* (New York: Piercy and Reed, 1843); Douglass, "Address, of the Colored National Convention, to the People of the United States," *Proceedings of the Colored National Convention, Held in Rochester, July 6th, 7th and 8th, 1853* (Rochester: Office of Frederick Douglass' Paper, 1853), 11, 40.

14. *Proceedings of the National Convention of Colored Men, Held in the City of Syracuse, N.Y., October 4, 5, 6, 7, 1864; with the Bill of Wrongs and Rights, and the Address to the American People* (Boston: J. R. Rock and Geo. L. Ruffin, 1864), 15, 25, 42. On the importance of the Syracuse convention to Black Reconstruction, see Hugh Davis, *"We Will Be Satisfied with Nothing Less": The African American Struggle for Equal Rights in the North during Reconstruction* (Ithaca, NY: Cornell University Press, 2011), 2–5; and David W. Blight, *Frederick Douglass: Prophet of Freedom* (New York: Simon & Schuster, 2018), 440–44. Over the years, the National Equal Rights League expanded to include white and Black par-

ticipants, and it remained a functioning organization working for Blacks' rights until 1921.

15. Douglass, "Address of the Colored National Convention to the People of the United States," *Proceedings of the National Convention of Colored Men*, 44, 46, 58, 61.

16. Douglass, "Address of the Colored National Convention," 54.

17. Douglass, 52.

18. B. F. Wade and H. Winter Davis, "The President's Suppression of the Bill for Reconstruction in the Rebellious States," in Henry Winter Davis, *Speeches and Addresses Delivered in the Congress of the United States, and on Several Public Occasions* (New York: Harper & Brothers, 1867), 422; "General News," *New York Times*, August 9, 1864; Wade and Davis, "The President's Suppression," 423. For a still useful discussion of the Wade-Davis Bill, see H. L. Trefousse, *Benjamin Franklin Wade: Radical Republican from Ohio* (New York: Twayne Publishers, 1963), 218–32. On the abolitionists' objection to Lincoln's Louisiana Ten Percent Plan and support for the Wade-Davis Bill, see James M. McPherson, *The Struggle for Equality: Abolitionists and the Negro in the Civil War and Reconstruction* (Princeton, NJ: Princeton University Press, 1964), 243–46; and on the specifics of the Ten Percent Plan and Reconstruction in Louisiana, see Eric Foner, *The Fiery Trial: Abraham Lincoln and American Slavery* (New York: W. W. Norton, 2010), 271–84.

19. Douglass to Mary Browne Carpenter, letter of June 1864, *FDP: Correspondence*, II, 442, 443. The letter first appeared in the Leeds (Eng.) *Mercury*, and was reprinted in the *Liberator*, September 16, 1864. Garrison ran the letter in an effort to embarrass Douglass for not fully supporting Lincoln.

20. Douglass to Theodore Tilton, letter of October 15, 1864, *FDP: Correspondence*, II, 462.

21. "What the Black Man Wants: An Address Delivered in Boston, Massachusetts, on 26 January 1865," *FDP: Speeches, Debates, and Interviews*, IV, 62.

3. "Abraham Lincoln Dies, the Republic Lives"

1. Frederick Douglass, *Life and Times of Frederick Douglass*, ed. Raymond W. Logan (1881, 1891–1892; New York: Collier Books, 1962), 364, 365.

2. "Remarks at Vice-Presidential Swearing In" (March 4, 1865), *PAJ*, VII, 505 (*Congressional Globe*) and 506 (*New York Times*); Howard K. Beale and Alan W. Brownsword, eds., *Diary of Gideon Welles, Secretary of the Navy under Lincoln and Johnson* (New York: W. W. Norton, 1960), II, 252; "Remarks at Vice-Presidential Swearing In," 506; "From Washington," *Chicago Tribune*, March 6, 1865. The material in this and the next paragraph draws on Hans L. Trefousse, *Andrew Johnson: A Biography* (New York: W. W. Norton, 1989), 190–92.

3. Hugh McCulloch, *Men and Measures of Half a Century: Sketches and Comments* (New York: Charles Scribner's Sons, 1888), 373; Charles Sumner to Wendell Phillips, letter of March 12, 1865, in *The Selected Letters of Charles Sumner*, ed. Beverly Wilson Palmer (Boston: Northeastern University Press, 1990), 272; Sumner to Francis Lieber, letter of March 13, 1865, in Palmer, *Selected Letters of Charles Sumner*, II, 275. See the March 9, 1865, *Independent* (New York) for one of several calls for Johnson to resign.

4. On this point, see Trefousse, *Andrew Johnson*, 191.

5. Charles Sumner to Richard Cobden, letter of March 27, 1865, in Palmer, *Selected Letters of Charles Sumner*, II, 279. On the January 1865 meeting of the Massachusetts Anti-Slavery Society, see the *Liberator*, January 13, 1865, and February 3, 1865.

6. Lincoln, "Last Public Address," in *The Collected Works of Abraham Lincoln*, ed. Roy P. Basler (Springfield, IL: Abraham Lincoln Association, 1953), VIII, 400, 403. For a comprehensive study, see Louis P. Masur, *Lincoln's Last Speech: Wartime Reconstruction and the Crisis of Reunion* (New York: Oxford University Press, 2015).

7. Lincoln, "Last Public Address," 403. Eric Foner writes that, had he not been assassinated, "Lincoln's ideas would undoubtedly have continued to evolve" (*The Fiery Trial: Abraham Lincoln and American Slavery* [New York: W. W. Norton, 2010], 334–35), though of course it is impossible to say how and when the evolution would have occurred. Foner's comments on Lincoln and Reconstruction are worth keeping in mind: "Unlike Sumner and other Radicals, Lincoln did not see Reconstruction as an opportunity for sweeping political and social revolution beyond emancipation. He had long made clear his opposition to the confiscation and redistribution of land. He believed, as most Republicans did in April 1865, that voting requirements should be determined by the states" (*Fiery Trial*, 225). At the time, Johnson was not such an outlier.

8. Martha Hodes, *Mourning Lincoln* (New Haven, CT: Yale University Press, 2015), 38. Booth's remarks were reported by one of his co-conspirators.

9. Douglass, "Our Martyred President: An Address Delivered in Rochester, New York, on 15 April 1865," *FDP: Speeches, Debates, and Interviews*, IV, 76.

10. Johnson, "Remarks on Assuming the Presidency" (April 15, 1865), *PAJ*, VII, 554.

4. "There Is No Such Thing as Reconstruction"

1. James M. Thompson to Andrew Johnson, letter of May 5, 1865, *PAJ*, VIII, 33.

2. "George W. Julian's Journal—the Assassination of Lincoln" (entry of April 15, 1865), *Indiana Magazine of History* 11, no. 4 (1915): 335.

3. Allan Nevins and Milton Halsey Thomas, eds., *The Diary of George Templeton Strong: The Civil War, 1860–1865* (New York: Macmillan, 1952), 591 (entry of April 21, 1865).

4. "George W. Julian's Journal" (entry of April 16, 1865), 335; Johnson, "Response to District of Columbia Ministers" (April 17, 1865), *PAJ*, VII, 576. Julian would have a second meeting with Johnson, on April 24, 1865; according to his journal, that did not go well, with Johnson "indulging in bad grammar, bad pronunciation and much incoherency of thought" ("George W. Julian's Journal," 337).

5. Charles Sumner to John Andrew, letter of September 10, 1864, in *The Selected Letters of Charles Sumner*, ed. Beverly Wilson Palmer (Boston: Northeastern University Press, 1990), II, 251.

6. Charles Sumner to Francis Lieber, letter of April 17, 1865, in Palmer, *Selected Letters*, II, 294; Edward Pierce, *Memoirs and Letters of Charles Sumner* (Boston: Roberts Brothers, 1893), IV, 245 (Pierce's biography drew on Sumner's notes and comments); Sumner to the Duchess of Argyll, letter of April 24, 1865, in Palmer, *Selected Letters*, II, 295; Sumner to John Bright, letter of April 12, 1865, in Palmer, II, 297.

7. Charles Sumner to Lieber, letter of May 2, 1865, in Palmer, II, 299.

8. Carl Schurz, "The Treason of Slavery," in *Speeches, Correspondence, and Political Papers of Carl Schurz*, ed. Frederic Bancroft (New York: G. P. Putnam's Sons, 1913), I, 232; Schurz to Charles Sumner, letter of May 9, 1865, in Bancroft, *Speeches, Correspondence*, I, 255.

9. Gerrit Smith to Andrew Johnson, letter of April 19, 1865, *PAJ*, VII, 593; Wendell Phillips, "Abraham Lincoln Assassinated" (April 23, 1865), in *Wendell Phillips on Civil Rights and Freedom*, ed. Louis Filler (Washington, D.C.: University Press of America, 1982), 189.

10. [William Lloyd Garrison], "Andrew Johnson, President of the United States," *Liberator*, April 28, 1865.

11. Johnson, "Amnesty Proclamation" (May 29, 1865), *PAJ*, VIII, 129. Johnson did support executing some of the conspirators involved with Lincoln's assassination, including the boardinghouse owner Mary Surratt, who was hanged July 7, 1865.

12. That said, Gregory P. Downs makes a good case that Johnson "was actually quite bold" in the spring and summer of 1865, blocking "white Southerners' dreams of complete restoration." He elaborates: "To a surprising degree, Johnson regularly sustained the military throughout 1865 and 1866" (*After Appomattox: Military Occupation and the Ends of War* [Cambridge, MA: Harvard University Press, 2015], 34).

13. "Gallery of Portraits of Past and Present Members of Congress," *New York Sunday Times*, May 21, 1849, *PAJ*, I, 678.

14. "Interview with John A. Logan" (May 31, 1865), *Washington Morning Chronicle*, June 1, 1865, *PAJ*, VIII, 153, 154. On the oddness and even ludicrousness

of Johnson's view of the impossibility of secession, see Brenda Wineapple, *The Impeachers: The Trial of Andrew Johnson and the Dream of a Just Nation* (New York: Random House, 2019), 34–36.

15. African Americans were typically left out of the rhetoric, rituals, and politics of sectional reunion. See Nina Silber, *The Romance of Reunion: Northerners and the South, 1865–1900* (Chapel Hill: University of North Carolina Press, 1993); and David W. Blight, *Race and Reunion: The Civil War in American Memory* (Cambridge, MA: Harvard University Press, 2001).

16. Sumner to John Bright, letter of June 5, 1865, in Pierce, *Memoirs and Letters of Charles Sumner*, IV, 253; Sumner to Salmon Chase, letter of July 1, 1865, in Palmer, *Selected Letters of Charles Sumner*, II, 312; Sumner to John Bright, letter of November 5, 1865, in Palmer, II, 342. In a letter of July 20, 1865, a disillusioned Sumner confided to his friend Henry Dawes, "I had every reason to believe that Presdt. Johnson would incline to the side of Equal Rights" (Palmer, II, 318).

17. Sumner to Andrew Johnson, letter of November 11, 1865, in Palmer, II, 344–45.

18. Thaddeus Stevens to Andrew Johnson, letter of July 6, 1865, in *The Selected Papers of Thaddeus Stevens*, ed. Beverly Wilson Palmer and Holly Byers Ochoa (Pittsburgh, PA: University of Pittsburgh Press, 1998), II, 7–8.

19. Thaddeus Stevens, "Reconstruction," speech delivered September 6, 1865, in Lancaster, Pennsylvania, in Palmer and Ochoa, *Selected Papers of Thaddeus Stevens*, II, 16.

20. Stevens, "Reconstruction," 18.

21. Carl Schurz to Andrew Johnson, letter of July 28, 1865, in *Advice after Appomattox: Letters to Andrew Johnson, 1865–1866*, ed. Brooks D. Simpson, Leroy P. Graf, and John Muldowny (Knoxville: University of Tennessee Press, 1987), 79; Schurz to Johnson, letter of August 13, 1865, in Simpson, Graf, and Muldowny, *Advice after Appomattox*, 90; Schurz to Johnson, letter of August 29, 1865, in Simpson, Graf, and Muldowny, 106.

22. Charles Sumner to the Duchess of Argyll, letter of December 25, 1865, in Palmer, *Selected Letters of Charles Sumner*, II, 349.

23. Douglass to James M. McKim, letter of May 2, 1865, *FDP: Correspondence*, II, 482. In his not always reliable final autobiography, Douglass, who remained actively engaged with the cause of Blacks' civil rights, claimed that he faced a vocational crisis at the end of the Civil War, thinking that he had come "to the end of the noblest and best part of my life." He asked himself: "Where should I go, and what should I do?" As it turned out—or so he said—Douglass's future was decided for him by his admirers: "Invitations began to pour in upon me from colleges, lyceums, and literary societies, offering me one hundred and even two hundred dollars for a single lecture" (several thousand dollars per lecture in today's value). Douglass concluded the discussion on a triumphal note: "Here, then, was a new vocation before

me, full of advantages mentally and pecuniarily" (*Life and Times of Frederick Douglass*, ed. Rayford W. Logan [1881, 1891–1892; New York: Collier Books, 1962], 373, 374, 376). On Douglass as a lecturer during this period, see John R. McKivigan, "'A New Vocation before Me': Frederick Douglass's Post-Civil War Lyceum Career," *Howard Journal of Communications* 29, no. 3 (2018): 268–81.

24. On the question of citizenship and Black rights, see Eric Foner, *The Second Founding: How the Civil War and Reconstruction Remade the Constitution* (New York: W. W. Norton, 2019); Carrie Hyde, *Civic Longing: The Speculative Origins of U.S. Citizenship* (Cambridge, MA: Harvard University Press, 2018), esp. chap. 1; and Christopher James Bonner, *Remaking the Republic: Black Politics and the Creation of American Citizenship* (Philadelphia: University of Pennsylvania Press, 2020).

25. Douglass, "In What New Skin Will the Old Snake Come Forth? An Address Delivered in New York, New York, on 10 May 1865," *FDP: Speeches, Debates, and Interviews*, IV, 83. Transcriptions of debates and speeches at the meeting can be found in the May 13, 20, 1865, issues of the *National Anti-Slavery Standard*. The American Anti-Slavery Society dissolved in 1870 after the ratification of the Fifteenth Amendment.

26. Douglass, "Eulogy on Abraham Lincoln," June 1, 1865, Frederick Douglass Papers, Library of Congress, Manuscript Division.

27. Martha W. Greene to Frederick Douglass, letter of August 2, 1865, General Correspondence, Frederick Douglass Papers, Library of Congress.

5. A Moses in the White House

1. *A Memorial Discourse; by Rev. Henry Highland Garnet, Delivered in the Hall of the House of Representatives, Washington City, D.C., on Sabbath, February 12, 1865, with an Introduction by James McCune Smith, M.D.* (Philadelphia: Joseph M. Wilson, 1865), 89. Garnet's 1843 "An Address to the Slaves of the United States" was included in this edition. On activist Blacks in Washington, D.C., see Kate Masur, *An Example for All the Land: Emancipation and the Struggle over Equality in Washington, D.C.* (Chapel Hill: University of North Carolina Press, 2010).

2. John Mercer Langston, *From the Virginia Plantation to the National Capitol* (Harford, CT: American Publishing Company, 1894), 229.

3. Langston, *From the Virginia Plantation*, 226, 227. (Langston gave the lecture on January 2, 1865.) See also William Cheek and Aimee Lee Cheek, *John Mercer Langston and the Fight for Black Freedom, 1829–65* (Urbana: University of Illinois Press, 1989), 443–46.

4. Langston, *From the Virginia Plantation*, 227.

5. Langston, 230, 231. Such was Langston's admiration for Johnson that he chose not to discuss the president's impeachment in his autobiography.

6. "Response to John Mercer Langston," *Philadelphia Press*, April 21, 1865, *PAJ*, VII, 585–86.
7. "Reply to the Delegation of Black Ministers," *Washington Morning Chronicle*, May 12, 1865, *PAJ*, VIII, 63, 62.
8. "Reply to the Delegation of Black Ministers," 63. Johnson's presentation of himself as a Moses to Black people was not yet viewed ironically or critically; see the celebration of Johnson as Moses in the article "A Moses to the Slave," published in the abolitionist *National Anti-Slavery Standard*, May 6, 1865.
9. "From Delegation Representing the Black People of Kentucky," *Chicago Tribune*, June 15, 1865, *PAJ*, VIII, 204; "From Committee of Richmond Blacks," *Washington Morning Chronicle*, June 17, 1865, *PAJ*, VIII, 211; "From Delegation Representing the Black People of Kentucky," *PAJ*, VIII, 205; "From the Committee of Richmond Blacks," *PAJ*, VIII, 213.
10. *Celebration of the Colored People's Educational Monument Association in Memory of Abraham Lincoln, on the Fourth of July, 1865, in the Presidential Grounds, Washington, D.C.* (Washington, D.C.: McGill & Witherow, 1865), 5, 9.
11. *Celebration of the Colored People's Educational Monument*, 31.
12. Johnson to William L. Sharkey, letter of August 15, 1865, *PAJ*, VIII, 599–600.
13. Sharkey to Johnson, letter of August 20, 1865, *PAJ*, VIII, 628.
14. George L. Stearns to Andrew Johnson, letter of May 17, 1865, *PAJ*, VIII, 85; "Interview with George L. Stearns," *New York Times*, October 23, 1865, *PAJ*, IX, 180. See also Stearns's pamphlet *The Equality of All Men before the Law, Claimed and Defended; in Speeches by Hon. William D. Kelley, Wendell Phillips, and Frederick Douglass, and Letters from Elizur Wright and Wm. Heighton* (Boston: Geo. C. Rand & Avery, 1865). Stearns printed over ten thousand copies of this pamphlet. On Stearns and Douglass, see David W. Blight, *Frederick Douglass: Prophet of Freedom* (New York: Simon & Schuster, 2018), 296, 315, 391, 404, 406, 410.
15. Henry Ward Beecher to Andrew Johnson, letter of October 23, 1865, *PAJ*, IX, 269.
16. "Andrew Johnson," *Christian Recorder*, October 14, 1865; Johnson, "Speech to First Regiment, USCT" (October 10, 1865), *New York Times*, October 11, 1865, *PAJ*, IX, 221, 222.
17. P. V. G., "Letter from Washington," *Christian Recorder*, October 14, 1865. For somewhat more critical pieces on Johnson, see "The Question of the Hour," *Christian Recorder*, July 15, 1865; "What Shall Be Done with the Negro?," *Christian Recorder*, July 29, 1865; and "Reconstruction," *Christian Recorder*, September 2, 1865. On the *Christian Recorder*, which had close ties to the African Methodist Episcopal Church, see Eric Gardner, *Black Print Unbound: The Christian Recorder, African American Literature, and Periodical Culture* (New York: Oxford University Press, 2015).

18. Douglass, "The Assassination and Its Lessons: Speech Delivered 24 October 1865, Parker Fraternity Lecture, Music Hall, Boston, Massachusetts," *FDP: Speeches, Debates, and Interviews*, IV, 593.

19. Douglass, "The Douglass Institute: An Address Delivered in Baltimore, Maryland, on 29 September, 1865," *FDP: Speeches, Debates, and Interviews*, IV, 90, 91. On Douglass's suspicion of all-Black organizations earlier in his career, see Robert S. Levine, *Martin Delany, Frederick Douglass, and the Politics of Representative Identity* (Chapel Hill: University of North Carolina Press, 1997), chap. 2. For a discussion of Black reading societies and schools during the antebellum period and beyond, see Elizabeth McHenry, *Forgotten Readers: Recovering the Lost History of African American Literary Societies* (Durham, NC: Duke University Press, 2002), chaps. 1–2. Nick Bromell forcefully argues that Douglass's challenge to whites' anti-Black racism informed his political and philosophical work from the late 1840s to the time of his death; see his *The Powers of Dignity: The Black Political Philosophy of Frederick Douglass* (Durham, NC: Duke University Press, 2021).

20. *Proceedings of the First Annual Meeting of the National Equal Rights League, Held in Cleveland, Ohio, October 19, 20, and 21, 1865* (Philadelphia: E. C. Markely & Son, 1865), 20, 28, 39.

21. "Convention of the Colored People of New England, Boston, December 1, 1865," *National Anti-Slavery Standard*, December 9, 1865.

22. "Convention of the Colored People of New England."

23. George Bancroft to Andrew Johnson, letter of December 1, 1865, *PAJ*, IX, 449.

24. Johnson, "Message to Congress" (December 4, 1865), *PAJ*, IX, 474, 475, 474.

25. Johnson, "Message to Congress," 473, 474.

26. Johnson, "Message to Congress," 470, 472.

27. Douglass, "Abraham Lincoln: A Speech" (December 1865), Frederick Douglass Papers, Manuscript/Mixed Materials, Library of Congress. The speech survives in manuscript; the venue is unclear.

6. The Black Delegation Visits a Moses of Their People

1. Stephen Kantrowitz, *More than Freedom: Fighting for Black Citizenship in a White Republic* (New York: Penguin Press, 2012), 348. See also S. A. M. Washington, *George Thomas Downing: Sketch of His Life and Times* (Newport, RI: Milne Printery, 1910). For a range of perspectives on the Black delegation's meeting with Johnson, see W. E. B. Du Bois, *Black Reconstruction in America* (1935; New York: Simon & Schuster, 1998), 296–301; Garrett Epps, *Democracy Reborn: The Fourteenth Amendment and the Fight for Equal Rights in Post-Civil War America* (New York: Henry Holt, 2006), 144–49; James Oakes, *The Radical and the Republican: Frederick Douglass, Abraham Lincoln, and the Triumph of Antislavery*

Politics (New York: W. W. Norton, 2007), 249–55; David W. Blight, *Frederick Douglass: Prophet of Freedom* (New York: Simon & Schuster, 2018), 472–76; and Brenda Wineapple, *The Impeachers: The Trial of Andrew Johnson and the Dream of a Just Nation* (New York: Random House, 2019), 107–11.

2. George T. Downing, Lewis H. Douglass, Frederick Douglass, William Whipper, William E. Mathews, A. J. Ransier, A. W. Ross, John Jones, and Joseph E. Oates, letter to Hon. Charles Sumner (n.d.), ALS in the Walter O. and Linda Evans Collection. For additional background on the Black delegation, see Hugh Davis, *"We Will Be Satisfied with Nothing Less": The African American Struggle for Equal Rights in the North during Reconstruction* (Ithaca, NY: Cornell University Press, 2011), 55–58.

3. Charles Sumner, "The Equal Rights of All: The Great Guaranty and Present Necessity, for the Sake of Security, and to Maintain a Republican Government: Speech in the Senate, on the Proposed Amendment of the Constitution Fixing the Basis of Representation, February 5 and 6, 1866," in *The Works of Charles Sumner* (Boston: Lee and Shepard, 1874), X, 135, 221, 222, 235. In a letter of February 13, 1866, Sumner responded to the Black delegates' praise of his speech, thanking them for their kind words, pledging his allegiance to their cause, and urging them to remain "patient and determined" (ALS in the Walter O. and Linda Evans Collection). In his 1852 *The Condition, Elevation, Emigration and Destiny of the Colored People of the United States*, Martin R. Delany had anticipated Sumner's argument about whites constituting a minority of the world's population.

4. George T. Downing, Lewis H. Douglass, Frederick Douglass, William Whipper, William E. Mathews, A. J. Ransier, A. W. Ross, John Jones, and Joseph E. Oates to Charles Sumner, letter of February 13, 1866, ALS in the Walter O. and Linda Evans Collection.

5. On James O. Clephane, see *Men and Women of America: A Biographical Dictionary of Contemporaries* (New York: L. R. Hamersly & Company, 1910), 361; and Frank Romano, *History of the Linotype Company* (Rochester, NY: RIT Press, 2014), 1–13.

6. "Important Expression of Views by the President. Interview with a Colored Delegation," *Washington Evening Star*, February 7, 1866. This report on the meeting in the *Star* is available online via the Library of Congress's Chronicling America website. For the rest of the chapter, I will be working with the February 8, 1866, report in the *Washington Morning Chronicle*, which Clephane revised for accuracy. That version is available in *PAJ*, X, 41–48.

7. "Interview with Delegation of Blacks," *Washington Morning Chronicle*, February 8, 1866, *PAJ*, X, 41.

8. "Interview with Delegation of Blacks," 41.

9. "Interview with Delegation of Blacks," 42. Douglass's argument for the privileges of citizenship, based in part on African Americans' military service going back to the time of the Revolutionary War, echoed that of Black

activist William C. Nell's *Services of Colored Americans, in the Wars of 1776 and 1812* (Boston: Robert F. Wallcut, 1851).

10. Douglass, *Life and Times of Frederick Douglass*, ed. Rayford W. Logan (1881, 1891–1892; New York: Collier Books, 1962), 382.
11. "Interview with Delegation of Blacks," 42, 43.
12. "Interview with Delegation of Blacks," 43.
13. "Interview with Delegation of Blacks," 43. For clarity, boldface has been added here and below.
14. Douglass, "Eulogy on Abraham Lincoln," June 1, 1865, Frederick Douglass Papers, Library of Congress, Manuscript Division; Douglass, *Life and Times*, 382.
15. "Interview with Delegation of Blacks," 44.
16. "Interview with Delegation of Blacks," 45; "Interview with James Dixon" (January 28, 1866), *Washington Morning Chronicle*, January 29, 1866, *PAJ*, IX, 648; "Interview with Delegation of Blacks," 45.
17. "Interview with Delegation of Blacks," 46.
18. "Interview with Delegation of Blacks," 46, 47.
19. "Interview with Delegation of Blacks," 47.
20. "Interview with Delegation of Blacks," 47–48. On enslaved persons having illusory freedom during the holidays, see Douglass, *Narrative of the Life of Frederick Douglass, An American Slave* (1845; New York: Penguin Books, 1982), 114–16.
21. "Interview with Delegation of Blacks," 48.
22. "Interview with Delegation of Blacks," 48. On colonization, see Phillip W. Magness, *Colonization after Emancipation: Lincoln and the Movement for Black Resettlement* (Columbia: University of Missouri Press, 2011).
23. "Interview with Delegation of Blacks," 48.
24. The "Interview with Delegation of Blacks," in various forms, appeared in the *National Intelligencer*, February 8, 1866; *New York Times*, February 8, 1865; *Baltimore Sun*, February 8, 1866; *Richmond Examiner*, February 9, 1866; *Rochester Union and Advertiser*, February 12, 1866; *Illinois State Register*, February 13, 1866; *Salt Lake Daily Telegraph*, February 14, 1866; *San Francisco Evening Bulletin*, February 14, 1866; *Bennington Banner*, February 15, 1866; *Daily Iowa State Register*, February 16, 1866; *Boston Commonwealth*, February 17, 1866; *Christian Recorder*, February 17, 1866; and other newspapers across the country.
25. Paul H. Bergeron, *Andrew Johnson's Civil War and Reconstruction* (Knoxville: University of Tennessee Press, 2011), 104, 205. Marble's comments on the meeting appeared in the February 10, 1865, issue of the *New York World*. The secretary's letter to Marble can be found in the Marble Papers at the Library of Congress.
26. Douglass, *Life and Times*, 382.
27. Douglass, *Life and Times*, 382.
28. "Reply of the Black Delegates to the President" (February 7, 1866), *Washington Morning Chronicle*, February 8, 1866, *PAJ*, X, 53, 54.

29. *New York Times*, February 9, 1866; anonymous letter to Douglass, February 16, 1866, ALS in the Walter O. and Linda Evans Collection; "Your Friends" to Douglass and five other members of the delegation, letter of February 19, 1866, ALS in the Walter O. and Linda Evans Collection.

30. M. R. Delany to G. T. Downing, William Whipper, Frederick Douglass, John Jones, L. H. Douglass, and others, letter of February 22, 1866, in Frank [Frances] A. Rollin, *Life and Public Services of Martin R. Delany* (Boston: Lee and Shepard, 1868), 281–82.

31. "Our 'Poor White' President," *National Anti-Slavery Standard*, February 17, 1866.

32. "The President and the Colored Delegation," *Christian Recorder*, February 17, 1866.

33. "Letter from Washington," *Christian Recorder*, March 3, 1866.

34. "Further Remarks in Response to Black Delegates," *New York Times*, February 11, 1866, *PAJ*, X, 58, 59. On Raymond, see *PAJ*, X, 59, n. 2.

35. William L. Hodge to Andrew Johnson, letter of February 8, 1866, *PAJ*, X, 60; Charles Dement to Andrew Johnson, letter of February 19, 1866, *PAJ*, X, 119; Ralph Phinny to Andrew Johnson, letter of February [15] 1866, *PAJ*, X, 102.

36. James H. Embry to Andrew Johnson, letter of February 9, 1866, *PAJ*, X, 63, 62.

37. Embry to Johnson, 62, 63.

38. "Administration Friend" to Johnson, letter of March 10, 1866, *PAJ*, X, 232; Douglass, "The Assassination and Its Lessons: An Address Delivered in Washington, D.C., on 13 February 1866," *FDP: Speeches, Debates, and Interviews*, IV, 112. For the citation from the February 14, 1866, *New York Tribune*, see *FDP: Speeches, Debates, and Interviews*, IV, 107.

39. On Johnson's increasing paranoia and inability to see differences between the moderate and Radical Republicans, see Michael Les Benedict, *A Compromise of Principle: Congressional Republicans and Reconstruction, 1863–1869* (New York: W. W. Norton, 1974), 14–25; and Mark Wahlgren Summers, *A Dangerous Stir: Fear, Paranoia, and the Making of Reconstruction* (Chapel Hill: University of North Carolina Press, 2009), 97–99.

7. The President's Riots

1. See Eric Foner, *Reconstruction: America's Unfinished Revolution, 1863–1877* (New York: Harper & Row, 1988), 142–44, et passim; and Paul A. Cimbala and Randall M. Miller, eds., *The Freedmen's Bureau and Reconstruction: Reconsiderations* (New York: Fordham University Press, 1999).

2. Johnson, "Freedmen's Bureau Veto Message" (February 19, 1866), *PAJ*, X, 120.

3. Johnson, "Washington's Birthday Address" (February 22, 1866), *PAJ*, X, 147, 152, 150, 152, 151.

4. Johnson, "Washington's Birthday Address," 157; "President Johnson," *Christian Recorder*, March 3, 1866. Hans L. Trefousse terms the speech a "tactless harangue" that "horrified even the most moderate Republicans" (*Andrew Johnson: A Biography* [New York W. W. Norton, 1989], 244).

5. Johnson, "Veto of Civil Rights Bill" (March 27, 1866), *PAJ*, X, 319, 320. On the veto further fracturing Johnson's relations with his own Republican Party, see Foner, *Reconstruction*, 249–52.

6. "The Veto—The Nation Aroused," *Christian Recorder*, March 31, 1866.

7. Douglass, "The Issues of the Day: An Address Delivered in Washington, D.C. on 10 March 1866," *New York Tribune*, March 12, 1866, *FDP: Speeches, Debates, and Interviews*, IV, 121, 123. One month later Charles Sumner wrote something similar about Johnson in a letter of April 3, 1866, to the Duchess of Argyll, stating that Johnson "is no Moses, but a Pharaoh to the colored race, & they now regard him so" (Beverly Wilson Palmer, ed., *The Selected Letters of Charles Sumner* [Boston: Northeastern University Press, 1990], II, 359).

8. Douglass, "The Issues of the Day," 121, 123.

9. Johnson, "Speech to Washington Blacks," *Washington Evening Star*, April 19, 1866, *PAJ*, X, 432.

10. Mark Wahlgren Summers, *The Ordeal of the Reunion: A New History of Reconstruction* (Chapel Hill: University of North Carolina Press, 2014), qt. 96. See also Stephen V. Ash, *A Massacre in Memphis: The Race Riot That Shook the Nation One Year after the Civil War* (New York: Hill and Wang, 2013).

11. James B. Bingham to Andrew Johnson, letter of May 17, 1866, *PAJ*, X, 513, 514.

12. "The Riot in Memphis," *New York Times*, May 12, 1866.

13. "The Moral of the Memphis Riots," *Nation*, May 15, 1866. Initial reports blamed the Blacks of New Orleans for the riot; see, for example, "Negro Riot in Memphis," *New York Herald*, May 3, 1866; "Serious Riot in Memphis," *Philadelphia Inquirer*, May 3, 1866; "The Riot of Memphis," *Daily Constitutional Union* (Washington, D.C.), May 3, 1866; and "The Memphis Negro Riots," *New York Herald*, May 5, 1866.

14. "Interview with Paschal B. Randolph" (July 21, 1866), *New York Times*, July 26, 1866, *PAJ*, X, 710, 711.

15. "Interview with Paschal B. Randolph," 711.

16. "Interview with Paschal B. Randolph," 711, 712.

17. Martin R. Delany to Andrew Johnson, letter of July 25, 1866, in Frank [Frances] A. Rollin, *Life and Public Services of Martin R. Delany* (Boston: Lee and Shepard, 1868), 278, 279, 280.

18. See James G. Hollandsworth Jr., *An Absolute Massacre: The New Orleans Race Riot of July 30, 1866* (Baton Rouge: Louisiana State University Press, 2001);

and Summers, *The Ordeal of the Reunion*, 96. On Memphis and New Orleans in the larger context of white violence against Blacks in the South, see Douglas R. Egerton, *The Wars of Reconstruction: The Brief, Violent History of America's Most Progressive Era* (New York: Bloomsbury Press, 2014), chap. 8.

19. Philip H. Sheridan to Andrew Johnson, letter of August 6, 1866, *PAJ*, XI, 36, 37.

20. But as historian Carole Emberton points out, in most newspaper articles and political speeches "nothing was said of the trauma, grief, and dislocations that white violence inflicted on Black victims and their families." Instead, the emphasis was on "the precariousness of federal authority and the threat of general disorder" (*Beyond Redemption: Race, Violence, and the American South after the Civil War* [Chicago: University of Chicago Press, 2013], 51, 50).

21. Wendell Phillips, "The President's Riot at New Orleans," *National Anti-Slavery Standard*, August 16, 1866.

22. "New Orleans during the Riot," *Christian Recorder*, August 25, 1866; *New Orleans Tribune*, September 1, 1866. See also "New Orleans Correspondence," *Christian Recorder*, August 18, 1866.

23. Douglass, "Let No One Be Excluded from the Ballot-Box: An Address Delivered in Albany, New York, on 20 November 1866," *FDP: Speeches, Debates, and Interviews*, IV, 147.

8. Shadowing Johnson, Defying the Loyalists

1. I am influenced here by Toni Morrison's account of how Blacks had a haunting presence in the imaginations of nineteenth-century American white writers (*Playing in the Dark: Whiteness and the Literary Imagination* [New York: Vintage Books, 1993]).

2. Wendell Phillips, "The Great Rebel Convention," *National Anti-Slavery Standard*, August 28, 1866; "The Press on the Johnson Convention," rpt. from the *New York Tribune*, *National Anti-Slavery Standard*, September 1, 1866; Johnson, "Reply to Committee from Philadelphia National Union Convention" (August 18, 1866), *National Intelligencer*, August 20, 1866, *PAJ*, XI, 93.

3. For lively accounts of Johnson's "Swing around the Circle," see Hans L. Trefousse, *Andrew Johnson: A Biography* (New York: W. W. Norton, 1989), 262–66; and Brenda Wineapple, *The Impeachers: The Trial of Andrew Johnson and the Dream of a Just Nation* (New York: Random House, 2019), chap. 10.

4. Johnson, "Speech in Cleveland" (September 3, 1866), *Cleveland Plain Dealer*, September 4, 1866, *PAJ*, XI, 176, 177.

5. Johnson, "Speech in Cleveland," 180.

6. Johnson, "Speech at St. Louis" (September 8, 1866), *Missouri Democrat*, September 10, 1866, *PAJ*, XI, 193, 194, 195.

7. Johnson, "Speech at St. Louis," 196, 194, 195.

8. Johnson, "Speech at St. Louis," 199.

9. "Andrew Johnson at St. Louis," *Chicago Tribune*, September 11, 1866; Howard K. Beale and Alan W. Brownsword, eds., *Diary of Gideon Welles, Secretary of the Navy under Lincoln and Johnson* (New York: W. W. Norton, 1960), II, 589, 590.

10. Douglass, *Life and Times of Frederick Douglass*, ed. Rayford W. Logan (1881, 1891–1892; New York: Collier Books, 1962), 387. On Douglass at the Southern Loyalists' Convention, see also David W. Blight, *Frederick Douglass: Prophet of Freedom* (New York: Simon & Schuster, 2018), 484–88.

11. On the Southern Loyalists' Convention, see Eric Foner, *Reconstruction: America's Unfinished Revolution, 1863–1877* (New York: Harper & Row, 1988), 270–71; and Kurt T. Lash, *The Fourteenth Amendment and the Privileges and Immunities of American Citizenship* (Cambridge: Cambridge University Press, 2014), 205–8.

12. Douglass, *Life and Times*, 387, 388.

13. Douglass, *Life and Times*, 389. Douglass can overdramatize in his retrospective autobiographies, but a reporter for the *New York Herald* summarized Douglass's 1866 statement at the convention on his refusal to withdraw, and it corresponds with his 1881 recollection, though with a different constituency. The reporter writes that Douglass "had been approached by members of the Louisiana delegation, not to walk in the procession or enter the Convention, as it would hurt the cause and would endanger the election in one or two of the Northern States. They might as well ask him to put a pistol to his head as to abdicate his manhood" ("The Altered State of the Negro: An Address Delivered in Philadelphia, Pennsylvania, on 5 September 1866," *FDP: Speeches, Debates, and Interviews*, IV, 137).

14. Douglass, *Life and Times*, 390.

15. Douglass, *Life and Times*, 390, 391.

16. Samuel Shoch to Thaddeus Stevens, letter of August 27, 1866, in *The Selected Papers of Thaddeus Stevens*, ed. Beverly Wilson Palmer and Holly Byers Ochoa (Pittsburgh, PA: University of Pittsburgh Press, 1998), II, 189; Stevens to William D. Kelley, letter of September 6, 1866, in Palmer and Ochoa, *Selected Papers of Thaddeus Stevens*, II, 192. (The letter appeared in the September 6, 1866, issue of the *New York Times*.)

17. Douglass, "We Are Here and Want the Ballot-Box: An Address Delivered in Philadelphia, Pennsylvania, on 4 September 1866," *FDP: Speeches, Debates, and Interviews*, IV, 127, 129; Douglass, "The Altered State of the Negro," 138.

18. Douglass, "Govern with Magnanimity and Courage: An Address Delivered in Philadelphia, Pennsylvania, on 6 September 1866," *FDP: Speeches, Debates, and Interviews*, IV, 143–44, 145.

19. Douglass, "We Are Here and Want the Ballot-Box," 131; Douglass, "Govern with Magnanimity," 143.

20. "The Southern Loyalists' Convention, etc.," *Christian Recorder*, September 15, 1866; "The Southern Loyalists' Convention," *Christian Recorder*, September 8, 1866; *New York Herald*, September 5, 1866. On the politics of the con-

vention, see James M. McPherson, *The Struggle for Equality: Abolitionists and the Negro in the Civil War and Reconstruction* (Princeton, NJ: Princeton University Press, 1964), 360–63.

9. Sources of Danger to the Republic

1. Douglass to "William Tichnor [*sic*] and James Field," letter of October 22, 1866, ALS, Norcross Manuscripts, Massachusetts Historical Society.
2. The quotation is from Ira Dworkin's "The Black *Atlantic Monthly*: Rethinking Literary Citizenship." My thanks to Dworkin for sharing this draft chapter from his book-in-progress on Nicholas Said. On the *Atlantic*, see also Richard H. Brodhead, *Cultures of Letters: Scenes of Reading and Writing in Nineteenth-Century America* (Chicago: University of Chicago Press, 1993), 79–82.
3. In his October 22, 1865, letter to Ticknor and Fields, Douglass suggested that the title of the overall essay could be "An Appeal to Congress for Impartial Suffrage."
4. Douglass, "Reconstruction," *Atlantic Monthly* 18 (December 1866): 761, 764.
5. Douglass, "Reconstruction," 763, 764, 762, 763.
6. "Letter from Frederick Douglass," *National Anti-Slavery Standard*, July 7, 1866; Douglass, "Reconstruction," 765. Historians have come to celebrate the Radical Republicans for their idealism, but in late 1866 Douglass, as he had with Lincoln during much of the Civil War, saw timidity in Congress's pragmatism. On the idealism of the Radical Republicans, see Eric Foner's influential *Reconstruction: America's Unfinished Revolution, 1863–1867* (New York: Harper & Row, 1988). For a recent work that emphasizes that idealism, see Brenda Wineapple, *The Impeachers: The Trial of Andrew Johnson and the Dream of a Just Nation* (New York: Random House, 2019), esp. 420–21. In *The Second Founding: How the Civil War and Reconstruction Remade the Constitution* (New York: W. W. Norton, 2019), Eric Foner writes that one aim of the Fourteenth Amendment was "to guarantee the rights of black Americans," but another was to "extend the Republican party into the South" (57). Douglass believed that many Republicans saw that second aim as outweighing the first; hence their reluctance to make Black suffrage part of the amendment.
7. Douglass, "An Appeal to Congress for Impartial Suffrage," *Atlantic Monthly* 19 (January 1867): 112.
8. George Sewell Boutwell, "The Usurpation," *Atlantic Monthly* 18 (October 1866): 510, 513, 509. Boutwell may have had in mind the compromises at the 1787 Constitutional Convention that ensured the South's political dominance, in terms of presidents and congressional representation, up to the time of the Civil War.
9. Douglass, "An Appeal to Congress," 117.

10. Johnson, "Message to Congress" (December 3, 1866), *PAJ*, XI, 503, 504.
11. Johnson, "District of Columbia Franchise Law Veto Message" (January 5, 1867), *PAJ*, XI, 588, 577.
12. A month after speaking in Philadelphia, Douglass presented "Sources of Danger" to a predominantly white audience in St. Louis. That remains the best-known version of the speech. The Yale University Press *Frederick Douglass Papers* uses a transcript of that speech, drawn from the *Daily Missouri Democrat*, February 8, 1867. See John R. McKivigan, Julie Husband, and Heather L. Kaufman, eds., *The Speeches of Frederick Douglass: A Critical Edition* (New Haven, CT: Yale University Press, 2018), 217–46.
13. An announcement of the lecture series can be found in the November 24, 1866, issue of the *Christian Recorder*.
14. Douglass and Harper spoke together or were part of the same lecture series on a number of occasions. The Thirty-Eighth Course of Lectures, 1866–1867, at the Salem Lyceum, for example, featured Douglass with a lecture titled "On Some Dangers to the Republic" and Harper with a lecture called "Our National Salvation" (*Historical Sketch of the Salem Lyceum, with a List of the Officers and Lecturers since Its Formation in 1830* [Salem, MA: Press of the Salem Gazette, 1879], 61). My thanks to Eric Gardner for calling this series to my attention. See also "Equal Rights Convention for the State of New York," *National Anti-Slavery Standard*, November 10, 1866; the meeting of the American Anti-Slavery Society in New York City on May, 11, 1869 (*FDP: Speeches, Debates, and Interviews*, IV, 199); the May 12–13, 1869, meeting of the American Equal Rights Association in New York City (*FDP: Speeches, Debates, and Interviews*, IV, 219); and the April 14, 1875, centennial anniversary of the Pennsylvania Society for Promoting the Abolition of Slavery (*FDP: Speeches, Debates, and Interviews*, IV, 407).
15. "Harvest Home at Princeton," *Christian Recorder*, September 15, 1866. The writer went on to say that Douglass "is more massive than Mrs. H., but she is more polished than he, and fully his equal in warm and glowing eloquence." My thanks to Eric Gardner for calling this article to my attention.
16. "Speech of Frances Ellen Watkins Harper," *Proceedings of the Eleventh National Woman's Rights Convention, Held at the Church of the Puritans, New York, May 10, 1866* (New York: Robert J. Johnston, Printer, 1866), 46. See also the version in Frances Smith Foster, ed., *A Brighter Coming Day: A Frances Ellen Watkins Harper Reader* (New York: Feminist Press, 1990), 217–19, which Foster titles "We Are All Bound Up Together."
17. "National Salvation: A Lecture Delivered Last Evening at National Hall, by Mrs. F. E. W. Harper, with Some Account of the Lecturer," *Philadelphia Daily Evening Telegraph*, February 1, 1867. See also Eric Gardner's invaluable "Frances Watkin Harper's 'National Salvation': A Rediscovered Lecture on Reconstruction," *Commonplace: The Journal of Early American Life*, Summer 2017, http://commonplace.online.

18. "National Salvation."
19. "National Salvation."
20. "National Salvation." For a bracing study of racism in the North, see Paul D. Escott, *The Worst Passions of Human Nature: White Supremacy in the Civil War North* (Charlottesville: University of Virginia Press, 2020).
21. "National Salvation"; "Matters in General," *Christian Recorder*, February 2, 1867.
22. Douglass, "The Future of the Colored Race," *North American Review*, May 1866, in *The Life and Writings of Frederick Douglass*, ed. Philip S. Foner (New York: International Publishers, 1955), IV, 195. David W. Blight is eloquent on Douglass as a prophet; see his *Frederick Douglass: Prophet of Freedom* (New York: Simon & Schuster, 2018).
23. "'Sources of Danger to the Republic': Frederick Douglass' Great Lecture Last Night," *Philadelphia Daily Evening Telegraph*, January 4, 1867; *National Anti-Slavery Standard*, January 12, 1867.
24. "'Sources of Danger to the Republic.'"
25. "'Sources of Danger to the Republic.'"
26. "'Sources of Danger to the Republic.'"
27. "'Sources of Danger to the Republic.'"
28. "'Sources of Danger to the Republic.'"
29. Douglass to Charles Sumner, letter of October 19, 1866, in Foner, *Life and Writings of Frederick Douglass*, IV, 197–98; Sumner, "The One Man Power *vs.* Congress: The Present Situation: Address at the Opening of the Annual Lectures of the Parker Fraternity, at the Music Hall, Boston, October 2, 1866," in *The Works of Charles Sumner* (Boston: Lee and Shepard, 1875), XI, 3, 27, 9.
30. "'Sources of Danger to the Republic.'" Johnson was hardly the first president to take advantage of the patronage power.
31. "'Sources of Danger to the Republic.'"
32. "'Sources of Danger to the Republic.'"
33. "'Sources of Danger to the Republic.'"
34. "'Sources of Danger to the Republic.'"
35. "'Sources of Danger to the Republic.'"
36. "'Sources of Danger to the Republic.'"
37. "'Sources of Danger to the Republic.'"
38. "'Sources of Danger to the Republic.'"
39. "'Sources of Danger to the Republic.'"
40. For accounts of the speech, see, for example, the *New York Herald*, December 18, 1866; *Cincinnati Enquirer*, January 11, 1867, which noted that tickets cost fifty cents; *Boston Commonwealth*, January 12, 1867; *Daily Missouri Democrat*, February 8, 1867; *Chicago Tribune*, March 23, 1867, which reported, "We anticipate a full house and a most interesting lecture"; and *Newark Daily Advertiser*, October 23, 1867.

41. Cited in *FDP: Speeches, Debates, and Interviews*, IV, 218. The newspaper reported that there were "a goodly number of colored people" in the audience as well, but that number was undoubtedly small.
42. Douglass, "Sources of Danger to the Republic: An Address Delivered in St. Louis, Missouri, 7 February 1867," *FDP: Speeches, Debates, and Interviews*, IV, 152.
43. Douglass, "Sources of Danger to the Republic: An Address Delivered in St. Louis," 171, 172.
44. For instance, when Douglass traveled to Washington, D.C., shortly after the National Loyalists' Convention to lecture at Black churches, Frederick Koones, a white chief clerk and navy agent in Washington, wrote Johnson about those lectures. According to Koones, Reverend Byron Sunderland of the District's First Presbyterian Church, whom he termed "one of the most ultra woolly heads," had given "his pulpit to Fred Douglass much to the disgust and disapprobation of the congregation." Koones himself may have been disgusted, but if the Black church had been led by an "ultra"— Koones's term for a radical Black activist—Douglass probably found a wholly receptive audience. See Koones to Johnson, letter of October 16, 1866, *PAJ*, XI, 356–57.

10. A Job Offer

1. Eric Foner, *Reconstruction: America's Unfinished Revolution, 1863–1877* (New York: Harper & Row, 1988), 278. See also Foner's *The Second Founding: How the Civil War and Reconstruction Remade the Constitution* (New York: W. W. Norton, 2019), 89–91.
2. In the Second Reconstruction Act of March 25, for instance, Congress mandated that the military commanders create a registry of eligible voters. As Allen C. Guelzo notes, "The registration process would identify 1.3 million voters in the five military districts—and to the horror of white Southerners, 700,000 were black, with black majorities in five states" (*Reconstruction: A Concise History* [New York: Oxford University Press, 2018], 50). See also Brenda Wineapple, *The Impeachers: The Trial of Andrew Johnson and the Dream of a Just Nation* (New York: Random House, 2019), 194–98.
3. Montgomery Blair to Andrew Johnson, letter of February 26, 1867, *PAJ*, XII, 67; Johnson, "Veto of the First Military Reconstruction Act" (March 2, 1867), *PAJ*, XII, 84; Johnson, "Veto of the Second Military Reconstruction Act" (March 23, 1867), *PAJ*, XII, 179, 178.
4. *Congressional Globe*, "Statutes at Large," Thirty-Ninth Congress, Sess. II, Chaps. 153, 154 (1867), 430.
5. *Congressional Globe*, "Statutes at Large," 431.
6. Johnson, "Veto of the Tenure of Office Act" (March 2, 1867), *PAJ*, XII, 95.

7. Johnson, "Freedmen's Bureau Veto" (July 16, 1866), *PAJ*, X, 698.
8. Thaddeus Stevens, "Reconstruction" (speech to Congress, January 3, 1867), in *The Selected Papers of Thaddeus Stevens*, ed. Beverly Wilson Palmer and Holly Byers Ochoa (Pittsburgh, PA: University of Pittsburgh Press, 1998), II, 212.
9. Samuel Johnson to Andrew Johnson, letter of March 25, 1867, *PAJ*, XII, 183.
10. Andrew Johnson to John P. Holtsinger, letter of April 27, 1867, *PAJ*, XII, 237; Frederick G. Edwards to Andrew Johnson, letter of April 12, 1867, *PAJ*, XII, 227.
11. J. McClary Perkins to Andrew Johnson, letter of August 16, 1867, *PAJ*, XII, 486, 488.
12. James G. Randall, ed., *The Diary of Orville Hickman Browning* (Springfield: Illinois State Historical Society, 1933), II, 151. I have preserved the misspellings and ungrammatical phrasings as they appear in the diary.
13. Randall, *Diary of Orville Hickman Browning*, II, 151.
14. Charles Remond Douglass to Frederick Douglass, letter of May 25, 1867; Charles Remond Douglass to Frederick Douglass, letter of May 9, 1867. The paragraph also draws on Charles Remond Douglass to Frederick Douglass, letter of July 14, 1867. These letters are available in General Correspondence, Frederick Douglass Papers, Library of Congress. See also William S. McFeely, *Frederick Douglass* (New York: W. W. Norton, 1991), 259–61.
15. Charles Remond Douglass to Frederick Douglass, letter of August 21, 1867, General Correspondence, Frederick Douglass Papers, Library of Congress.
16. Charles Remond Douglass to Frederick Douglass, letter of July 18, 1867, General Correspondence, Frederick Douglass Papers, Library of Congress.
17. Howard K. Beale and Alan W. Brownsword, eds., *Diary of Gideon Welles, Secretary of the Navy under Lincoln and Johnson* (New York: W. W. Norton, 1960), III, 142.
18. William Slade to Frederick Douglass, letter of July 29, 1867, General Correspondence, Frederick Douglass Papers, Library of Congress.
19. Frederick Douglass to William Slade, letter of August 12, 1867, General Correspondence, Frederick Douglass Papers, Library of Congress. Douglass biographer McFeely writes about the Freedmen's Bureau position: "There was no job, short of president or pope, that Frederick Douglass would have liked better" (*Frederick Douglass*, 260). But McFeely overestimates Douglass's willingness to work with Johnson and misreads Douglass's ironic response to Slade as a sincere effort to determine whether he would have the support of Johnson.
20. William Slade to Frederick Douglass, letter of August 18, 1867, General Correspondence, Frederick Douglass Papers, Library of Congress; Charles Remond Douglass to Frederick Douglass, letter of August 21, 1867, General Correspondence, Frederick Douglass Papers, Library of Congress; Charles Remond Douglass to Frederick Douglass, letter of September 2, 1867, General Correspondence, Frederick Douglass Papers, Library of Congress. See

also Benjamin Quarles, *Frederick Douglass* (1948; New York: Athenaeum, 1968), 237–40; and David W. Blight, *Frederick Douglass' Civil War: Keeping Faith in Jubilee* (Baton Rouge: Louisiana State University Press, 1989), 198.

21. Frederick Douglass to Theodore Tilton, letter of September 2, 1867, Miscellaneous Manuscripts, New York Historical Society.

22. "Frederick Douglass," *Independent*, September 12, 1867; Frederick Douglass to Gerrit Smith, letter of September 19, 1867, in *The Life and Writings of Frederick Douglass*, ed. Philip Foner (New York: International Publishers, 1955), IV, 206.

23. John Mercer Langston, *From the Virginia Plantation to the National Capitol; or, The First and Only Negro Representative in Congress from the Old Dominion* (Hartford, CT: American Publishing Company, 1894), 275–76.

24. Charles Remond Douglass to Frederick Douglass, letter of September 2, 1867, General Correspondence, Frederick Douglass Papers, Library of Congress; "A Letter Addressed by Wendell Phillips to Robert Purvis, September 13, 1867," ed. Joseph Alfred Boromé, *The Journal of Negro History* 42, no. 4 (1977): 294.

25. Robert Purvis to Wendell Phillips, letter of September 18, 1867, qtd. in Margaret Hope Bacon, *But One Race: The Life of Robert Purvis* (Albany: State University of New York Press, 2007), 170. Howard served as president of Howard University from 1869 to 1874, with several of those years overlapping with his job as commissioner of the Freedmen's Bureau. Howard's admirer John Langston became the founding dean of Howard's law school in 1868.

26. Langston, *From the Virginia Plantation to the National Capitol*, 276.

27. Ulysses S. Grant to Andrew Johnson, letter of August 1, 1867, *PAJ*, XII, 447; Grant to Johnson, letter of August 17, 1867, *PAJ*, XII, 489. See also Gideon Welles to Andrew Johnson, letter of August 4, 1867, *PAJ*, XII, 453–56.

28. Johnson to Edwin M. Stanton, letter of August 5, 1867, *PAJ*, XII, 461; Johnson to Ulysses S. Grant, letter of August 12, 1867, *PAJ*, XII, 475; Stanton to Johnson, letter of August 12, 1867, *PAJ*, XII, 477. See also Stanton to Johnson, letter of August 5, 1867, *PAJ*, XII, 461. Johnson removed another popular military commander, Major General Daniel Sickles, later that month, again because he didn't like his politics.

11. The Trials of Impeachment

1. "Frederick Douglass upon National Affairs," *National Anti-Slavery Standard*, November 9, 1867.

2. "Hon. Ben. Wade on the Late Elections," *Daily Columbus Enquirer*, November 13, 1867.

3. There are no extant essays or lectures by Douglass commenting on the Tenure of Office Act. But Douglass gave numerous lectures for which we do not

have newspaper transcriptions. In all likelihood, he had something to say about the act in lectures of February and March 1868.

4. Johnson, "To the Cabinet" (November 30, 1867), *PAJ*, XIII, 269, 270.

5. Eric Foner, *Reconstruction: America's Unfinished Revolution, 1863–1877* (New York: Harper & Row, 1988), 180; Johnson, "Third Annual Message" (December 3, 1867), *PAJ*, XIII, 286, 289, 287, 289. The message was ghostwritten by the Pennsylvanian Jeremiah Black, who had been part of Democratic president James Buchanan's cabinet and had written Johnson's unsuccessful vetoes of the Reconstruction Acts. The words of the message may have been Black's, but he wrote them for Johnson, who readily presented them.

6. Johnson, "Third Annual Message," 288–89.

7. "Interview with *Cincinnati Commercial* Correspondent" (December 31, 1867), *PAJ*, XIII, 396.

8. "The President's Message," *Elevator: A Weekly Journal of Progress*, December 13, 1867; "The President's Message," *Christian Recorder*, December 7, 1867.

9. Ulysses S. Grant to Andrew Johnson, letter of February 3, 1868, *PAJ*, XIII, 524. See also Grant to Johnson, letter of January 28, 1868, *PAJ*, XIII, 498–500.

10. "Grant, Meade, and Congress," *Christian Recorder*, January 25, 1868; "Congress at Work," *Christian Recorder*, January 25, 1868.

11. On Blacks in Washington, D.C., see Kate Masur, *An Example for All the Land: Emancipation and the Struggle over Equality in Washington, D.C.* (Chapel Hill: University of North Carolina Press, 2010).

12. Charles Remond Douglass to Frederick Douglass, letter of February 14, 1868, General Correspondence, Frederick Douglass Papers, Library of Congress.

13. Brenda Wineapple, *The Impeachers: The Trial of Andrew Johnson and the Dream of a Just Nation* (New York: Random House, 2019), 249.

14. Charles Remond Douglass to Frederick Douglass, letter of February 24, 1868, General Correspondence, Frederick Douglass Papers, Library of Congress. The Supreme Court confirmed Johnson's position on the unconstitutionality of the Tenure of Office Act in 1887.

15. *Loyal Georgian*, February 15, 1868, qt. in Douglas R. Egerton, *The Wars of Reconstruction: The Brief, Violent History of America's Most Progressive Era* (New York: Bloomsbury Press, 2014), 232; "Impeachment: The Congressional Charge against the President," *New York Herald*, March 2, 1868; Thaddeus Stevens to Benjamin F. Butler, letter of February 28, 1868, in *The Selected Papers of Thaddeus Stevens*, ed. Beverly Wilson Palmer and Holly Byers Ochoa (Pittsburgh, PA: University of Pittsburgh Press, 1998), II, 366; Charles Sumner to Edward Atkinson, letter of February 27, 1868, and Sumner to John Bright, letter of March 24, 1868, in *The Selected Letters of Charles Sumner*, ed. Beverly Wilson Palmer (Boston: Northeastern University Press, 1990), II, 420, 421. In a February 28, 1868, article titled "Mass Meeting Called

in Cincinnati on Impeachment," the *Baltimore Sun* reported on a proposed gathering of "all who desire the preservation of the public peace . . . and who are opposed to the impeachment of a president of the United States."

16. "Great Noise over a Small Affair," *Baltimore Sun*, February 21, 1868; "The Assault upon the Editor of the Meriden Recorder," *New York Times*, February 23, 1868. See also "A Disgraceful Assault," *Hartford Daily Courant*, February 21, 1868.

17. "Washington: Presentation of the Articles of Impeachment," *New York Tribune*, March 5, 1868.

18. "The Press on the Troubles at Washington," *Baltimore Sun*, February 25, 1868. The Articles of Impeachment are available online at https://www.senate.gov/artandhistory/history/common/briefing/Impeachment_Johnson.htm#7.

19. See the reference to the online resource in the note above.

20. Charles Remond Douglass to Frederick Douglass, letter of March 27, 1868, General Correspondence, Frederick Douglass Papers, Library of Congress. Douglass may have also received letters from Washington from Ottilie Assing, the German journalist and translator who was often his companion during his travels (and may have been his paramour). According to her biographer, Assing, who usually spent time with Charles Remond Douglass when she visited Washington, "became fascinated with the impeachment hearings, following developments in Washington with 'pure delight'" (Maria Diedrich, *Love across the Color Lines: Ottilie Assing and Frederick Douglass* [New York: Hill and Wang, 1999], 279). The "pure delight" is from a letter of April 3, 1868, to her sister in Germany. Assing regularly lambasted Johnson in the way of her close friend Douglass. She told readers of the German magazine *Morgenblatt*, for instance, "The president has voiced his hatred of the Negroes; he has clearly expressed his unwillingness to confer civil equality on the only class of people in the South who from the beginning to the end of the war were loyal to the Union and its rightful government" ("Presidential Policies—Persecution of Negroes—Embittered Southerners," *Morgenblatt*, September 1865, rpt. in *Radical Passion: Ottilie Assing's Reports from America and Letters to Frederick Douglass*, ed. and trans. Christoph Lohmann [New York: Peter Lang, 1999], 319).

21. Charles Remond Douglass to Frederick Douglass, letter of March 27, General Correspondence, Frederick Douglass Papers, Library of Congress.

22. Salmon P. Chase to Dr. J. E. Snodgrass, letter of March 16, 1868, in Robert B. Warden, *An Account of the Private Life and Public Services of Salmon Portland Chase* (Cincinnati: Wilstach, Baldwin & Co., 1874), 681; Chase to Gerrit Smith, letter of April 19, 1868, in Warden, *An Account*, 685.

23. On Johnson's defense team, see Wineapple, *The Impeachers*, chap. 20.

24. *Trial of Andrew Johnson, President of the United States, before the Senate of the United States on Impeachment by the House of Representatives for High Crimes and Misdemean-*

ors (Washington, D.C.: Government Printing Office, 1868), I, 173 (March 31, 1868). For clarity, boldface has been added here and below.

25. *Trial of Andrew Johnson*, I, 304 (April 3, 1868).

26. "Affairs at the Capital," *Christian Recorder*, April 18, 1868. See also the "Affairs at the Capital" column in the *Christian Recorder*'s issues of April 4, 11, and 25, 1868.

27. *Trial of Andrew Johnson*, II, 219 (and see 219–30 for Stevens's entire speech of April 27, 1868); Stevens, "Remarks on Impeachment" (January 6, 1867), *Selected Papers of Thaddeus Stevens*, II, 235.

28. Some might object to my characterization of the Tenure of Office Act as focusing on relatively inconsequential details. But imagine a counterfactual: a Republican president from 1865 to 1868 intent on Reconstruction policies that enlarged Blacks' civil rights comes to be opposed by a Democratic-majority Congress that impeaches him for firing one of his cabinet officers. If that had been the case, we'd be talking about the Democrats' desperation tactics.

12. "Demented Moses of Tennessee"

1. "Impeachment: The Probable Result To-day," *New York Herald*, May 16, 1868. See the discussion of this article later in the chapter.

2. That is the argument that Brenda Wineapple develops, often compellingly, in *The Impeachers: The Trial of Andrew Johnson and the Dream of a Just Nation* (New York: Random House, 2019).

3. Charles Remond Douglass to Frederick Douglass, letter of April 24, 1868, General Correspondence, Frederick Douglass Papers, Library of Congress.

4. *Trial of Andrew Johnson, President of the United States, before the Senate of the United States on Impeachment by the House of Representatives for High Crimes and Misdemeanors* (Washington, D.C.: Government Printing Office, 1868), I, 589, 597, 600, 603 (April 16, 1868).

5. *Trial of Andrew Johnson*, I, 628–29 (April 16, 1868).

6. *Trial of Andrew Johnson*, I, 629–30 (April 16, 1868).

7. *Trial of Andrew Johnson*, I, 631, 632 (April 16, 1868). Butler's direct attack on Johnson for the the impact of his policies on the freedpeople was rare for the trial, but see House manager Thomas Williams's remarks of April 25, when he stated that Johnson "had in effect reopened the war, inaugurated anarchy, turned loose once more the incarnate devil of baffled treason and unappeasable hate, whom, as we fondly thought, our victories had overthrown and bound in chains, ordained rapine and murder from the Potomac to the Gulf, and deluged the streets of Memphis as well of New Orleans, and the green fields of the south, already dotted with so many patriot graves, with the blood of martyred citizens" (*Trial of Andrew Johnson*,

II, 233–34). By contrast, Thaddeus Stevens, who had doubts about the Articles of Impeachment, tended to focus on those articles. In his extended call for conviction on April 25, he stated that "the only question to be considered is: is the respondent violating the law?" He responded in the affirmative in terms of the Tenure of Office Act (*Trial of Andrew Johnson*, II, 220). On Stevens at the trial, see Hans L. Trefousse, *Thaddeus Stevens: Nineteenth-Century Egalitarian* (Chapel Hill: University of North Carolina Press, 1999), chap. 19.

8. Charles Remond Douglass to Frederick Douglass, letter of April 24, 1868, General Correspondence, Frederick Douglass Papers, Library of Congress; Douglass to Theodore Tilton, letter of October 15, 1864, in *The Life and Writings of Frederick Douglass*, ed. Philip Foner (New York: International Publishers, 1955), IV, 424.

9. "The Ku Klux Klan in Washington: Downing, the Oysterman, and Bob, the Bootblack, Doomed," *New York Herald*, April 13, 1868. For a complementary perspective on this article, see Wineapple, *The Impeachers*, 312–13.

10. "Impeachment: The Probable Result To-day," *New York Herald*, May 16, 1868. On African Americans' responses to the verdict, see David O. Stewart, *Impeached: The Trial of Andrew Johnson and the Fight for Lincoln's Legacy* (New York: Simon & Schuster, 2009), 272–74.

11. Douglass, "Equal Rights for All: Addresses Delivered in New York, New York, on 14 May 1868," *FDP: Speeches, Debates, and Interviews*, IV, 178. On George Francis Train as a showman and racist, see Holly Jackson, *American Radicals: How Nineteenth-Century Protest Shaped the Nation* (New York: Crown, 2019), 264–65.

12. Philip A. Bell, "The Inconsistencies of Reform Parties," *Elevator: A Weekly Journal of Progress*, May 15, 1868 (see also "The Cowardice of Republicanism" in the issue of May 8, 1868); Charles Remond Douglass to Frederick Douglass, letter of April 28, 1868, General Correspondence, Frederick Douglass Papers, Library of Congress; Douglass, "Equal Rights for All," 175. Douglass and Bell probably crossed paths during the 1840s and 1850s when Bell was based in New York and attended Black conventions. Douglass wrote Bell on April 28, 1868, to congratulate him on "battling bravely and hopefully" for African Americans in California (*Elevator*, June 5, 1868).

13. For James Grimes's statement, see the U.S. Senate website "The Impeachment of Andrew Johnson (1868) President of the United States" (https://www.senate.gov/artandhistory/history/common/briefing/Impeachment_Johnson.htm#1). Stewart argues for bribery, declaring "that dark men undertook dark deeds to keep Andrew Johnson in office" (*Impeached*, 241). As with U.S. politics going back to the 1780s and 1790s, horse-trading was probably at work during the deliberations. My own sense is that distrust of Wade and a desire to have Grant as the Republican presidential nominee were the most crucial factors leading to the acquittal. On the distrust of Wade at the time of the first impeachment vote, see H. L. Trefousse, *Benja-*

min Franklin Wade: Radical Republican from Ohio (New York: Twayne Publishers, 1963), 305–10.

14. "Senator Ben. Wade at Home: His Personal Manners and Habits—His Views on Labor," *New York Times,* July 1, 1867; "Ben Wade's Supposed Cabinet," *Flake's Bulletin,* March 4, 1868.

15. *National Anti-Slavery Standard,* May 16, 1868; F. E. W. Harper, "Minnie's Sacrifice," chap. XIX, *Christian Recorder,* September 11, 1869.

16. Charles Remond Douglass to Frederick Douglass, letter of May 29, 1868, General Correspondence, Frederick Douglass Papers, Library of Congress. On Chase and Johnson, see Wineapple, *The Impeachers,* 267–71.

17. Douglass, "Salmon P. Chase," *National Anti-Slavery Standard,* July 18, 1868. The essay also appeared in the *Elevator,* September 11, 1868, and several other newspapers.

18. Douglass, "Salmon P. Chase."

19. Douglass, "Salmon P. Chase."

20. Douglass, "Salmon P. Chase." By the time he wrote his 1881 *Life and Times of Frederick Douglass,* Douglass would appear to have forgiven Chase, for his portrayal of Chase in his final autobiography is highly positive. He says nothing about Chase's role as the presiding judge of Johnson's impeachment trial.

21. Douglass, "The Work before Us," *Independent,* August 27, 1868.

22. Douglass, "The Work before Us."

23. Douglass, "The Work before Us."

Epilogue: "We Have a Fight on Our Hands"

1. Johnson, "Farewell Address" (March 4, 1869), *PAJ,* XV, 508, 515.

2. "That Watch! Mr. President!," *Christian Recorder,* September 8, 1866. On the awarding of the gold watch in February 1865, see *PAJ, VII,* li, and the end of chapter 1 above.

3. Johnson, "Speech at Knoxville" (April 3, 1869), *PAJ,* XV, 570. Black voters had been added as a result of the Fourteenth Amendment and in anticipation of the probable ratification of the Fifteenth Amendment.

4. Johnson, "Speech at Knoxville," 570, 571.

5. Johnson, "Speech in Memphis" (April 15, 1869), *PAJ,* XV, 609, 610, 611.

6. Johnson, "Speech in Memphis," 612.

7. Johnson, "Speech in U.S. Senate" (March 22, 1875), *PAJ,* XVI, 737; "Interview with *New York Herald* Correspondent" (March 7, 1875), *PAJ,* XVI, 711.

8. On this point, see Eric Foner, *The Second Founding: How the Civil War and Reconstruction Remade the Constitution* (New York: W. W. Norton, 2019).

9. W. E. B. Du Bois, *Black Reconstruction in America* (1935; New York: Simon & Schuster, 1998), 322. For a fuller discussion of Du Bois's historical interpre-

tation of Johnson, see Christina Zwarg, *The Archive of Fear: White Crisis and Black Freedom in Douglass, Stowe, and Du Bois* (New York: Oxford University Press, 2020), 112–30.

10. To be precise, this phrase was coined by the character Clifford in Nathaniel Hawthorne's *The House of the Seven Gables*, ed. Robert S. Levine (1851; New York: W. W. Norton, 2020), 185.

11. Douglass, "Addresses Delivered in New York, New York, on 14 May 1868," *FDP: Speeches, Debates, and Interviews*, IV, 174; Douglass, "Seeming and Real," *New National Era*, October 6, 1870, in *The Life and Writings of Frederick Douglass*, ed. Philip S. Foner (New York: International Publishers, 1955), IV, 226; Douglass, "Give Us the Freedom Intended for Us," *New National Era*, December 5, 1872, in Foner, *Life and Writings*, IV, 299; Douglass, "Introduction to *The Reason Why the Colored American Is Not in the World's Columbia Exposition*" (1893), in Foner, IV, 471.

12. Douglass, "Looking the Republican Party Squarely in the Face: An Address Delivered in Cincinnati, Ohio, on 14 June 1876," *FDP: Speeches, Debates, and Interviews*, IV, 441.

13. Douglass, "Our National Capital: An Address Delivered in Baltimore, Maryland, on 8 May 1877," *FDP: Speeches, Debates, and Interviews*, IV, 467, 456–57.

14. Douglass, "The Lessons of Emancipation to the New Generation: An Address Delivered in Elmira, New York, on 3 August 1880," *FDP: Speeches, Debates, and Interviews*, IV, 572–73.

15. Douglass, "This Decision Has Humbled the Nation: An Address Delivered in Washington, D.C., on 22 October 1883," *FDP: Speeches, Debates, and Interviews*, V, 114–15.

16. Douglass, "The Nation's Problem: An Address Delivered in Washington, D.C., on 16 April 1889," *FDP: Speeches, Debates, and Interviews*, V, 406, 411, 423, 407, 425, 406.

17. Douglass, *Life and Times of Frederick Douglass*, ed. Rayford W. Logan (1881, 1891–1892; New York: Collier Books, 1962), 512, 539, 544.

18. Douglass, "Lessons of the Hour: An Address Delivered in Washington, D.C., on 9 January 1894," *FDP: Speeches, Debates, and Interviews*, V, 596, 598.

19. Douglass, "'To Mr. De Witt Miller,' Signed Anacostia, D.C., January 22, 1893," in Foner, *Life and Writings*, IV, 477. On the *Plessy v. Ferguson* Supreme Court case, see Steve Luxenberg, *Separate: The Story of* Plessy v. Ferguson, *and America's Journey from Slavery to Segregation* (New York: W. W. Norton, 2019).

20. "'Sources of Danger to the Republic': Frederick Douglass' Great Lecture Last Night," *Philadelphia Daily Evening Telegraph*, January 4, 1867. For one of many examples of recent op-ed pieces on Johnson and Trump, see Manisha Sinha, "Donald Trump, Meet Your Precursor," *New York Times*, November 29, 2019.

21. On this topic, see Heather Cox Richardson, *How the South Won the Civil War: Oligarchy, Democracy, and the Continuing Fight for the Soul of America* (New York: Oxford University Press, 2020).

22. Abraham Lincoln, "First Inaugural Address" (March 4, 1861), in *The Portable Abraham Lincoln*, ed. Andrew Delbanco (New York: Penguin Books, 1992), 204; Douglass, "Lessons of the Hour," 607.

INDEX

Page numbers in *italics* refer to illustrations. Page numbers beginning with 265 refer to endnotes.